The LOCOMOTIVES
that BALDWIN built

SOME JOBS were so rushed that occasionally the lettering had to be done as the locomotive was being steamed up for its trial runs. This view of the neat little three-foot gauge, American 4-4-0 type Yucatan locomotive built September 1945, is an instance of this procedure. In the background a giant Baltimore & Ohio single-expansion articulated is steaming up.

Cylinders, 13″ × 28″   Boiler, diameter, 44″
Drivers, 46″   Weight, total engine, 65,500 lb.

(Collection of Frederick Westing)

The LOCOMOTIVES that BALDWIN built

By Fred Westing

OLD IRONSIDES, the locomotive that started it all. Built by Matthias William Baldwin in person. The financial bickering that followed its sale almost drove Baldwin away from locomotives; fortunately it didn't. (Collection of Frederick Westing)

BONANZA BOOKS · NEW YORK

517R01617

COPYRIGHT MCMLXVI BY SUPERIOR PUBLISHING COMPANY, SEATTLE, WASHINGTON

*This edition published by Bonanza Books,
a division of Crown Publishers, Inc.,
by arrangement with Superior Publishing Company.*
d   e   f   g   h

Library of Congress Catalogue Card Number 66-25422

PRINTED IN THE UNITED STATES OF AMERICA

Dedication

To My Esteemed Friend Paul T. Warner

THE PHOTOGRAPHER and one of his more than 25,000 subjects. Fred Haines was Baldwin's official photographer for over 25 years, during which time he photographed most of the locomotives seen in this book. Florence McIntyre his assistant is under the focusing cloth. (C. A. Brown photo)

Foreword

This book is due greatly to the efforts and enthusiasm of John F. Kirkland, Regional Manager, Pacific Coast, Baldwin-Lima-Hamilton, Corporation, and Albert P. Salisbury, President, Superior Publishing Company, Seattle, Washington.

It does not represent a complete coverage of every Baldwin locomotive, nor is it a complete history of the Works, but contains ample material to show much that Baldwin accomplished in over 120 years of locomotive building covering 70,000 locomotives. It also illustrates the versatility and variety that went into Baldwin's design and construction.

What is shown are many interesting Baldwin engines built between 1831 and 1954. Pertinent sidelights in text and captions provide data which we hope will be of added interest to the locomotive and railroad devotee.

An outstanding feature is the reproduced facsimile of the old Baldwin History, covering the period from 1831 to 1923, and long out of print. Much of that book was written by Paul T. Warner, the greatest American locomotive historian, from my viewpoint. Paul was Librarian at Baldwin's when I was there and just about every day we'd find time to "talk shop." I never knew Paul to be stumped on a question concerning a Baldwin engine, and his knowledge of all the "old timers" regardless of builder was phenomenal.

Some new pictures supplement those already in the facsimile section. For this, thanks are due to Charles A. Brown, who supplied these older locomotive photographs from his collection.

One thing for sure, never in such variety have so many Baldwin built engines appeared between the covers of a book. On that point we can satisfy the reader—just a quick perusal should indicate that.

To those to whom the steam locomotive remains the most human of all man-made machines, happy viewing and reading.

Frederick Westing

Drexel Hill, Penn.
1966

CONTENTS

THE FOUNDER

THE PRESIDENT, 1923

VAUCLAIN'S FAVORITE POSE was at the throttle. On one of his private car railroad trips, he stopped at the plant of the St. Louis Car Co., and inspected one of the gas-electric cars he sold to Mexico on a previous trip. Sale was made by Vauclain for the Electro Motive Corp., who subcontracted the building of the car to the St. Louis Car Co. (Collection of C. A. Brown)

MAIN OFFICE AND WORKS, PHILADELPHIA PLANT

HISTORY
OF
THE BALDWIN LOCOMOTIVE WORKS

1831—1923

SOME of the early photos, like this one, taken in 1869 of Saucon Iron Company's "Jacob Riegel" reveal the tranquil street scene of Broad St., Philadelphia, just after the close of the Civil War. (Collection of C. A. Brown)

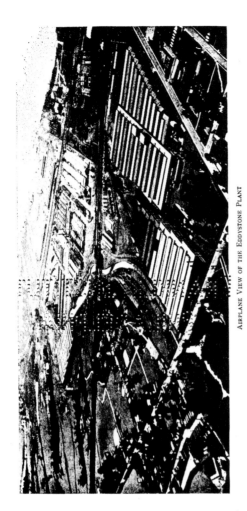

AIRPLANE VIEW OF THE EDDYSTONE PLANT

THE BALDWIN LOCOMOTIVE WORKS

1831
MATTHIAS W. BALDWIN

1839
BALDWIN, VAIL & HUFTY
M. W. BALDWIN*   GEORGE VAIL*   GEORGE W. HUFTY*

1841
BALDWIN & VAIL
M. W. BALDWIN*   GEORGE VAIL*

1842
BALDWIN & WHITNEY
M. W. BALDWIN*   ASA WHITNEY*

1846
M. W. BALDWIN

1854
M. W. BALDWIN & CO.
M. W. BALDWIN*   MATTHEW BAIRD*

1867
M. BAIRD & CO.
MATTHEW BAIRD*   GEORGE BURNHAM*   CHARLES T. PARRY*

1870
M. BAIRD & CO.
MATTHEW BAIRD*   GEORGE BURNHAM*   CHARLES T. PARRY*
EDWARD H. WILLIAMS*   WILLIAM P. HENSZEY*   EDWARD LONGSTRETH*

1873
BURNHAM, PARRY, WILLIAMS & CO.
GEORGE BURNHAM*   CHARLES T. PARRY*   EDWARD H. WILLIAMS*
WILLIAM P. HENSZEY*   EDWARD LONGSTRETH*   JOHN H. CONVERSE*

1886
BURNHAM, PARRY, WILLIAMS & CO.
GEORGE BURNHAM*   CHARLES T. PARRY*   EDWARD H. WILLIAMS*
WILLIAM P. HENSZEY*   JOHN H. CONVERSE*   WILLIAM C. STROUD*
WILLIAM H. MORROW*   WILLIAM L. AUSTIN

1891
BURNHAM, WILLIAMS & CO.
GEORGE BURNHAM*   EDWARD H. WILLIAMS*   WILLIAM P. HENSZEY*
JOHN H. CONVERSE*   WILLIAM C. STROUD*   WILLIAM L. AUSTIN

1896
BURNHAM, WILLIAMS & CO.
GEORGE BURNHAM*   EDWARD H. WILLIAMS*   WILLIAM P. HENSZEY*
JOHN H. CONVERSE*   WILLIAM L. AUSTIN   SAMUEL M. VAUCLAIN
ALBA B. JOHNSON   GEORGE BURNHAM, JR.

1901
BURNHAM, WILLIAMS & CO.
GEORGE BURNHAM*   WILLIAM P. HENSZEY*   JOHN H. CONVERSE*
WILLIAM L. AUSTIN   SAMUEL M. VAUCLAIN   ALBA B. JOHNSON
GEORGE BURNHAM, JR.

1907
BURNHAM, WILLIAMS & CO.
GEORGE BURNHAM*   WILLIAM P. HENSZEY*   JOHN H. CONVERSE*
WILLIAM L. AUSTIN   SAMUEL M. VAUCLAIN   ALBA B. JOHNSON

1909
Incorporated under the Laws of Pennsylvania as
BALDWIN LOCOMOTIVE WORKS

1911
Incorporated under the Laws of Pennsylvania as
THE BALDWIN LOCOMOTIVE WORKS

*NOW DECEASED

THEY DON'T GROW MUSHROOMS like that any more: Grand Trunk No. 283 was outshopped in May 1870. (Collection of C. A. Brown)

MARIETTA AND PITTSBURGH R.R. "Marietta" blocks Broad Street traffic in July 1870. (Collection of C. A. Brown)

ST. LOUIS, VANDALIA AND TERRE HAUTE R.R. No. 22, Aug. 1870. Note the ornate builders plate between the driving wheel splashers. (Collection of C. A. Brown)

"ALERT" OF THE GLENDON IRON CO. used the ancient practice of running the water pump from the cylinder rod a practice which made it necessary to run the locomotive to get water in the boiler even though there was no other reason to move the locomotive. History neglected to record the identity of the possessor of the beard. (1870). (Collection of C. A. Brown)

Organization, 1923

DIRECTORS

WILLIAM L. AUSTIN, Rosemont, Pa.
SAMUEL M. VAUCLAIN, Rosemont, Pa.
SAMUEL F. PRYOR, New York, N. Y.
WILLIAM E. COREY, New York, N. Y.
SYDNEY E. HUTCHINSON, Philadelphia, Pa.
SIDNEY F. TYLER, Philadelphia, Pa.
B. DAWSON COLEMAN, Lebanon, Pa.
HAROLD T. WHITE, New York, N. Y.
THOMAS G. ASHTON, Philadelphia, Pa.
ARTHUR W. SEWALL, Philadelphia, Pa.
THOMAS S. GATES, Philadelphia, Pa.
JOHN M. HANSEN, Pittsburgh, Pa.

OFFICERS

SAMUEL M. VAUCLAIN	President
JOHN P. SYKES	Senior Vice-President in Charge of Plants and Manufacture
WILLIAM deKRAFFT	Vice-President in Charge of Finance, and Treasurer
GRAFTON GREENOUGH	Vice-President in Charge of Domestic Sales
F. de ST. PHALLE	Vice-President in Charge of Foreign Sales
JAMES McNAUGHTON	Vice-President in Charge of the New York Office
CHARLES A. BOURGEOIS	Vice-President in Charge of Manufacture
JACQUES L. VAUCLAIN	Vice-President in Charge of Plant and Equipment
HARRY GLAENZER	Vice-President in Charge of Engineering
WILLIAM A. RUSSELL	Vice-President in Charge of Purchases
HENRY V. WILLE	Consulting Vice-President Concerning Engineering and Metallurgy
ARTHUR L. CHURCH	Secretary and Assistant Treasurer
A. B. EHST	Comptroller

General Counsel

MORGAN, LEWIS and BOCKIUS
934 Land Title Building, Philadelphia

CONTENTS

CAMDEN AND ATLANTIC'S "Camden" was a classic 4-4-0 of the early 70's. (Collection of C. A. Brown)

The Baldwin Locomotive Works

CHAPTER I.

THE FIRST BALDWIN LOCOMOTIVE

THE Baldwin Locomotive Works dates its origin from the inception of steam railroads in America. Called into existence by the early requirements of the railroad interests of the country, it has grown with their growth and kept pace with their progress. It has reflected in its career the successive stages of American railroad practice, and has itself contributed largely to the development of the locomotive as it exists today. A history of The Baldwin Locomotive Works, therefore, is in a great measure, a record of the progress of locomotive engineering in this country, and as such cannot fail to be of interest to those who are concerned in this important element of our material progress.

At the present date, the Works occupy 19 6 acres in the heart of Philadelphia and 616 acres at Eddystone, on the Delaware River, twelve miles below the city. The offices and principal machine shops are situated in the rectangle bounded on the north by Spring Garden Street, on the east by Broad Street, on the south by the Philadelphia and Reading Railway Subway and on the west by Nineteenth Street. There are also shops located on the line of the Philadelphia and Reading Railway at Twenty-sixth to Twenty-ninth Streets.

MATTHIAS W. BALDWIN, the founder of the establishment, learned the trade of a jeweler, and entered the service of Fletcher & Gardiner, Jewelers and Silversmiths, Philadelphia, in 1817. Two years later he opened a small shop, in the same line of business, on his own account. The demand for articles of this character falling off, however, he formed a partnership in 1825, with David Mason, a machinist, in the manufacture of bookbinders' tools and cylinders for calico printing. Their shop was in "Coffee-House Alley," which ran north from Walnut Street, above Fourth. They afterward removed to Minor Street, below Sixth. The business was so successful that steam power became necessary in carrying on their manufacture, and an engine was bought for the purpose. This proving unsatisfactory, Mr. Baldwin decided to design and construct one which should be specially

adapted to the requirements of his shop. One of these requirements was that it should occupy the least possible space, and this was met by the construction of an upright engine on a novel and ingenious plan. On a bed-plate about five feet square an upright

MR. BALDWIN'S FIRST ENGINE

cylinder was placed; the piston rod connected to a cross-bar having two legs turned downward, and sliding in grooves on the sides of the cylinder, which thus formed the guides. To the sides of these legs, at their lower ends, was connected by pivots an U-shaped frame, prolonged at the arch into a single rod, which took hold of the crank of a fly wheel carried by upright standards on the bed-plate. It will be seen that the length of the ordinary separate guide-bars was thus saved, and the whole engine was

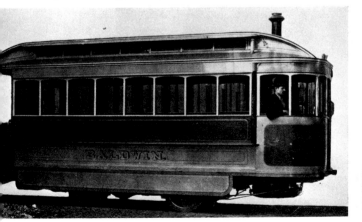

A BALDWIN STEAM CAR of the 1870's. Bowing to steam locomotive tradition, a bell may be seen on the roof above the derby hatted engineer. (Collection of C. A. Brown)

ANOTHER VERSION of the resort dummy was this type with most of the machinery enclosed to avoid frightening the horses. "George" was built by Baldwin in 1871 for the Brooklyn Bath and Coney Island R.R. (Collection of C. A. Brown)

brought within the smallest possible compass. The design of the machine was not only unique, but its workmanship was so excellent, and its efficiency so great, as readily to procure for Mr. Baldwin orders for additional stationary engines. His attention was thus turned to steam engineering, and the way was prepared for his grappling with the problem of the locomotive when the time should arrive.

This original stationary engine, constructed prior to 1830, is still in good order and carefully preserved at the Works. It has successively supplied the power in six different departments as they have been opened, from time to time, in the growth of the business.

The manufacture of stationary steam engines thus took a prominent place in the establishment, and Mr. Mason shortly afterward withdrew from the partnership.

In 1829-30 the use of steam as a motive power on railroads had begun to engage the attention of American engineers. A few locomotives had been imported from England, and one (which, however, was not successful) had been constructed at the West Point Foundry, in New York City. To gratify the public interest in the new motor, Mr. Franklin Peale, then proprietor of the Philadelphia Museum, applied to Mr. Baldwin to construct a miniature locomotive for exhibition in his establishment. With the aid only of the imperfect published descriptions and sketches of the locomotives which had taken part in the Rainhill competition in England, Mr. Baldwin undertook the work, and on the 25th of April, 1831, the miniature locomotive was put in motion on a circular track made of pine boards covered with hoop iron, in the rooms of the Museum. Two small cars, containing seats for four passengers, were attached to it, and the novel spectacle attracted crowds of admiring spectators. Both anthracite and pine-knot coal were used as fuel, and the exhaust steam was discharged into the chimney, thus utilizing it to increase the draught.

The success of the model was such that, in the same year, Mr. Baldwin received an order for a locomotive from the Philadelphia, Germantown and Norristown Railroad Company, whose short line of six miles to Germantown was operated by horse

power. The Camden and Amboy Railroad Company had shortly before imported a locomotive from England, which was stored in a shed at Bordentown. It had not yet been put together; but Mr. Baldwin, in company with his friend Mr. Peale, visited the spot, inspected the detached parts, and made a few memoranda of some of its principal dimensions. Guided by these figures and his experience with the Peale model, Mr. Baldwin commenced the task. The difficulties to be overcome in filling the order can hardly be appreciated at this day. There were few mechanics competent to do any part of the work on

THE "OLD IRONSIDES," 1832

a locomotive. Suitable tools were with difficulty obtainable. Cylinders were bored by a chisel fixed in a block of wood and turned by hand. Blacksmiths able to weld a bar of iron exceeding one and one-quarter inches in thickness were few, or not to be had. It was necessary for Mr. Baldwin to do much of the work with his own hands, to educate the workmen who assisted him, and to improvise tools for the various processes.

The work was prosecuted, nevertheless, under all these difficulties, and the locomotive was fully completed, christened "Old Ironsides," and tried on the road, November 23, 1832. The circumstances of the trial are fully preserved, and are given,

OUT THE BACK DOOR of the Broad St. works poses No. 15, pride and joy of the St. Louis Vandalia and Terre Haute in 1870. (Collection of C. A. Brown)

farther on, in the extracts from the journals of the day. Despite some imperfections, naturally occurring in a first effort, and afterward to a great extent remedied, the engine was, for that early day, a marked and gratifying success. It was put at once into service, as appears from the Company's advertisement three days after the trial, and did duty on the Germantown road and others for over a score of years.

The "Ironsides" was a four-wheeled engine, modeled essentially on the English practice of that day, as shown in the "Planet" class, and weighed, in running order, something over five tons. The rear or driving wheels were 54 inches in diameter on a crank axle placed in front of the firebox. The cranks were 39 inches from center to center. The front wheels, which were simply carrying wheels, were 45 inches in diameter, on an axle placed just back of the cylinders. The cylinders were 9½ inches in diameter by 18 inches stroke, and were attached horizontally to the outside of the smokebox, which was **D**-shaped, with the sides receding inwardly, so as to bring the center line of each cylinder in line with the center of the crank. The wheels were made with heavy cast-iron hubs, wooden spokes and rims, and wrought-iron tires. The frame was of wood, placed outside the wheels. The boiler was 30 inches in diameter, and contained 72 copper tubes, 1½ inches in diameter and seven feet long. The tender was a four-wheeled platform, with wooden sides and back, carrying an iron box for a water tank, inclosed in a wooden casing, and with a space for fuel in front. The engine had no cab. The valve motion was at first given by a single loose eccentric for each cylinder, placed on the axle between the crank and the hub of the wheel. On the inside of the eccentric was a half-circular slot, running half way around. A stop was fastened to the axle at the arm of the crank, terminating in a pin which projected into the slot. The engine was reversed by changing the position of the eccentric on the axle by a lever operated from the footboard. This form of valve motion was, however, shortly afterward changed, and a single fixed eccentric for each cylinder substituted. The rock shafts, which were under the footboard, had arms above and below, and the eccentric straps had each a forked rod, with a hook, or an upper and

lower latch or pin, at their extremities, to engage with the upper or lower arm of the rock shaft. The eccentric rods were raised or lowered by a double treadle, so as to connect with the upper or lower arm of the rock shaft, according as forward or backward gear was desired. A peculiarity in the exhaust of the "Ironsides" was that there was only a single straight pipe running across from one cylinder to the other, with an opening in the upper side of the pipe, midway between the cylinders, to which was attached at right angles the perpendicular pipe into the chimney. The cylinders, therefore, exhausted against each other; and it was found, after the engine had been put in use, that this was a serious objection. This defect was afterward remedied by turning each exhaust pipe upward into the chimney substantially as it is now done. The steam joints were made with canvas and red lead, as was the practice in English locomotives, and in consequence much trouble was caused, from time to time, by leaking.

The price of the engine was to have been $4000, but some difficulty was found in procuring a settlement. The Company claimed that the engine did not perform according to contract; and objection was also made to some of the defects alluded to. After these had been corrected as far as possible, however, Mr. Baldwin finally succeeded in effecting a compromise settlement, and received from the Company $3500 for the machine.

The results of the trial and the impression produced by it on the public mind may be gathered from the following extracts from the newspapers of the day:

The *United States Gazette*, of November 24, 1832, remarked:

"A most gratifying experiment was made yesterday afternoon on the Philadelphia, Germantown and Norristown Railroad. The beautiful locomotive engine and tender, built by Mr. Baldwin, of this city, whose reputation as an ingenious machinist is well known, were for the first time placed on the road. The engine traveled about six miles, working with perfect accuracy and ease in all its parts, and with great velocity."

The *Chronicle* of the same date noticed the trial more at length, as follows:

"It gives us pleasure to state that the locomotive engine built by our townsman, M. W. Baldwin, has proved highly successful. In the presence of several gentlemen of science and information on such subjects, the engine

A TYPICAL RESORT ENGINE of the 1870's was this trim little 2-4-2, built in 1871 for the Savanah, Skidaway and Seabound R.R. Tiny double enders like this were popular for hauling passengers (sometimes in open cars) along the fashionable beaches of the East Coast. Much hand painted striping embellished the tank and driving wheels. (Collection of C. A. Brown)

THIS NEAT 4-4-0 was built in 1876 for Daniel Messmore to Mr. Weston's design. That's probably Mr. Weston in the gangway. This was said to be a very successful locomotive. (Collection of C. A. Brown)

NOTE: *A Mr. Weston—seen on the tender—had Baldwin build this engine in January 1873 to his design. Featured were double valves in each steam chest which Weston claimed enabled his engine to outhaul any other locomotive for her size and weight. The Weston engine ran coal to Amboy, N.J. against Camdon & Amboy engine No. 659 which was similar in size and type. and the Weston engine to quote New York division engineer Martin Lee, "ran all around No. 659." Then they ran the Weston engine against two ten-wheel freight engines just new from Baldwins, Nos. 556 and 569. The Weston engine hauled more cars and made better time.*

After proving herself for a month in the Amboy coal runs, Weston's engine went on the Pennsylvania Railroad running between Harrisburg and Philadelphia. The locomotive then went westward and obscurity in May 1873. According to Martin Lee, this engine burned her smoke, had a vacuum gauge on front of the boiler, and was the first engine ever turned out of Baldwin's with a driver brake on wheels.

Cylinders, 17½" × 24"	Boiler pressure 130 lb.
Drivers, 66"	Tender capacity, Water, 2,800 gallons
	Coal, 10,000 lb.

Regarding reference to D. Messmore, this gentleman probably purchased this locomotive from Weston (whose name prominently appears on the cab sides) and a check on extra orders probably revealed that Messmore requested some spare parts. But I'd be inclined to credit this engine to Mr. Weston's ownership originally. Then again Mr. Messmore may have financed the invention but nothing is available to explain this discrepancy in ownership. My information comes from a former railroader who personally knew Mr. Vauclain and kept accurate records of events "at the time they happened." (Frederick Westing)

LONG ISLAND'S "METEOR", No. 71, made her debut in 1879, and a handsome debutante, too! (Collection of C. A. Brown)

was yesterday placed upon the road for the first time. All her parts had been previously highly finished and fitted together in Mr. Baldwin's factory. She was taken apart on Tuesday, and removed to the Company's depot, and yesterday morning she was completely together, ready for travel. After the regular passenger cars had arrived from Germantown in the afternoon, the tracks being clear, preparation was made for her starting. The placing fire in the furnace and raising steam occupied 20 minutes. The engine (with her tender) moved from the depot in beautiful style, working with great ease and uniformity. She proceeded about half a mile beyond the Union Tavern, at the township line, and returned immediately, a distance of six miles, at a speed of about 28 miles to the hour, her speed having been slackened at all the road crossings, and it being after dark, but a portion of her power was used. It is needless to say that the spectators were delighted. From this experiment there is every reason to believe this engine will draw 30 tons gross, at an average speed of 40 miles an hour, on a level road. The principal superiority of the engine over any of the English ones known consists in the light weight — which is but between four and five tons — her small bulk, and the simplicity of her working machinery. We rejoice at the result of this experiment, as it conclusively shows that Philadelphia, always famous for the skill of her mechanics, is enabled to produce steam engines for railroads combining so many superior qualities as to warrant the belief that her mechanics will hereafter supply nearly all the public works of this description in the country."

On subsequent trials, the "Ironsides" attained a speed of 30 miles per hour, with its usual train attached. So great were the wonder and curiosity which attached to such a prodigy, that people flocked to see the marvel, and eagerly bought the privilege of riding after the strange monster. The officers of the road were not slow to avail themselves of the public interest to increase their passenger receipts, and the advertisement on page 14, from *Poulson's American Daily Advertiser*, of November 26, 1832, will show that as yet they regarded the new machine rather as a curiosity and a bait to allure travel than as a practical every-day servant.

This announcement did not mean that in wet weather horses *would be attached to the locomotive* to aid it in drawing the train, but that the usual horse cars would be employed in making the trips upon the road without the engine.

Upon making the first trip to Germantown with a passenger train with the "Ironsides," one of the drivers slipped upon the axle, causing the wheels to track less than the gauge of the road and drop in between the rails. It was also discovered that the valve arrangement of the pumps was defective, and they failed

to supply the boiler with water. The shifting of the driving wheel upon the axle fastened the eccentric, so that it would not operate in backward motion. These mishaps caused delay, and prevented the engine from reaching its destination, to the great disappointment of all concerned. They were corrected in a few days, and the machine was used in experimenting upon its efficiency, making occasional trips with trains to Germantown. The road had an ascending grade, nearly uniform, of 32 feet per mile, and for the last half mile of 45 feet per mile, and it was found that the engine was too light for the business of the road upon these grades.

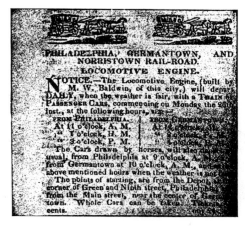

Such was Mr. Baldwin's first locomotive; and it is related of him that his discouragement at the difficulties which he had undergone in building it, and in finally procuring a settlement for it, was such that he remarked to one of his friends, with much decision, "That is our last locomotive."

It was some time before he received an order for another, but meanwhile the subject had become singularly fascinating to him, and occupied his mind so fully that he was eager to work out his new ideas in a tangible form.

FITCHBURG R.R. No. 90, outshopped in 1881 was a straight forward freight hauler for the hills of Western Massachusetts. (Collection of C. A. Brown)

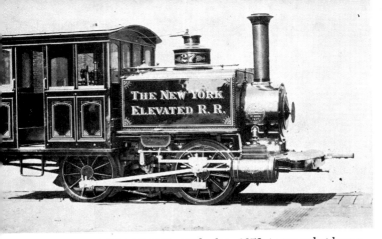

NEW YORK ELEVATED'S No. 27 built in 1878, is somewhat larger in all dimensions than No. 24. (Collection of C. A. Brown)

NEW YORK ELEVATED R.R. No. 24 was a tiny engine for standard gauge tracks. Built in 1878. (Collection of C. A. Brown)

NORTHERN PACIFIC No. 280, delivered in 1883. (Collection of C. A. Brown)

NORFOLK & WESTERN No. 95, Baldwin built in 1883, sported an early Belpaire Firebox. (Collection of C. A. Brown)

CHAPTER II.

EARLY IMPROVEMENTS IN THE LOCOMOTIVE

Shortly after the "Ironsides" had been placed on the Germantown road, Mr. E. L. Miller, of Charleston, S. C., came to Philadelphia and made a careful examination of the machine. Mr. Miller had, in 1830, contracted to furnish a locomotive to the Charleston and Hamburg Railroad Company, and accordingly the engine "Best Friend" had been built under his direction at the West Point Foundry, New York. After inspecting the "Ironsides," he suggested to Mr. Baldwin to visit the Mohawk and Hudson Railroad, and examine an English locomotive which had been placed on that road in July, 1831, by Messrs. Robert Stephenson & Co., of Newcastle, England. It was originally a four-wheeled engine of the "Planet" type, with horizontal cylinders and crank axle. The front wheels of this engine were removed about a year after the machine was put at work, and a four-wheeled swiveling or "bogie" truck substituted. The result of Mr. Baldwin's investigations was the adoption of this design, but with some important improvements. Among these was the "half-crank," which he devised on his return from this trip, and which he patented September 10, 1834. In this form of crank, the outer arm is omitted, and the wrist is fixed in a spoke of the wheel. In other words, the wheel itself formed one arm of the crank. The result sought and gained was that the cranks were strengthened, and, being at the extremities of the axle, the boiler could be made larger in diameter and placed lower. The driving axle could also be placed back of the firebox; the connecting rods passing by the sides of the firebox and taking hold inside of the wheels. This arrangement of the crank also involved the placing of the cylinders outside the smokebox, as was done on the "Ironsides."

By the time the order for the second locomotive was received, Mr. Baldwin had matured this device and was prepared

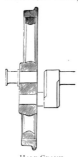

HALF-CRANK

to embody it in practical form. The order came from Mr. E. L. Miller, in behalf of the Charleston and Hamburg Railroad Company, and the engine bore his name, and was completed February 18, 1834. It was on six wheels; one pair being drivers, 54 inches in diameter, with half-crank axle placed back of the firebox as above described, and the four front wheels combined in a swiveling truck. The driving wheels, it should be observed, were cast in solid bell metal. The combined wood and iron wheels used on the "Ironsides" had proved objectionable, and Mr. Baldwin, in his endeavors to find a satisfactory substitute, had recourse to brass. June 29, 1833, he took out a patent for a cast-brass wheel, his idea being that by varying the hardness of the metal the adhesion of the drivers on the rails could be increased or diminished at will. The brass wheels on the "Miller," however, soon wore out, and the experiment with this metal was not repeated. The "E. L. Miller" had cylinders ten inches in diameter; stroke of piston, sixteen inches; and weighed, with water in the boiler, seven tons eight hundred-weight. The boiler had a high dome over the firebox; and this form of construction, it may be noted, was followed, with a few exceptions, for many years.

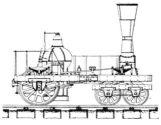

BALDWIN LOCOMOTIVE, 1834

The valve motion was given by a single fixed eccentric for each cylinder. Each eccentric strap had two arms attached to it, one above and the other below, and, as the driving axle was back of the firebox, these arms were prolonged backward under the footboard, with a hook on the inner side of the end of each. The rock shaft had arms above and below its axis, and the hooks of the two rods of each eccentric were moved by hand levers so as to engage with either arm, thus producing backward or forward gear. This form of single eccentric, peculiar to Mr. Baldwin, was in the interest of simplicity in the working parts,

JACKSONVILLE, TAMPA & KEY WEST No. 5 was built in 1884 as a 5'0" gauge locomotive just before the roads in the south converted to the northern standard of 4'8½" gauge. (Collection of C. A. Brown)

and was adhered to for some years. It gave rise to an animated controversy among mechanics as to whether, with its use, it was possible to get a lead on the valve in both directions. Many maintained that this was impracticable; but Mr. Baldwin demonstrated by actual experience that the reverse was the case.

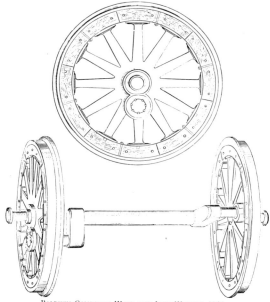

BALDWIN COMPOUND WOOD AND IRON WHEELS, 1834

Meanwhile the Commonwealth of Pennsylvania had given Mr. Baldwin an order for a locomotive for the State Road, as it was then called, from Philadelphia to Columbia, which, up to that time, had been worked by horses. This engine, called the "Lancaster," was completed in June, 1834. It was similar to the "Miller," and weighed 17,000 pounds. After it was placed in service, the records show that it hauled at one time nineteen loaded burden cars over the highest grades between Philadelphia

and Columbia. This was characterized at that time by the officers of the road as an "unprecedented performance." The success of the machine on its trial trips was such that the Legislature decided to adopt steam power for working the road, and Mr. Baldwin received orders for several additional locomotives. Two others were accordingly delivered to the State in September and November respectively of that year, and one was also built and delivered to the Philadelphia and Trenton Railroad Company during the same season. This latter engine, which was put in service October 21, 1834, averaged 21,000 miles per year to September 15, 1840.

Five locomotives were thus completed in 1834, and the new business was fairly under way. The building in Lodge Alley, to which Mr. Baldwin had removed from Minor Street, and where these engines were constructed, began to be found too contracted, and another removal was decided upon. A location on Broad and Hamilton Streets (the site, in part, of the present works) was selected, and a three-story L-shaped brick building, fronting on both streets, erected. This was completed and the business removed to it during the following year (1835). Mr. Baldwin's stationary engine, described on page 8, was placed in service in the new shop by Mr. Andrew C. Vauclain, father of Mr. Samuel M. Vauclain, who is now President of the Company. The original building was partially destroyed by fire in 1884, and was replaced by a four-story brick structure.

These early locomotives, built in 1834, were the types of Mr. Baldwin's practice for some years. All, or nearly all of them, embraced several important devices, which were the results of his study and experiments up to that time. The devices referred to were patented September 10, 1834, and the same patent covered the following four inventions, *viz.*:

1. The half-crank, and method of attaching it to the driving wheel. (This has already been described.)

2. A new mode of constructing the wheels of locomotive engines and cars. In this the hub and spokes were of cast iron, cast together. The spokes were cast without a rim, and terminated in segment flanges, each spoke having a separate flange disconnected from its neighbors. By this means, it was claimed,

THE "NIP AND N" (New York, Philadelphia and Norfolk) was a subsidiary of the Pennsylvania R.R., but had its own motive power identity when No. 7 was built in 1884, to standard PRR designs. (Collection of C. A. Brown)

the injurious effect of the unequal expansion of the materials composing the wheels was lessened or altogether prevented. The flanges bore against wooden felloes, made in two thicknesses, and put together so as to break joints. Tenons or pins projected from the flanges into openings made in the wooden felloes, to keep them in place. Around the whole the tire was passed and secured by bolts. The sketch on page 17 shows the device.

3. A new mode of forming the joints of steam and other tubes. This was Mr. Baldwin's invention of ground joints for steam pipes, which was a very valuable improvement over previous methods of making joints with red-lead packing, and which rendered it possible to carry a much higher pressure of steam.

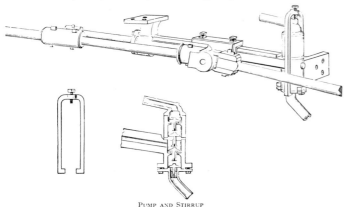

PUMP AND STIRRUP

4. A new mode of forming the joints and other parts of the supply pump, and of locating the pump itself. This invention consisted in making the single guide bar hollow and using it for the pump barrel. The pump plunger was attached to the piston rod at a socket or sleeve formed for the purpose, and the hollow guide bar terminated in the vertical pump chamber. This chamber was made in two pieces, joined about midway between the induction and eduction pipes. This joint was ground steam-tight, as were also the joints of the induction pipe with the

bottom of the lower chamber, and the flange of the eduction pipe with the top of the upper chamber. All these parts were held together by a stirrup with a set-screw in its arched top, and the arrangement was such that by simply unscrewing this set-screw the different sections of the chamber, with all the valves, could be taken apart for cleaning or adjusting. The cut on page 19 illustrates the device.

It is probable that the five engines built during 1834 embodied all, or nearly all, these devices. They all had the half-crank, the ground joints for steam pipes (which were first made by Mr. Baldwin in 1833), and the pump formed in the guide bar, and all had the four-wheeled truck in front, and a single pair of drivers back of the firebox. On this position of the driving wheels Mr. Baldwin laid great stress, as it made a more even distribution of the weight, throwing about one-half on the drivers and one-half on the four-wheeled truck. It also extended the wheel base, making the engine much steadier and less damaging to the track. Mr. William Norris, who had established a locomotive works in Philadelphia in 1832, was at this time building a six-wheeled engine with a truck in front and the driving wheels placed in front of the firebox. Considerable rivalry naturally existed between the two manufacturers as to the comparative merits of their respective plans. In Mr. Norris's engine, the position of the driving axle in front of the firebox threw on it more of the weight of the engine, and thus increased the adhesion and the tractive power. Mr. Baldwin, however, maintained the superiority of his plan, as giving a better distribution of the weight and a longer wheel base, and consequently rendering the machine less destructive to the track. As the iron rails then in use were generally light, and much of the track was of wood, this feature was of some importance.

To the use of the ground joint for steam pipes, however, much of the success of his early engines was due. The English builders were making locomotives with canvas and red-lead joints, permitting a steam pressure of only 60 pounds per square inch to be carried, while Mr. Baldwin's machines were worked at 120 pounds with ease. Several locomotives imported from England at about this period by the Commonwealth of Pennsylvania

THE GOVERNMENT OF QUEENSLAND took delivery of this 3'6" 4-4-0 with the odd visored roof in 1885. (Collection of C. A. Brown)

for the State Road, which were built by Robert Stephenson & Co., had canvas and red-lead joints, and their efficiency was so much less than that of the Baldwin engines, on account of this and other features of construction, that they were soon laid aside or sold.

In June, 1834, a patent was issued to Mr. E. L. Miller, by whom Mr. Baldwin's second engine was ordered, for a method of increasing the adhesion of a locomotive by throwing a part of the weight of the tender on the rear of the engine, thus increasing the weight on the drivers. Mr. Baldwin adopted this device on an engine built for the Philadelphia and Trenton Railroad Company, May, 1835, and thereafter used it largely, paying $100 royalty for each engine. Eventually (May 6, 1839) he bought the patent for $9,000, evidently considering that the device was especially valuable, if not indispensable, in order to render his engine as powerful, when required, as other patterns having the driving wheels in front of the firebox, and therefore utilizing more of the weight of the engine for adhesion.

In making the truck and tender wheels of these early locomotives, the hubs were cast in three pieces and afterward banded with wrought iron, the interstices being filled with spelter. This method of construction was adopted on account of the difficulty then found in casting a chilled wheel in one solid piece.

Early in 1835, the new shop on Broad Street was completed and occupied. Mr. Baldwin's attention was thenceforward given to locomotive building exclusively, except that a stationary engine was occasionally constructed.

In May, 1835, his eleventh locomotive, the "Black Hawk," was delivered to the Philadelphia and Trenton Railroad Company. This was the first outside connected engine of his build. It was also the first engine on which the Miller device of attaching part of the weight of the tender to the engine was employed. On the eighteenth engine, the "Brandywine," built for the Philadelphia and Columbia Railroad Company, brass tires were used on the driving wheels, for the purpose of obtaining more adhesion; but they wore out rapidly and were replaced with iron.

April 3, 1835, Mr. Baldwin took out a patent for certain improvements in the wheels and tubes of locomotive engines. That relating to the wheels provided for casting the hub and spokes together, and having the spokes terminate in segments of a rim, as described in his patent of September 10, 1834. Between the ends of the spokes and the tires, wood was interposed, and the tire might be either of wrought iron or of chilled cast iron. The intention was expressed of making the tire usually of cast iron chilled. The main object, however, was declared to be the interposition between the spokes and the rim of a layer of wood or other substance possessing some degree of elasticity. This method of making driving wheels was followed for several years, the tires being made with a shoulder, as illustrated below.

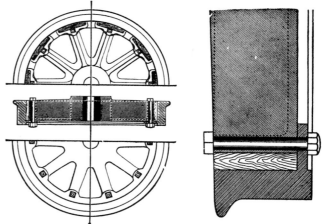

DRIVING WHEELS, PATENTED SEPTEMBER, 1834

The improvement in locomotive tubes consisted in driving a copper ferrule or thimble on the outside of the end of the tube, and soldering it in place, instead of driving a ferrule into the tube as had previously been the practice. The object of the latter method had been to make a tight joint with the tube sheet; but by putting the ferrule on the outside of the tube, not only was the joint made as tight as before, but the tube was strengthened, and left unobstructed throughout to the full extent of its diam-

THE R.F. AND P. didn't always have big engines. No. 18 did the honors between Richmond and Washington starting in 1885. (Collection of C. A. Brown)

eter. This method of setting tubes has been generally followed in the Works from that date to the present, the only difference being that, at this time, with iron or steel tubes, the end is swedged down, the copper ferrule brazed on, and the end of the tube turned or riveted over against the copper thimble and the flue sheet to make the joint perfect.

Fourteen engines were constructed in 1835; 40 in 1836; 40 in 1837; 23 in 1838; 26 in 1839, and nine in 1840. During all these years the general design continued the same; but, in compliance with the demand for more power, three sizes were furnished, as follows:

First class—Cylinders, 12½"×16"; weight loaded, 26,000 pounds.
Second class—   "   12" ×16";   "   "   23,000   "
Third class—   "   10½"×16";   "   "   20,000   "

Mr. Baldwin fully believed, in 1838, that the first class engine was as heavy as would be called for, and he declared that it was as large as he intended to build. Most of the engines had the half-crank, but occasionally an outside-connected machine was turned out. These latter, however, failed to give as complete satisfaction as the half-crank machine. The drivers were generally 54 inches in diameter.

A patent was issued to Mr. Baldwin, August 17, 1835, for his device of cylindrical pedestals. In this method of construction, the pedestal was of cast iron, and was bored in a lathe so as to form two concave jaws. The boxes were also turned in a lathe so that their vertical ends were cylindrical, and they were thus fitted in the pedestals. This method of fitting up pedestals and boxes was cheap and effective, and was used for some years for the driving and tender wheels.

As showing the estimation in which these early engines were held, it may not be out of place to refer to the opinions of some of the railroad managers of that period.

Mr. L. A. Sykes, engineer of the New Jersey Transportation Company, under date of June 12, 1838, wrote that he could draw with his engines 20 four-wheeled cars with 26 passengers each, at a speed of 20 to 25 miles per hour, over grades of 26 feet per mile. "As to simplicity of construction," he adds, "small liability to get out of order, economy of repairs, and ease to the road, I fully believe Mr. Baldwin's engines stand unrivalled. I consider the simplicity of the engine, the arrangement of the working parts, and the distribution of the weight, far superior to any engine I have ever seen, either of American or English manufacture, and I have not the least hesitation in saying that Mr. Baldwin's engine will do the same amount of work with much less repairs, either to the engine or the track, than any other engine in use."

L. G. Cannon, President of the Rensselaer and Saratoga Railroad Company, writes: "Your engines will, in performance and cost of repairs, bear comparison with any other engine made in this or any other country."

Some of Mr. Baldwin's engines on the State Road, in 1837, cost, for repairs, only from 1.2 to 1.6 cents per mile. It is noted that the engine "West Chester," on the same road, weighing 20,735 pounds (10,475 on drivers), drew 51 cars (four-wheeled), weighing 289 net tons, over the road, some of the track being of wood covered with strap-rail.

The financial difficulties of 1836 and 1837, which brought ruin upon so many, did not leave Mr. Baldwin unscathed. His embarrassments became so great that he was unable to proceed, and was forced to call his creditors together for a settlement. After offering to surrender all his property, his shop, tools, house and everything, if they so desired—all of which would realize only about 25 per cent. of their claims—he proposed to them that they should permit him to go on with the business, and in three years he would pay the full amount of all claims, principal and interest. This was finally acceded to, and the promise was in effect fulfilled, although not without an extension of two years beyond the time originally proposed.

In May, 1837, the number of hands employed was 300, but this number was reduced weekly, owing to the falling off in the demand for engines.

These financial troubles had their effect on the demand for locomotives, as will be seen in the decrease in the number built in 1838, 1839 and 1840; and this result was furthered by the establishment of several other locomotive works, and the introduction of other patterns of engines.

NO. 94 WAS BUILT for the Wisconsin Central Lines in 1886. She later became Chicago & Great Western 624, and finally ended up on the Baltimore and Ohio. (Collection of C. A. Brown)

The changes and improvements in details made during these years may be summed up as follows:

The subject of burning anthracite coal had engaged much attention. In October, 1836, Mr. Baldwin secured a patent for a grate or fireplace which could be detached from the engine at pleasure, and a new one with a fresh coal fire substituted. The intention was to have the grate with freshly ignited coal all ready for the engine on its arrival at a station, and placed between the rails over suitable levers, by which it could be attached quickly to the firebox. It is needless to say that this was never practiced. In January, 1838, however, Mr. Baldwin was experimenting with the consumption of coal on the Germantown road, and in July of the same year the records show that he was making a locomotive to burn coal, part of the arrangement being to blow the fire with a fan.

The first locomotives for export were built during this year. They were shipped to Cuba, to the order of Alfred Cruger, and bore the builder's numbers 104 and 105. These locomotives were completed in the spring and summer, and were followed by a third later in the year.

Up to 1838, Mr. Baldwin had made both driving and truck wheels with wrought tires, but during that year chilled wheels for engine and tender trucks were adopted. His tires were furnished by Messrs. S. Vail & Son, Morristown, N. J., who made the only tires then obtainable in America. They were very thin, being only one inch to 1½ inches thick; and Mr. Baldwin, in importing some tires from England at that time, insisted on their being made double the ordinary thickness. The manufacturers at first objected and ridiculed the idea, the practice being to use two tires when extra thickness was wanted, but finally they consented to meet his requirements.

All his engines thus far had the single eccentric for each valve, but at about this period double eccentrics were adopted, each terminating in a straight hook, and reversed by hand levers.

At this early period, Mr. Baldwin had begun to feel the necessity of making all like parts of locomotives of the same class in such manner as to be absolutely interchangeable. Steps were taken in this direction, but it was not until many years afterward that the system of standard gauges was perfected, which became a distinguishing feature in the establishment.

In March, 1839, Mr. Baldwin's records show that he was building a number of outside-connected engines, and had succeeded in making them strong and durable. He was also making a new chilled wheel, and one which he thought would not break.

On the 136th locomotive, completed October 18, 1839, for the Philadelphia, Germantown and Norristown Railroad, the old pattern of wooden frame was abandoned, and no outside frame whatever was employed—the machinery, as well as the truck and the pedestals of the driving axles, being attached directly to the naked boiler. The wooden frame thenceforward disappeared gradually, and an iron frame took its place. Another innovation was the adoption of eight-wheeled tenders, the first of which was built at about this period.

On April 8, 1839, Mr. Baldwin associated with himself Messrs. Vail & Hufty, and the business was conducted under the firm name of Baldwin, Vail & Hufty until 1841, when Mr. Hufty withdrew, and Baldwin & Vail continued the copartnership until 1842.

THE P & NY RR went into the Lehigh Valley after this 4-8-0 was delivered by Baldwin in 1887. (Collection of C. A. Brown)

CHAPTER III.

INCREASING LOCOMOTIVE CAPACITY

The time had now arrived when the increase of business on railroads demanded more powerful locomotives. It had for some years been felt that for freight traffic the engine with one pair of drivers was insufficient. Mr. Baldwin's engine had the single pair of drivers placed back of the firebox; that made by Mr. Norris, one pair in front of the firebox. An engine with two pairs of drivers, one pair in front and one pair behind the firebox, was the next logical step, and Mr. Henry R. Campbell, of Philadelphia, was the first to carry this design into execution. Mr. Campbell was the Chief Engineer of the Germantown Railroad when the "Ironsides" was placed on that line, and had since given much attention to the subject of locomotive construction. February 5, 1836, Mr. Campbell secured a patent for an eight-wheeled engine with four drivers connected, and a four-wheeled truck in front; and subsequently contracted with James Brooks, of Philadelphia, to build for him such a machine. The work was begun March 16, 1836, and the engine was completed May 8, 1837. This was the first eight-wheeled engine of this design, and from it the American type of locomotive of today takes its origin. The engine lacked, however, one essential feature; there were no equalizing beams between the drivers, and nothing but the ordinary steel springs over each journal of the driving axles to equalize the weight upon them. It remained for Messrs. Eastwick & Harrison to supply this deficiency; and in 1837 that firm constructed at their shop in Philadelphia, a locomotive on this plan, but with the driving axles running in a separate square frame, connected to the main frame above it by a single central bearing on each side. This engine had 12 x 18-inch cylinders and four coupled driving wheels 44 inches in diameter, carrying eight of the twelve tons constituting the total weight. Subsequently, Mr. Joseph Harrison, Jr., of the same firm, substituted "equalizing beams" on engines of this plan afterward constructed by them, substantially in the same manner as since generally employed.

In the *American Railroad Journal* of July 30, 1836, a woodcut showing Mr. Campbell's engine, together with an elaborate calculation of the effective power of an engine on this plan, by William J. Lewis, Esq., Civil Engineer, was published, with a table showing its performance upon grades ranging from a dead level to a rise of 100 feet per mile. Mr. Campbell stated that his experience at that time (1835-36) convinced him that grades of 100 feet rise per mile would, if roads were judiciously located, carry railroads over any of the mountain passes in America, without the use of planes with stationary steam power, or, as a general rule, of costly tunnels—an opinion very extensively verified by the experience of the country since that date.

A step had thus been taken toward a plan of locomotive having more adhesive power. Mr. Baldwin, however, was slow to adopt the new design. He naturally regarded innovations with distrust. He had done much to perfect the old pattern of engine, and had built over 100 of them, which were in successful operation on various railroads. Many of the details were the subjects of his several patents, and had been greatly simplified in his practice. In fact, simplicity in all the working parts had been so largely his aim, that it was natural that he should distrust any plan involving additional machinery, and he regarded the new design as only an experiment at best. In November, 1838, he wrote to a correspondent that he did not think there was any advantage in the eight-wheeled engine. There being three points in contact, it could not turn a curve, he argued, without slipping one or the other pair of wheels sideways. Another objection was in the multiplicity of machinery and the difficulty in maintaining four driving wheels all of exactly the same size. Some means, however, of getting more adhesion must be had, and the result of his reflections upon this subject was the project of a "geared engine." In August, 1839, he took steps to secure a patent for such a machine, and December 31, 1840, letters patent were granted him for the device. In this engine an independent shaft or axle was placed between the two axles of the truck, and connected by cranks and coupling rods with cranks on the outside of the driving wheels. This shaft had a central cog-wheel engaging on each side with intermediate

CALIFORNIA SOUTHERN No. 15 was built in 1887. (Collection of C. A. Brown)

cog-wheels, which in turn geared into cog-wheels on each truck axle. The intermediate cog-wheels had wide teeth, so that the truck could pivot while the main shaft remained parallel with the driving axle. The diameters of the cog-wheels were, of course, in such proportion to the driving and truck wheels that the latter should revolve as much oftener than the drivers as their smaller size might require. Of the success of this machine for freight service, Mr. Baldwin was very sanguine. One was put in hand at once, completed in August, 1841, and eventually sold to the Sugarloaf Coal Company. It was an inside-connected engine, weighing 30,000 pounds, of which 11,775 pounds were on the drivers, and 18,335 on the truck. The driving wheels were 44 and the truck wheels 33 inches in diameter. The cylinders were 13 inches in diameter by 16 inches stroke. On a trial of the engine upon the Philadelphia and Reading Railroad, it hauled 590 tons from Reading to Philadelphia—a distance of 54 miles—in five hours and 22 minutes. The superintendent of the road, in writing of the trial, remarked that this train was unprecedented in length and weight both in America and Europe. The performance was noticed in favorable terms by the Philadelphia newspapers, and was made the subject of a report by the Committee on Science and Arts of the Franklin Institute, who strongly recommended this plan of engine for freight service. The success of the trial led Mr. Baldwin at first to believe that the geared engine would be generally adopted for freight traffic; but in this he was disappointed. No further demand was made for such machines, and no more of them were built.

In 1840, Mr. Baldwin received an order, through August Belmont, Esq., of New York, for a locomotive for Austria, and had nearly completed one which was calculated to do the work required, when he learned that only 60 pounds pressure of steam was admissible, whereas his engine was designed to use steam at 100 pounds and over. He accordingly constructed another, meeting this requirement, and shipped it in the following year. This engine, it may be noted, had a kind of link motion, agreeably to the specification received, and was the first of his make upon which the link was introduced.

Mr. Baldwin's patent of December 31, 1840, already referred to as covering his geared engine, embraced several other devices, as follows:

1. A method of operating a fan, or blowing wheel, for the purpose of blowing the fire. The fan was to be placed under the footboard, and driven by the friction of a grooved pulley in contact with the flange of the driving wheel.

2. The substitution of a metallic stuffing consisting of wire, for the hemp, wool, or other material which had been employed in stuffing boxes.

3. The placing of springs of the engine truck so as to obviate the evil of the locking of the wheels when the truck frame vibrates from the center pin vertically. Spiral as well as semi-elliptic springs, placed at each end of the truck frame, were specified. The spiral spring is described as received in two cups, one above and one below. The cups were connected together at their centers, by a pin upon one and a socket in the other, so that the cups could approach toward or recede from each other and still preserve their parallelism.

4. An improvement in the manner of constructing the iron frames of locomotives, by making the pedestals in one piece with, and constituting part of, the frames.

5. The employment of spiral springs in connection with cylindrical pedestals and boxes. A single spiral was at first used, but, not proving sufficiently strong, a combination or nest of spirals curving alternately in opposite directions was afterward employed. Each spiral had its bearing in a spiral recess in the pedestal.

In the specification of this patent a change in the method of making cylindrical pedestals and boxes is noted. Instead of boring and turning them in a lathe, they were cast to the required shape in chills. This method of construction was used for a time, but eventually a return was made to the original plan, as giving a more accurate job.

In 1842, Mr. Baldwin constructed, under an arrangement with Mr. Ross Winans, three locomotives for the Western Railroad of Massachusetts, on a plan which had been designed by that gentleman for freight traffic. These machines had upright

CENTRAL VERMONT No. 99, class of 1887. (Collection of C. A. Brown)

boilers and horizontal cylinders, which worked cranks on a shaft bearing cog-wheels engaging with other cog-wheels on an intermediate shaft. This latter shaft had cranks coupled to four driving wheels on each side. These engines were constructed to burn anthracite coal. Their peculiarly uncouth appearance earned for them the name of "crabs," and they were but short-lived in service.

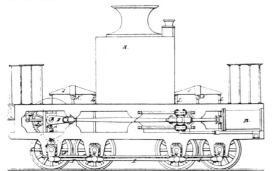

WINANS' LOCOMOTIVE, AS BUILT FOR WESTERN RAILROAD OF MASSACHUSETTS, 1842
(From the Original Patent Specification)

But to return to the progress of Mr. Baldwin's locomotive practice. Only eight engines were built in 1841. The geared engine had not proved a success. It was unsatisfactory, as well to its designer as to the railroad community. The problem of utilizing more or all of the weight of the engine for adhesion remained, in Mr. Baldwin's view, yet to be solved. The plan of coupling four or six wheels had long before been adopted in England, but on the short curves prevalent on American railroads he felt that something more was necessary. The wheels must not only be coupled, but at the same time must be free to adapt themselves to a curve. These two conditions were apparently incompatible, and to reconcile these inconsistencies was the task which Mr. Baldwin set himself to accomplish. He undertook it, too, at a time when his business had fallen off greatly and he was involved in the most serious financial embarrassments. The problem was constantly before him, and at length, during a

sleepless night, its solution flashed across his mind. The plan so long sought for, and which subsequently, more than any other of his improvements or inventions, contributed to the foundation of his fortune, was his well-known six-wheels-connected locomo-

BALDWIN SIX-WHEELS-CONNECTED LOCOMOTIVE, 1842

tive with the four front drivers combined in a flexible truck. For this machine Mr. Baldwin secured a patent, August 25, 1842. Its principal characteristic features are now matters of history, but they deserve here a brief mention. The engine was on six wheels, all connected as drivers. The rear wheels were placed rigidly in the frames, usually behind the firebox, with inside

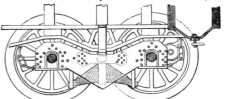

BALDWIN FLEXIBLE BEAM TRUCK, 1842—ELEVATION

bearings. The cylinders were inclined, and with outside connections. The four remaining wheels had inside journals running in boxes held by two wide and deep wrought-iron beams, one on each side. These beams were unconnected, and entirely independ-

PHILADELPHIA & READING No. 965 was rather typical of the passenger engines built in the late eighties. (Collection of C. A. Brown)

ent of each other. The pedestals formed in them were bored out cylindrically, and into them cylindrical boxes, as patented by him in 1835, were fitted. The engine frame on each side was directly over the beam, and a spherical pin, running down from the frame, bore in a socket in the beam midway between the two axles. It will thus be seen that each side beam independently could turn horizontally or vertically under the spherical pin, and the cylindrical boxes could also turn in the pedestals. Hence, in passing a curve, the middle pair of drivers could move laterally in one

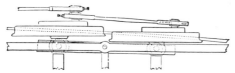

BALDWIN FLEXIBLE BEAM TRUCK, 1842—HALF PLAN

direction—say to the right—while the front pair could move in the opposite direction, or to the left; the two axles all the while remaining parallel to each other and to the rear driving axle. The operation of these beams was therefore like that of the parallel ruler. On a straight line the two beams and the two axles formed a rectangle; on curves, a parallelogram, the angles varying with the degree of curvature. The coupling rods were made with cylindrical brasses, thus forming ball-and-socket joints, to enable them to accommodate themselves to the lateral movements of the wheels. Colburn, in his "Locomotive Engineering," remarks of this arrangement of rods as follows:

"Geometrically, no doubt, this combination of wheels could only work properly around curves by a lengthening and shortening of the rods which served to couple the principal pair of driving wheels with the hind truck wheels. But if the coupling rods from the principal pair of driving wheels be five feet long, and if the beams of the truck frame be four feet long (the radius of curve described by the axle boxes around the spherical side bearings being two feet), then the total corresponding lengthening of the coupling rods, in order to allow the hind truck wheels to move one inch to one side, and the front wheels of the truck one inch to the other side of their normal position on a straight line would be $\sqrt{60^2+1^2}-60+24-\sqrt{24^2-1^2}=0.0275$ inch, or less than 1/32-inch. And if only one pair of driving wheels were thus coupled with a four-wheeled truck, the total wheel base being nine feet, the motion

permitted by this slight elongation of the coupling rods (an elongation provided for by a trifling slackness in the brasses) would enable three pairs of wheels to stand without binding in a curve of only 100 feet radius."

The first engine of the new plan was finished early in December, 1842, being one of fourteen engines constructed in that year, and was sent to the Georgia Railroad, on the order of Mr. J. Edgar Thomson, then Chief Engineer and Superintendent of that line. It weighed twelve tons, and drew, besides its own weight, 250 tons up a grade of 36 feet to the mile.

Other orders soon followed. The new machine was received generally with great favor. The loads hauled by it exceeded anything so far known in American railroad practice, and sagacious managers hailed it as a means of largely reducing operating expenses. On the Central Railroad of Georgia, one of these 12-ton engines drew 19 eight-wheeled cars, with 750 bales of cotton, each bale weighing 450 pounds, over maximum grades of 30 feet per mile; and the manager of the road declared that it could readily take 1,000 bales. On the Philadelphia and Reading Railroad a similar engine of 18 tons weight drew 150 loaded cars (total weight of cars and lading, 1,130 tons) from Schuylkill Haven to Philadelphia, at a speed of seven miles per hour. The regular load was 100 loaded cars, which were hauled at a speed of from twelve to fifteen miles per hour on a level.

The following extract from a letter, dated August 10, 1844, of Mr. G. A. Nicolls, then superintendent of that line, gives the particulars of the performance of these machines, and shows the estimation in which they were held:

"We have had two of these engines in operation for about four weeks. Each engine weighs about 40,000 pounds with water and fuel, equally distributed on six wheels, all of which are coupled, thus gaining the whole adhesion of the engine's weight. Their cylinders are 15 by 18 inches.

"The daily allotted load of each of these engines is 100 coal cars, each loaded with 3.6 tons of coal, and weighing 2.15 tons each, empty; making a net weight of 360 tons of coal carried, and a gross weight of train of 575 tons, all of 2,240 pounds.

"This train is hauled over the 94 miles of the road, half of which is level, at the rate of 12 miles per hour; and with it the engine is able to make 14 to 15 miles per hour on a level.

"Were all the cars on the road of sufficient strength, and making the trip by daylight, nearly one-half being now performed at night, I have no

LARGE BOILERED 4-4-0 built for the New Haven in 1888. She later was renumbered 1405. (Collection of C. A. Brown)

doubt of these engines being quite equal to a load of 800 tons gross, as their average daily performance on any of the levels of our road, some of which are eight miles long.

"In strength of make, quality of workmanship, finish, and proportion of parts, I consider them equal to any, and superior to most, freight engines I have seen. They are remarkably easy on the rails, either in their vertical or horizontal action, from the equalization of their weight, and the improved truck under the forward part of the engine. This latter adapts itself to all the curves of the road, including some of 716 feet radius in the main track, and moves with great ease around our turning Y curves at Richmond, of about 300 feet radius.

"I consider these engines as near perfection, in the arrangement of their parts, and their general efficiency, as the present improvements in machinery and the locomotive engine will admit of. They are saving us 30 per cent. in every trip on the former cost of motive or engine power."

But the flexible beam truck also enabled Mr. Baldwin to meet the demand for an engine with four drivers connected. Other builders were making engines with four drivers and a four-wheeled truck, of the present American standard type. To compete with this design, Mr. Baldwin modified his six-wheels-connected engine by connecting only two of the three pairs of wheels as drivers, making the forward wheels of smaller diameter as leading wheels, but combining them with the front drivers in a flexible beam truck. The first engine on this plan was sent to the Erie and Kalamazoo Railroad, in October, 1843, and gave great satisfaction. The superintendent of the road was enthusiastic in its praise, and wrote to Mr. Baldwin that he doubted "if anything could be got up which would answer the business of the road so well." One was also sent to the Utica and Schenectady Railroad a few weeks later, of which the superintendent remarked that "it worked beautifully, and there were not wagons enough to give it a full load." In this plan the leading wheels were usually made 36 and the drivers 54 inches in diameter.

This machine, of course, came in competition with the eight-wheeled engine having four drivers, and Mr. Baldwin claimed for his plan a decided superiority. In each case about two-thirds of the total weight was carried on the four drivers, and Mr. Baldwin maintained that his engine, having only six instead of eight wheels, was simpler and more effective.

At about this period Mr. Baldwin's attention was called by Mr. Levi Bissell to an "Air-spring" which the latter had devised, and which it was imagined was destined to be a cheap, effective, and perpetual spring. The device consisted of a small cylinder placed above the frame over the axle box, and having a piston fitted air-tight into it. The piston rod was to bear on the axle box and the proper quantity of air was to be pumped into the cylinder above the piston, and the cylinder then hermetically closed. The piston had a leather packing which was to be kept moist by some fluid (molasses was proposed) previously introduced into the cylinder. Mr. Baldwin at first proposed to equalize the weight between the two pairs of drivers by connecting two air springs on each side by a pipe, the use of an equalizing beam being covered by Messrs. Eastwick & Harrison's patent. The air springs were found, however, not to work practically, and were never applied. It may be added that a model of an equalizing air spring was exhibited by Mr. Joseph Harrison, Jr., at the Franklin Institute, in 1838 or 1839.

With the introduction of the new machine, business began at once to revive, and the tide of prosperity turned once more in Mr. Baldwin's favor. Twelve engines were constructed in 1843, all but four of them of the new pattern; 22 engines in 1844, all of the new pattern; and 27 in 1845. Three of this number were of the old type, with one pair of drivers, but from that time forward the old pattern with the single pair of drivers disappeared from the practice of the establishment, save occasionally for exceptional purposes.

In 1842, the partnership with Mr. Vail was dissolved, and Mr. Asa Whitney, who had been superintendent of the Mohawk and Hudson Railroad, became a partner with Mr. Baldwin, and the firm continued as Baldwin & Whitney until 1846, when the latter withdrew to engage in the manufacture of car wheels, establishing the firm of A. Whitney & Sons, Philadelphia.

Mr. Whitney brought to the firm a railroad experience and thorough business talent. He introduced a system in many details of the management of the business, which Mr. Baldwin, whose mind was devoted more exclusively to mechanical subjects, had failed to establish or wholly ignored. The method at

PHILADELPHIA & READING 955 was a back cab consolidation built for the coal carrier in 1888. (Collection of C. A. Brown)

present in use in the establishment, of giving to each class of locomotives a distinctive designation, composed of a number and a letter, originated very shortly after Mr. Whitney's connection with the business. For the purpose of representing the different designs, sheets with engravings of locomotives were employed. The sheet showing the engine with one pair of drivers was marked B; that with two pairs, C; that with three, D; and that with four, E. Taking its rise from this circumstance, it became customary to designate as B engines those with one pair of drivers; as C engines, those with two pairs; as D engines, those with three pairs; and as E engines, those with four pairs. Shortly afterward, a number, indicating the weight in gross tons, was added. Thus the 12 D engine was one with three pairs of drivers and weighing twelve tons; the 12 C, an engine of same weight, but with only four wheels connected. A modification of this method of designating the several plans and sizes is still in use.

It will be observed that the classification as thus established began with the B engines. The letter A was reserved for an engine intended to run at very high speeds, and so designed that the driving wheels should make two revolutions for each reciprocation of the pistons. This was to be accomplished by means of gearing. The general plan of the engine was determined in Mr. Baldwin's mind, but was never carried into execution.

The adoption of the plan of six-wheels-connected engines opened the way at once to increasing their size. The weight being almost evenly distributed on six points, heavier machines were admissible, the weight on any one pair of drivers being little, if any, greater than had been the practice with the old plan of engine having a single pair of drivers. Hence, engines of 18 and 20 tons weight were shortly introduced, and in 1844, three of 20 tons weight, with cylinders 16½ inches diameter by 18 inches stroke, were constructed for the Western Railroad of Massachusetts, and six of 18 tons weight, previously referred to on page 34, for the Philadelphia and Reading Railroad. It should be noted that three of these latter engines had iron tubes. This was the first instance in which Mr. Baldwin had employed tubes of this material, although they had been previously used

by others. Lap-welded iron tubes were made by Morris, Tasker & Co., of Philadelphia, about 1838, and butt-welded iron tubes had previously been made by the same firm. Ross Winans, of Baltimore, had also made iron tubes by hand for locomotives of his manufacture, before 1838. The advantage found to result from the use of iron tubes, apart from their less cost, was that the tubes and boiler shell, being of the same material, expanded and contracted alike, while in the case of copper tubes, the expansion of the metal by heat varied from that of the boiler shell, and as a consequence there was greater liability to leakage at the joints with the tube sheets. The opinion prevailed largely at that time that some advantage resulted in the evaporation of water, owing to the superiority of copper as a conductor of heat. To determine this question, an experiment was tried with two of the six engines referred to above, one of which, the "Ontario," had copper tubes, and another, the "New England," iron tubes. In other respects they were precisely alike. The two engines were run from Richmond to Mount Carbon, August 27, 1844, each drawing a train of 101 empty cars, and returning from Mount Carbon to Richmond on the following day, each with 100 loaded cars. The quantity of water evaporated and wood consumed was noted, with the result shown in the following table:

	Up Trip, Aug. 27, 1844		Down Trip, Aug. 28, 1844	
	"Ontario" (Copper Tubes)	"New England" (Iron Tubes)	"Ontario" (Copper Tubes)	"New England" (Iron Tubes)
Time, running	9h. 7m.	7h. 41m.	10h. 44m.	8h. 19m.
Time, standing at stations	4h. 2m.	3h. 7m.	2h. 12m.	3h. 8m.
Cords of wood burned	6.68	5.50	6.94	6.00
Cubic feet of water evaporated	925.75	757.26	837.46	656.39
Ratio, cubic feet of water to a cord of wood	138.57	137.68	120.67	109.39

The conditions of the experiments not being absolutely the same in each case, the results could not of course be accepted as entirely accurate. They seemed to show, however, no considerable difference in the evaporative efficiency of copper and iron tubes.

NO. 440 WAS A HANDSOME ten-wheeler built for the Northern Pacific, in 1888. (Collection of C. A. Brown)

The period under consideration was marked also by the introduction of the French & Baird stack, which proved at once to be one of the most successful spark arresters thus far employed, and which was for years used almost exclusively wherever, as on the cotton-carrying railroads of the South, a thoroughly effective spark arrester was required. This stack was introduced by Mr. Baird, then a foreman in the Works, who purchased the patent right of what had been known as the Grimes stack, and combined with it some of the features of the stack made by Mr. Richard French, then Master Mechanic of the Germantown Railroad, together with certain improvements of his own. The cone over the straight inside pipe was made with volute flanges on its under side, which gave a rotary motion to the sparks. Around the cone was a casing about six inches smaller in diameter than the outside stack. Apertures were cut in the sides of the casing, through which the sparks in their rotary motion were discharged, and thus fell to the bottom of the space between the straight inside pipe and the outside stack. The opening in the top of the stack was fitted with a series of V-shaped iron circles perforated with numerous holes, thus presenting an enlarged area, through which the smoke escaped. The patent right for this stack was subsequently sold to Messrs. Radley & Hunter, and its essential principle is still used in the Radley & Hunter stack. The Rushton wood-burning stack, as now built, is a further improvement on the Radley & Hunter, in that the design has been simplified, the draft obstruction reduced, and the stack made more effective as a spark arrester.

During the year 1844 another important feature in locomotive construction—the cut-off valve—was added to Mr. Baldwin's practice. Up to that time the valve motion had been the two eccentrics, with the single flat hook for each cylinder. Since 1841, Mr. Baldwin had contemplated the addition of some device allowing the steam to be used expansively, and he now added the "half-stroke cut-off." In this device the steam chest was separated by a horizontal plate into an upper and a lower compartment. In the upper compartment, a valve, worked by a separate eccentric, and having a single opening, admitted steam through a port in this plate to the lower steam chamber. The

valve rod of the upper valve terminated in a notch or hook, which engaged with the upper arm of its rock shaft. When thus working, it acted as a cut-off at a fixed part of the stroke, determined by the setting of the eccentric. This was usually at half the stroke. When it was desired to dispense with the cut-off and work steam for the full stroke, the hook of the valve rod was lifted from the pin on the upper arm of the rock shaft by a lever worked from the footboard, and the valve rod was held in a notched rest fastened to the side of the boiler. This left the opening through the upper valve and the port in the partition plate open for the free passage of steam throughout the whole stroke. The first application of the half-stroke cut-off was made on the 20-ton six-wheeled locomotive "Atlantic," built for the Western Railroad of Massachusetts in 1844. It at once became the practice to apply the cut-off on all passenger engines, while the six and eight-wheels-connected freight engines were, with a few exceptions, built for a time longer with the single valve admitting steam for the full stroke.

In 1845, Mr. Baldwin built three locomotives for the Royal Railroad Company of Würtemberg. They were of 15 tons weight, on six wheels, four of them being 60 inches in diameter and coupled. The front drivers were combined by the flexible beams into a truck with the smaller leading wheels. The cylinders were inclined and outside, and the connecting rods took hold of a half-crank axle back of the firebox. It was specified that these engines should have the link motion which had shortly before been introduced in England by the Stephensons. Mr. Baldwin accordingly applied a link of a peculiar character to suit his own ideas of the device. The link was made solid, and of a truncated V-section, and the block was grooved so as to fit and slide on the outside of the link.

After building, during the years 1843, 1844 and 1845, ten four-wheels-connected engines on the plan above described, viz.: six wheels in all, the leading wheels and the front drivers being combined into a truck by the flexible beams, Mr. Baldwin finally adopted the present design of four drivers and a four-wheeled truck. Some of his customers who were favorable to the latter plan had ordered such machines of other builders, and Colonel

ON JUNE 22, 1889, Mr. Robert Coleman placed an order for a two-foot gauge 4-4-0 locomotive on the Baldwin Locomotive Works and specified delivery by July 4 in time for the rush of Independence Day picnickers on his Mt. Gretna narrow gauge line. Mr. Sam Vauclain, then shop superintendent, completed this little jewel in eight working days, on July 2, 1889. (Collection of C. A. Brown)

IN 1889, BALDWIN built this deluxe model 4-4-0 for the Cia de Caminios de Hierro de la Habana. (Collection of C. A. Brown)

Gadsden, President of the South Carolina Railroad Company, called on him in 1845 to build for that line some passenger engines of this pattern. He accordingly bought the patent right for this plan of engine of Mr. H. R. Campbell, and for the equaliz-

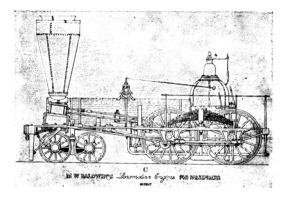

BALDWIN EIGHT-WHEELED, FOUR-COUPLED LOCOMOTIVE, 1845

ing beams used between the drivers, of Messrs. Eastwick & Harrison, and delivered to the South Carolina Railroad Company, in December, 1845, his first eight-wheeled engine with four drivers and a four-wheeled truck. This machine had cylinders 13¾ by 18 inches, and drivers 60 inches in diameter, with the springs between them arranged as equalizers. Its weight was 15 tons. It had the half-crank axle, the cylinders being inside the frame but outside the smokebox. The inside-connected engine, counterweighting being as yet unknown, was admitted to be steadier in running, and hence more suitable for passenger service. With the completion of the first eight-wheeled four-coupled engine, Mr. Baldwin's feelings underwent a revulsion in favor of this plan, and his partiality for it became as great as had been his antipathy before. Commenting on the machine, he recorded himself as "more pleased with its appearance and action than any engine he had turned out." In addition to the three engines of this description for the South Carolina

Railroad Company, a duplicate was sent to the Camden and Amboy Railroad Company, and a similar but lighter one to the Wilmington and Baltimore Railroad Company, shortly afterward. The engine for the Camden and Amboy Railroad Company, and perhaps the others, had the half-stroke cut-off.

From that time forward all of his four-wheels-connected machines were built on this plan, and the six-wheeled four-coupled engine was abandoned, except in the case of one built for the Philadelphia, Germantown and Norristown Railroad Company, in 1846, and this was afterward rebuilt into a six-wheels-connected machine. Three methods of carrying out the general design were, however, subsequently followed. At first the half-crank was used; then horizontal cylinders inclosed in the chimney seat and working a full-crank axle, which form of construction had been practiced at the Lowell Works; and eventually outside cylinders with outside connections.

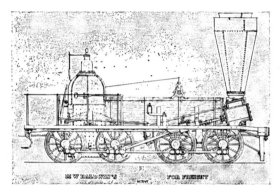

BALDWIN EIGHT-WHEELS-CONNECTED LOCOMOTIVE, 1846

Meanwhile, the flexible truck machine maintained its popularity for heavy freight service. All the engines thus far built on this plan had been six-wheeled, some with the rear driving axle back of the firebox, and others with it in front. The next step, following logically after the adoption of the eight-wheeled four-

BROOKLYN, BATH & WEST END 2-4-0 No. 3, built in 1889 later went to the Halifax & Yarmouth. (Collection of C. A. Brown)

BLUE RIDGE & ATLANTIC No. 1 "Pope Barrow" was completed in 1889. (Collection of C. A. Brown)

coupled engine, was to increase the size of the freight machine, and distribute the weight on eight wheels all connected, the two rear pairs being rigid in the frame, and the two front pairs combined into the flexible-beam truck. This was first done in 1846, when seventeen engines on this plan were constructed on one order for the Philadelphia and Reading Railroad Company. Fifteen of these were of 20 tons weight, with cylinders 15½ by 20 inches, and wheels 46 inches in diameter; and two of 25 tons weight, with cylinders 17¼ by 18 inches, and drivers 42 inches in diameter. These engines were the first on which Mr. Baldwin placed sand boxes, and they were also the first built by him with roofs. On all previous engines the footboard had only been inclosed by a railing. On these engines for the Reading Railroad four iron posts were carried up, and a wooden roof supported by them. The engine men added curtains at the sides and front, and Mr. Baldwin on subsequent engines added sides, with sash and glass. The cab proper, however, was of New England origin, where the severity of the climate demanded it, and where it had been used previous to this period.

Among the locomotives completed during 1846 and 1847, should be noted the "M. G. Bright," built for operating the inclined plane on the Madison and Indianapolis Railroad. The rise of this incline was one in seventeen, from the bank of the Ohio River at Madison. The engine had eight wheels, 42 inches in diameter, connected, and worked in the usual manner by outside inclined cylinders, 15½ inches diameter by 20 inches stroke. A second pair of cylinders, 17 inches in diameter with 18 inches stroke of piston, was placed vertically over the boiler, midway between the furnace and smoke arch. The connecting rods, worked by these cylinders, connected with cranks on a shaft under the boiler. This shaft carried a single cog-wheel at its center, and this cog-wheel engaged with another of about twice its diameter on a second shaft adjacent to it and in the same plane. The cog-wheel on this latter shaft worked in a rack-rail placed in the center of the track. The shaft itself had its bearings in the lower ends of two vertical rods, one on each side of the boiler, and these rods were united over the boiler by a horizontal bar, which was connected by means of a

bent lever and connecting rod to the piston worked by a small horizontal cylinder placed on top of the boiler. By means

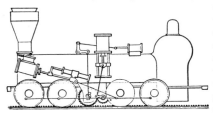

BALDWIN LOCOMOTIVE FOR RACK RAIL, 1847

of this cylinder, the yoke carrying the shaft and cog-wheel could be depressed and held down so as to engage the cogs with the rack-rail, or raised out of the way when only the ordinary drivers were re-quired. This device was designed by Mr. Andrew Cathcart, Master Mechanic of the Madison and Indianapolis Railroad. A similar machine, the "John Brough," for the same plane, was built by Mr. Baldwin in 1850. The incline was worked with a rack-rail and these engines until it was finally abandoned and a line with easier gradients substituted.

The use of iron tubes in freight engines grew in favor, and in October, 1847, Mr. Baldwin noted that he was fitting his tubes with copper ends, "for riveting to the boiler."

The subject of burning coal continued to engage much attention, but the use of anthracite had not as yet been generally successful. In October, 1847, the Baltimore and Ohio Railroad Company advertised for proposals for four engines to burn Cumberland coal, and the order was taken and partially filled by Mr. Baldwin with three eight-wheels-connected machines. These engines had a heater on top of the boiler for heating the feed water, and a grate with a rocking bar in the center, having fingers on each side which interlocked with projections on fixed bars, one in front and one behind. The rocking bar was operated from the footboard. This appears to have been the first instance of the use of a rocking grate in the practice of these Works.

The year 1848 showed a falling off in business, but in the following year there was a rapid recovery, and the Works were operating at full capacity by 1851. The engines of this period, with a few exceptions, were confined to three patterns.

OBSERVE THE ODD WHEEL spacing on this Marietta & North Georgia Railroad ten-wheeler. Baldwin product of 1889. (Collection of C. A. Brown)

the eight-wheeled four-coupled engine, from 12 to 19 tons in weight, for passengers and freight, and the six and eight-wheels-connected engines, for freight exclusively, the six-wheeled machine weighing from 12 to 17 tons, and the eight-wheeled from 18 to 27 tons. The drivers of these six and eight-wheels-connected machines were made generally 42, with occasional variations up to 48 inches in diameter.

The exceptions referred to above were the fast passenger engines built by Mr. Baldwin during this period. Early in 1848, the Vermont Central Railroad was approaching completion, and Governor Paine, the President of the Company, conceived the idea that the passenger service on the road required locomotives capable of running at very high speeds. Henry R. Campbell, Esq., was a contractor in building the line, and

THE "GOVERNOR PAINE," 1849

was authorized by Governor Paine to come to Philadelphia and offer Mr. Baldwin $10,000 for a locomotive which could run with a passenger train at a speed of 60 miles per hour. Mr. Baldwin at once undertook to meet these conditions. The work was begun early in 1848, and in March of that year Mr. Baldwin filed a caveat for his design. The engine was completed in 1849, and was named the "Governor Paine." It had one pair of driving wheels, 78 inches in diameter, placed back of the firebox. Another pair of wheels, but smaller and unconnected, was placed directly in front of the firebox, and a four-

wheeled truck carried the front of the engine. The cylinders were 17¼ inches diameter and 20 inches stroke, and were placed horizontally between the frames and the boiler at about the middle of the waist. The connecting rods took hold of "half-cranks" inside of the driving wheels. The object of placing the cylinders at the middle of the boiler was to lessen or obviate the lateral motion of the engine, produced when the cylinders were attached to the smoke arch. The bearings on the two rear axles were so contrived that by means of a lever, a part of the weight of the engine usually carried on the wheels in front of the firebox could be transferred to the driving axle. The "Governor Paine" was used for several years on the Vermont Central Railroad, and then rebuilt into a four-coupled machine. During its career, it was stated by the officers of the road that it had run a mile in 43 seconds. Three engines on the same plan, but with cylinders 14 by 20 inches, and six-feet driving wheels, the "Mifflin," "Blair" and "Indiana," were also built for the Pennsylvania Railroad Company in 1849. They weighed each about 47,000 pounds, distributed as follows: 18,000 on the drivers, 14,000 on the pair of wheels in front of the firebox, and 15,000 on the truck. By applying the lever, the weight on the drivers could be increased to about 24,000 pounds, the weight on the wheels in front of the firebox being correspondingly reduced. A speed of four miles in three minutes is recorded for them, and upon one occasion President Taylor was taken in a special train over the road by one of these machines at a speed of 60 miles an hour. One other engine of this pattern, the "Susquehanna," was built for the Hudson River Railroad Company in 1850. Its cylinders were 15 inches diameter by 20 inches stroke, and drivers six feet in diameter. All these engines, however, were short-lived, and died of insufficient adhesion.

Eight engines, with four drivers connected and half-crank axles, were built for the New York and Erie Railroad Company in 1849. These locomotives had 17 by 20-inch cylinders, and were among the last on which the half-crank axle was used. Thereafter, outside-connected engines were constructed almost exclusively.

EVERYBODY had suburban service in 1889. This is No. 4 of the Dallas and Oak Cliff. (Collection of C. A. Brown)

In May, 1848, Mr. Baldwin filed a caveat for a four-cylinder locomotive, but never carried the design into execution. The first instance of the use of steel axles in the practice of the establishment occurred during the same year—a set being placed as an experiment under an engine constructed for the Pennsylvania Railroad Company. In 1850, the old form of dome boiler, which had characterized the Baldwin engine since 1834, was abandoned, and the wagon-top form substituted.

The business in 1851 had reached the full capacity of the shop, a condition which continued during the following year. Contracts for work extended a year ahead, and to meet the demand, the facilities in the various departments were increased, and resulted in the construction of 60 engines in 1853, and 62 in 1854.

At the beginning of the latter year, Mr. Matthew Baird, who had been connected with the Works since 1836, as one of its foremen, entered into partnership with Mr. Baldwin, and the style of the firm was made M. W. Baldwin & Co.

The only novelty in the general plan of engines during this period was the addition of a ten-wheeled engine to the patterns of the establishment. The success of Mr. Baldwin's engines with all six or eight wheels connected, and the two front pairs combined by the parallel beams into a flexible truck, had been so marked that it was natural that he should oppose any other plan for freight service. The ten-wheeled engine, with six drivers connected, had, however, now become a competitor. This plan of engine was first patented by Septimus Norris, of Philadelphia, in 1846, and the original design was apparently to produce an engine which should have equal tractive power with the Baldwin six-wheels-connected machine. This the Norris patent sought to accomplish by proposing an engine with six drivers connected, and so disposed as to carry substantially the whole weight, the forward drivers being in advance of the center of gravity of the engine, and the truck only serving as a guide; the front of the engine being connected with it by a pivot pin, but without a bearing on the center plate. Mr. Norris's first engine on this plan was tried in April, 1847, and was found not to pass curves as readily as was expected. As the truck carried

little or no weight, it would not keep the track. The New York and Erie Railroad Company, of which John Brandt was then Master Mechanic, shortly afterward adopted the ten-wheeled engine, modified in plan so as to carry a part of the weight on the truck. Mr. Baldwin filled an order for this company, in 1850, of four eight-wheels-connected engines, and in making the contract he agreed to substitute a truck for the front pair of wheels if desired after trial. This, however, he was not called upon to do.

In February, 1852, Mr. J. Edgar Thomson, President of the Pennsylvania Railroad Company, invited proposals for a number of freight locomotives of 56,000 pounds weight each. They were to be adapted to burn bituminous coal, and to have six wheels connected and a truck in front, which might be either of two or four wheels. Mr. Baldwin secured the contract, and built twelve engines of the prescribed dimensions, *viz.:* cylinders, 18 by 22 inches; drivers, 44 inches diameter, with chilled tires. Several of these engines were constructed with a single pair of truck wheels in front of the drivers and under the cylinders. It was found, however, after the engines were put in service, that the two truck wheels carried 18,000 to 19,000 pounds, and this was objected to by the Company as too great a weight to be carried on a single pair of wheels. On the rest of the engines of the order, therefore, a four-wheeled truck in front was employed:

The ten-wheeled engine thereafter assumed a place in the Baldwin classification, but it was not until after 1860 that this type wholly superseded Mr. Baldwin's old plan of freight engine on six or eight wheels, all connected.

In 1855-56, two locomotives of 27 tons weight, with 19 by 22-inch cylinders and 48-inch drivers, were built for the Portage Railroad, and three for the Pennsylvania Railroad. In 1855, '56 and '57, fourteen of the same dimensions were built for the Cleveland and Pittsburgh Railroad; four for the Pittsburgh, Fort Wayne and Chicago Railroad; and one for the Marietta and Cincinnati Railroad. In 1858 and '59, one was constructed for the South Carolina Railroad, of the same size,

THREE FOOT GAUGE 4-4-0 built for the Potomac, Fredericksburg and Piedmont RR in 1889. (Collection of C. A. Brown)

THE ATLANTIC COAST line bought this cap stacked 4-4-0 for its Norfolk & Carolina subsidiary in 1889. (Collection of C. A. Brown)

and six lighter ten-wheelers, with cylinders 15½ by 22 inches, and 48-inch drivers, and two with cylinders 16 by 22 inches, and 48-inch drivers were sent out to railroads in Cuba.

On three locomotives—the "Clinton," "Athens," and "Sparta"—completed for the Central Railroad of Georgia in July, 1852, the driving boxes were made with a slot or cavity in the line of the vertical bearing on the journal. The object was to produce a more uniform distribution of the wear over the entire surface of the bearing. This was the first instance in which this device, which has since come into general use, was employed in the Works, and the boxes were so made by direction of Mr. Charles Whiting, then Master Mechanic of the Central Railroad of Georgia. He subsequently informed Mr. Baldwin that this method of fitting up driving boxes had been in use on the road for several years previous to his connection with the Company. As this device was subsequently made the subject of a patent by Mr. David Matthew, these facts may not be without interest.

In 1853, Mr. Charles Ellet, Chief Engineer of the Virginia Central Railroad, laid a temporary track across the Blue Ridge, at Rock Fish Gap, for use during the construction of a tunnel through the mountain. This track was 12,500 feet in length on the eastern slope, ascending in that distance 610 feet, or at the average rate of one in 20½ feet. The maximum grade was calculated for 296 feet per mile, and prevailed for half a mile. It was found, however, in fact, that the grade in places exceeded 300 feet per mile. The shortest radius of curvature was 238 feet. On the western slope, which was 10,650 feet in length, the maximum grade was 280 feet per mile, and the ruling radius of curvature 300 feet. This track was worked by two of the Baldwin six-wheels-connected flexible-beam truck locomotives constructed in 1853-54. From a description of this track, and the mode of working it, published by Mr. Ellet in 1856, the following is extracted:

"The locomotives mainly relied on for this severe duty were designed and constructed by the firm of M. W. Baldwin & Company, of Philadelphia. The slight modifications introduced at the instance of the writer, to adapt them better to the particular service to be performed in crossing the Blue Ridge, did not touch the working proportions or principle of the engines, the merits of which are due to the patentee, M. W. Baldwin, Esq.

"These engines are mounted on six wheels, all of which are drivers, and coupled, and 42 inches diameter. The wheels are set very close, so that the distance between the extreme points of contact of the wheels and the rail, of the front and rear drivers, is 9 feet 4 inches. This closeness of the wheels, of course, greatly reduces the difficulty of turning the short curves of the road. The diameter of the cylinders is 16½ inches, and the length of the stroke 20 inches. To increase the adhesion, and at the same time avoid the resistance of a tender, the engine carries its tank upon the boiler, and the footboard is lengthened out and provided with suspended side boxes, where a supply of fuel may be stored. By this means the weight of wood and water, instead of abstracting from the effective power of the engine, contributes to its adhesion and consequent ability to climb the mountain. The total weight of these engines is 55,000 pounds, or 27½ tons, when the boiler and tank are supplied with water, and fuel enough for a trip of eight miles is on board. The capacity of the tank is sufficient to hold 100 cubic feet of water, and it has storage room on top for 100 cubic feet of wood in addition to what may be carried in the side boxes and on the footboard.

"To enable the engines to better adapt themselves to the flexures of the road, the front and middle pairs of drivers are held in position by wrought iron beams, having cylindrical boxes in each end for the journal bearings, which beams vibrate on spherical pins fixed in the frame of the engine on each side, and resting on the centers of the beams. The object of this arrangement is to form a truck, somewhat flexible, which enables the drivers more readily to traverse the curves of the road.

"The writer has never permitted the power of the engines on this mountain road to be fully tested. The object has been to work the line regularly, economically, and above all, *safely*; and these conditions are incompatible with experimental loads subjecting the machinery to severe strains. The regular daily service of each of the engines is to make four trips, of eight miles, over the mountain, drawing one eight-wheel baggage car, together with two eight-wheel passenger cars, in each direction.

"In conveying freight, the regular train on the mountain is three of the eight-wheel house cars, fully loaded, or four of them when empty or partly loaded.

"These three cars when full, weigh with their loads, from 40 to 43 tons. Sometimes, though rarely, when the business has been unusually heavy, the loads have exceeded 50 tons.

"With such trains the engines are stopped on the track, ascending or descending, and are started again, on the steepest grades, at the discretion of the engineer.

"Water for the supply of the engines has been found difficult to obtain on the mountain; and since the road was constructed a tank has been established on the eastern slope, where the ascending engines stop daily on a grade of 280 feet per mile, and are there held by the brakes while the tank is being filled, and started again at the signal and without any difficulty.

DULUTH AND IRON RANGE 2-8-0 No. 7 was about as heavy as they came in 1883. (Collection of **C. A. Brown**)

TYPICAL ANTHRACITE ENGINE of the 1880's was Philadelphia and Reading No. 196, delivered in 1883. (Collection of C. A. Brown)

NOTE: *In 1877 when John E. Wootten, General Manager of the Philadelphia and Reading patented a boiler specifically designed to burn waste anthracite or culm, he inaugurated a breed of iron horse that to this day has a vast coterie of admirers. Large quantities of this material would collect at the mines and Wootten recognized the fact that if it could be burned in the firebox of a locomotive economical results would follow. This required a thin fire and a light draft to keep the fuel from blowing up the stack before sufficient combustion, and the solution was a larger grate than that used in burning lump anthracite. Wootten then placed the firebox above the drivers, with the grate width only limited by the loading gauge. This called for placing the cab on top of the firebox, but this arrangement was soon changed and the cab was placed ahead of the firebox straddling the boiler. Thus induced the name of "camelbacks" though some called them "Mother Hubbards." In any case they were not the original "camels" which were the invention of Ross Winans and had their cabs perched atop the boiler rather than straddling it.*

Engine No. 196 of the 4-4-0 type was typical of many built by Baldwin and the Reading itself in the eighties and nineties.

Cylinders 21″ × 22″	Weight, total engine, 103,000 lb.
Drivers 68½″	Tractive force, 16, 250 lb.

(Frederick Westing)

IN 1889, BALDWIN produced its first "Vauclain" compound locomotive. U. S. patents 406011 and 406012 were issued to Mr. Samuel Vauclain for this design as shown applied above to B & O No. 848. (Collection of C. A. Brown)

NO. 587 NORTHERN PACIFIC compound 2-6-0 participated in some tests which helped to prove conclusively that the compound use of steam was superior to the single expansion methods then available. Locomotive No. 587 and a single expansion mogul No. 584 were used for this comparison test. Both engines were of the same dimensions and weight, and differed only in cylinders and boiler pressure. In one test both locomotives carried 170 lbs. steam pressure. Another was made with the compound engine using 170 lbs. of pressure and the single expansion engine carrying 150 lbs. pressure. Another test was made with both engines carrying 150 lbs. pressure. The tests were run between Staples, North Dakota, and Fargo, North Dakota, a distance of 108.7 miles. Tests were regulated so that equal trains were assigned to each locomotive. On one of these trips the compound locomotive showed a saving of 53.5% in the consumption of fuel. The trip was made with the compound locomotive using its power to the greatest advantage. The average fuel advantage for the entire test period with varying loads, etc, showed the compound locomotive to have an overall advantage of 28% in fuel consumed. The compound locomotive operated at its best on the higher boiler pressure. For twenty years, until the use of superheated steam proved more effective with less mechanical gadgetry, Vauclain compounds were popular throughout the world. (Collection of C. A. Brown)

NEVER BASHFUL about trying new things, Baldwin, in 1886 built this "Soda Motor" for the Minneapolis, Lyndale and Minnetonka. History does not record what caused its demise, but it probably burped once too often.

"The ordinary speed of the engines, when loaded, is 7½ miles an hour on the ascending grades, and from 5½ to 6 miles an hour on the descent.

"When the road was first opened, it speedily appeared that the difference of 43 feet on the western side, and 58 on the eastern side, between the grades on curves of 300 feet radius and those on straight lines, was not sufficient to compensate for the increased friction due to such curvature. The velocity, with a constant supply of steam, was promptly retarded on passing from a straight line to a curve, and promptly accelerated again on passing from the curve to the straight line. But, after a little experience in the working of the road, it was found advisable to supply a small amount of grease to the flange of the engine by means of a sponge, saturated with oil, which, when needed, is kept in contact with the wheel by a spring. Since the use of the oil was introduced, the difficulty of turning the curves has been so far diminished that it is no longer possible to determine whether grades of 237.6 feet per mile on curves of 300 feet radius, or grades of 296 feet per mile on straight lines, are traversed most rapidly by the engine.

"When the track is in good condition, the brakes of only two of the cars possess sufficient power to control and regulate the movement of the train—that is to say, they will hold back the two cars and the engine. When there are three or more cars in the train, the brakes on the cars, of course command the train so much the more easily.

"But the safety of the train is not dependent on the brakes of the car. There is also a valve or air cock in the steam chest, under the control of the engineer. This air cock forms an independent brake, exclusively at the command of the engineer, and which can always be applied when the engine itself is in working order. The action of this power may be made ever so gradual, either slightly relieving the duty of the brakes on the cars, or bringing into play the entire power of the engine. The train is thus held in complete command."

The Mountain Top Track, it may be added, was worked successfully for several years by the engines described in the above extract, until it was abandoned on the completion of the tunnel. The exceptionally steep grades and short curves which characterized the line afforded a complete and satisfactory test of the adaptation of these machines to such peculiar service.

CHAPTER IV.

The Introduction of the Link Motion, and the Use of Coal as Fuel

The period now under consideration was marked by a most important step in the progress of American locomotive practice. We refer to the introduction of the link motion. Although this device was first employed by William T. James, of New York, in 1832, and eleven years later by the Stephensons, in England, and was by them applied thenceforward on their engines, it was not until 1849 that it was adopted in this country. In that year Mr. Thomas Rogers, of the Rogers Locomotive and Machine Company, introduced it in his practice. Other builders, however, strenuously resisted the innovation, and none more so than Mr. Baldwin. The theoretical objections which confessedly apply to the device, but which practically have been proved to be unimportant, were urged from the first by Mr. Baldwin as arguments against its use. The strong claim of the advocates of the link motion, that it gave a means of cutting off steam at any point of the stroke, could not be gainsaid, and this was admitted to be a consideration of the first importance. This very circumstance undoubtedly turned Mr. Baldwin's attention to the subject of methods for cutting off steam, and one of the first results was his "Variable Cut-off," patented April 27, 1852. This device consisted of two valves, the upper sliding upon the lower, and worked by an eccentric and rock shaft in the usual manner. The lower valve fitted steam-tight to the sides of the steam chest and the under surface of the upper valve. When the piston reached each end of its stroke, the full pressure of steam from the boiler was admitted around the upper valve, and transferred the lower valve instantaneously from one end of the steam chest to the other. The openings through the two valves were so arranged that steam was admitted to the cylinder only for a part of the stroke. The effect was, therefore, to cut off steam at a given point, and to open the induction and exhaust ports substantially at the same instant and to their full extent. The exhaust port, in addition, remained fully opened while the

WHICH WAY do you want to go? It makes no difference to this 0-10-0 tank engine built for the St. Clair Tunnel Co. when it opened in 1890. (Collection of C. A. Brown)

UNION PACIFIC had some camelbacks as represented by No. 1301, delivered in 1886. (Collection of C. A. Brown)

induction port was gradually closing, and after it had entirely closed. Although this device was never put in use, it may be noted in passing that it contained substantially the principle of the steam pump, as since patented and constructed.

Early in 1853 Mr. Baldwin abandoned the half-stroke cut-off previously described, and which he had been using since 1845, and adopted the variable cut-off, which was already employed by other builders. One of his letters, written in January, 1853, states his position as follows:

"I shall put on an improvement in the shape of a variable cut-off, which can be operated by the engineer while the machine is running, and which will cut off anywhere from six to twelve inches, according to the load and amount of steam wanted, and this without the link motion, which I could never be entirely satisfied with. I still have the independent cut-off, and the additional machinery to make it variable will be simple and not liable to be deranged."

This form of cut-off was a separate valve, sliding on a partition plate between it and the main steam valve, and worked by an independent eccentric and rock shaft. The upper arm of the rock shaft was curved so as to form a radius arm, on which a sliding block, forming the termination of the upper valve rod, could be adjusted and held at various distances from the axis, thus producing a variable travel of the upper valve. This device did not give an absolutely perfect cut-off, as it was not operative in backward gear, but when running forward it would cut off with great accuracy at any point of the stroke, was quick in its movement, and economical in the consumption of fuel.

After a short experience with this arrangement of the cut-off, the partition plate was omitted, and the upper valve was made to slide directly on the lower. This was eventually found objectionable, however, as the lower valve would soon cut a hollow in the valve face. Several unsuccessful attempts were made to remedy this defect by making the lower valve of brass, with long bearings, and making the valve face of the cylinder of hardened steel; finally, however, the plan of one valve on the other was abandoned, and recourse was again had to an interposed partition plate, as in the original half-stroke cut-off.

Mr. Baldwin did not adopt this form of cut-off without some modification of his own, and the modification in this instance consisted of a peculiar device, patented September 13, 1853, for raising and lowering the block on the radius arm. A quadrant was placed so that its circumference bore nearly against a curved arm projecting down from the sliding block, and which curved in the reverse direction from the quadrant. Two connections in the form of steel straps or chains, placed side by side, were interposed between the quadrant and this curved arm. One of the straps was connected to the lower end of the quadrant and the upper end of the curved arm; the other, to the upper end of the quadrant and the lower end of the curved arm. The effect was the same as if the quadrant and arm geared into each other in any position by teeth, and theoretically the block

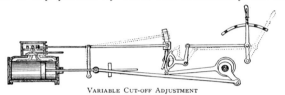

VARIABLE CUT-OFF ADJUSTMENT

was kept steady in whatever position placed on the radius arm of the rock shaft. This was the object sought to be accomplished, and was stated in the specification of the patent as follows:

"The principle of varying the cut-off by means of a vibrating arm and sliding pivot block has long been known, but the contrivances for changing the position of the block upon the arm have been very defective. The radius of motion of the link by which the sliding block is changed on the arm, and the radius of motion of that part of the vibrating arm on which the block is placed, have, in this kind of valve gear, as heretofore constructed, been different, which produced a continual rubbing of the sliding block upon the arm while the arm is vibrating; and as the block, for the greater part of the time, occupies one position on the arm, and only has to be moved toward either extremity occasionally, that part of the arm on which the block is most used soon becomes so worn that the block is loose, and jars."

This form of cut-off is shown on a drawing of a 15-ton locomotive for the Western and Atlantic Railroad, dated as early as July, 1852; and the device was used on a large number of locomotives built by Mr. Baldwin during 1853 and 1854. It was found, however, in practice, that both the steel straps and chains proved unsatisfactory. The straps would stretch suffi-

A PR MAN'S DREAM OF 1892. This classic photo shows Baldwin compound demonstrator No. 82 at Belmont yard, Philadelphia with 20 0-4-4T compound engines destined for the Chicago elevated. (Collection of C. A. Brown)

ciently to allow them to buckle and break, while the chains in turn proved little better, as they lengthened, allowing lost motion, or broke altogether. Eventually, therefore, the quadrant was wholly abandoned, and recourse was finally had to the lever and link for raising and lowering the sliding block. As thus arranged, the cut-off was substantially what was known as the "Cuyahoga Cut-off," as introduced by Mr. Ethan Rogers, of the Cuyahoga Works, Cleveland, Ohio, except that Mr. Baldwin used a partition plate between the upper and the lower valve.

BALDWIN PASSENGER LOCOMOTIVE WITH VARIABLE CUT-OFF, 1853

But while Mr. Baldwin in common with many other builders was thus resolutely opposing the link motion, it was nevertheless rapidly gaining favor with railroad managers. Engineers and master mechanics were everywhere learning to admire its simplicity, and were manifesting an enthusiastic preference for engines so constructed. At length, therefore, he was forced to succumb; and the link was applied to the "Pennsylvania," one of two engines completed for the Central Railroad of Georgia, in February, 1854. The other engine of the order, the "New Hampshire," had the variable cut-off, and Mr. Baldwin, while yielding to the demand in the former engine, was undoubtedly sanguine that the working of the latter would demonstrate the inferiority of the new device. In this, however, he was dis-

appointed, for in the following year the same company ordered three more engines, on which they specified the link motion. In 1856 seventeen engines for nine different companies had this form of valve gear, and its use was thus incorporated in his practice. It was not, however, until 1857 that he was induced to adopt it exclusively.

February 14, 1854, Mr. Baldwin and Mr. David Clark, Master Mechanic of the Mine Hill Railroad, took out conjointly a patent for a feed-water heater, placed at the base of a locomotive chimney, and consisting of one large vertical flue, surrounded by a number of smaller ones. The exhaust steam was discharged from the nozzles through the large central flue, creating a draft of the products of combustion through the smaller surrounding flues. The pumps forced the feed water into the chamber around these flues, whence it passed to the boiler by a pipe from the back of the stack. This heater was applied on several engines for the Mine Hill Railroad, and on a few other roads; but its use was exceptional, and lasted only for a year or two.

In December of the same year, Mr. Baldwin filed a caveat for a variable exhaust, operated automatically by the pressure of steam, so as to close when the pressure was lowest in the boiler, and open with the increase of pressure. The device was never put in service.

The use of coal, both bituminous and anthracite, as a fuel for locomotives, had by this time become a practical success. The economical combustion of bituminous coal, however, engaged considerable attention. It was felt that much remained to be accomplished in consuming the smoke and deriving the maximum of useful effect from the fuel. Mr. Baird, who was now associated with Mr. Baldwin in the management of the business, made this matter a subject of careful study and investigation. An experiment was conducted under his direction, by placing a sheet iron deflector in the firebox of an engine on the Germantown and Norristown Railroad. The success of the trial was such as to show conclusively that a more complete combustion resulted. As, however, a deflector formed by a single plate of iron would soon be destroyed by the action of the fire, Mr. Baird proposed to use a water-leg projecting upward and backward

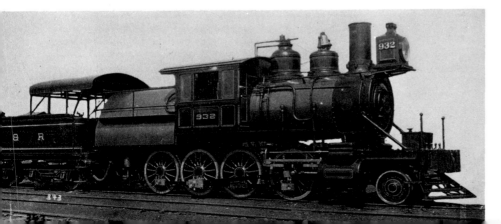

PHILADELPHIA & READING camel-back consolidation No. 932 sported a carport for the fireman in 1887. (Collection of C. A. Brown)

from the front of the firebox under the flues. Drawings and a model of the device were prepared, with a view of patenting it, but subsequently the intention was abandoned, Mr. Baird concluding that a firebrick arch as a deflector to accomplish the same object was preferable. This was accordingly tried on two locomotives built for the Pennsylvania Railroad Company in 1854, and was found so valuable an appliance that its use was at once established, and it was put on a number of engines built for railroads in Cuba and elsewhere. For several years the firebricks were supported on side plugs; but in 1858, in the "Media," built for the West Chester and Philadelphia Railroad Company, water-pipes extending from the crown obliquely downward and curving to the sides of the firebox at the bottom, were successfully used for the purpose.

The adoption of the link motion may be regarded as the dividing line between the present and the early and transitional stage of locomotive practice. Changes since that event have been principally in matters of detail, but it is the gradual perfection of these details which has made the locomotive the symmetrical, efficient, and wonderfully complete piece of mechanism it is today.

The greater number of locomotives built during the years 1855-1860 were of the ordinary type with four drivers coupled, and a four-wheeled truck, and varying in weight from 15-ton engines, with cylinders 12 by 22 inches, to 27-ton engines, with cylinders 16 by 24 inches. A few ten-wheeled engines were built, as has been previously noted, and the remainder were the Baldwin flexible truck six and eight-wheels-connected engines. The demand for these, however, was now rapidly falling off, the ten-wheeled and heavy four-coupled engines taking their place, and by 1859 they ceased to be built, save in exceptional cases, as for some foreign roads, from which orders for this pattern were still occasionally received.

A few novelties characterizing the engines of this period may be mentioned. Several built in 1855 had cross-tubes placed in the firebox, under the crown, in order to increase the heating surface. This feature, however, was found impracticable and was soon abandoned. The intense heat to which the tubes were

exposed converted the water contained in them into highly superheated steam, which would force its way out through the water around the firebox with violent ebullitions. Four engines, the "Tiger," "Leopard," "Hornet" and "Wasp," were built for the Pennsylvania Railroad Company, in 1856-57, with straight boilers and two domes. The "Delano" grate, by means of which the coal was forced into the firebox from below, was applied on four ten-wheeled engines for the Cleveland and Pittsburgh Railroad in 1857. In 1859 several engines were built with the form of boiler introduced on the Cumberland Valley

M.W. BALDWIN & CO., LOCOMOTIVE BUILDERS.

THE "TIGER"
Built for the Pennsylvania Railroad in 1856

Railroad, in 1851, by Mr. A. F. Smith, and which consisted of a combustion chamber in the waist of the boiler next the firebox. This form of boiler was for some years thereafter largely used in engines for soft coal. It was at first constructed with the "water-leg" which was a vertical water space, connecting the top and bottom sheets of the combustion chamber, but eventually this feature was omitted, and an unobstructed combustion chamber employed. Several engines were built for the Philadelphia, Wilmington and Baltimore Railroad Company, in 1859 and thereafter, with the "Dimpfel" boiler, in which the tubes contained water, and starting downward from the crown sheet, were

A **COMPOUND** brute of 1892. (Collection of C. A. Brown)

NOTE: *Small drivers on Vauclain compounds necessitated locating the large low-pressure cylinders above the smaller high-pressure cylinders to clear the rail top. On some larger drivered freight and on passenger engines the reverse arrangement was used; namely, the smaller or low-pressure cylinders were on top of the high-pressure cylinders.* (Frederick Westing)

curved to the horizontal, and terminated in a narrow water space next to the smokebox. The whole waist of the boiler, therefore, formed a combustion chamber, and the heat and gases, after passing for their whole length along and around the tubes, emerged into the lower part of the smokebox.

In 1860 an engine was built for the Mine Hill Railroad, with a boiler of a peculiar form. The top sheets sloped upward from both ends toward the center, thus making a raised part or hump in the center. The engine was designed to work on heavy grades, and the object sought by Mr. Wilder, the superintendent of the Mine Hill Railroad, was to have the water always at the same height in the space from which steam was drawn, whether going up or down grade.

All these experiments are indicative of the interest then prevailing upon the subject of coal burning. The result of experience and study had meantime satisfied Mr. Baldwin that to burn soft coal successfully required no peculiar devices; that the ordinary form of boiler with plain firebox was right, with perhaps the addition of a firebrick deflector; and that the secret of the economical and successful use of coal was in the mode of firing, rather than in a different form of furnace.

CHAPTER V.

THE CIVIL WAR PERIOD, MR. BALDWIN'S DEATH, AND SUBSEQUENT EVENTS UP TO THE CLOSE OF 1879

The year 1861 witnessed a marked falling off in the production. The breaking out of the Civil War at first unsettled business, and by many it was thought that railroad traffic would be so largely reduced that the demand for locomotives must cease altogether. A large number of hands were discharged from the Works, and only 40 locomotives were turned out during the year. It was even seriously contemplated to turn the resources of the establishment to the manufacture of shot and shell, and other munitions of war, the belief being entertained that the building of locomotives would have to be altogether suspended. So far was this from being the case, however, that after the first excitement had subsided, it was found that the demand for transportation by the General Government, and by the branches of trade and production stimulated by the War, was likely to tax the carrying capacity of the principal Northern railroads to the fullest extent. The Government itself became a large purchaser of locomotives, and it is noticeable, as indicating the increase of travel and freight transportation, that heavier machines than had ever before been built became the rule. The production during the War period reached a maximum of 130 locomotives in 1864; and from May, 1862, to June, 1864, 33 engines were built for the United States Military Railroads.

The demand from the various coal-carrying roads in Pennsylvania and vicinity was particularly active, and large numbers of ten-wheeled engines, and of the heaviest eight-wheeled four-coupled engines, were built. Of the latter class, the majority had 15 and 16-inch cylinders; and of the former, 17 and 18-inch cylinders.

The introduction of several important features in construction marks this period. Early in 1861 four 18-inch cylinder freight locomotives, with six coupled wheels, 52 inches in diameter, and a Bissell pony truck with radius bar in front, were sent to the Louisville and Nashville Railroad Company. This

THE CAB AND TENDER of "La Plata" of the Western R.R. of Buenos Aires almost look British. And note those domes: 5'6" gauge, built in 1884. (Collection of C. A. Brown)

BIG CAMELBACK. Not many 2-10-0 camelbacks were built. This one was for the New York, Lake Erie & Western. (Collection of C. A. Brown)

NOTE: *A real big one in its day. Again note the low-pressure cylinder of this Valclain compound on top of the smaller high-pressure cylinder to provide clearance. (Frederick Westing)*

1894 BROUGHT SOME INNOVATIONS. Note the odd slope of the cylinders and the 6-wheel rigid frame tender of this camelback Mogul for the Erie & Wyoming Valley. This was the first 3-cylinder engine built by a recognized locomotive builder. (Collection of C. A. Brown)

CLASSY COMPOUND COLUMBIA. With splashers on engine truck wheels, drivers and trailing truck wheels, No. 13350 had plenty of everything except tractive force. 1894. (Collection of C. A. Brown)

was the first instance of the use of the Bissell truck in the Baldwin Works. These engines, however, were not of the regular Mogul type, as they were only modifications of the ten-wheeler, the drivers retaining the same position well back, and a pair of pony wheels on the Bissell plan taking the place of the ordinary four-wheeled truck. Other engines of the same pattern, but with 18½-inch cylinders, were built in 1862-63 for the same company, and for the Dom Pedro II. Railway of Brazil.

FREIGHT LOCOMOTIVE
Dom Pedro II. Ry., Brazil
Cylinders, 18½" x 22"   Driving Wheels, Diam., 50½"
Weight, Total Engine, 63,000 lb.

The introduction of steel in locomotive construction was a distinguishing feature of the period. Steel tires were first used in the Works in 1862, on some engines for the Dom Pedro II. Railway of Brazil. Their general adoption on American railroads followed slowly. No tires of this material were then made in this country, and it was objected to their use that, as it took from 60 to 90 days to import them, an engine in case of a breakage of one of its tires, might be laid up useless for several months. To obviate this objection, M. W. Baldwin & Co. imported 500 steel tires, most of which were kept in stock, from which to fill orders. The steel tires as first used in 1862, on the locomotives for the Dom Pedro Segundo Railway, were made with a shoulder at one edge of the internal periphery, and were shrunk on the wheel centers. The accompanying sketch shows a section of the tire as then used.

Steel fireboxes were first built for some engines for the Pennsylvania

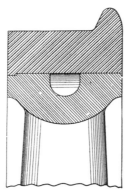

STEEL TIRE WITH SHOULDER

Railroad Company, in 1861. English steel of a high temper was used, and at the first attempt the fireboxes cracked in fitting them in the boilers, and it became necessary to take them out and substitute copper. American homogeneous cast steel was then tried on engines 231 and 232, completed for the Pennsylvania Railroad in January, 1862, and it was found to work successfully. The fireboxes of nearly all engines thereafter built for that road were of this material, and in 1866 its use for the purpose became general. It may be added that while all steel sheets for fireboxes or boilers are required to be thoroughly annealed before delivery, those which are flanged or worked in the process of boiler construction are a second time annealed before riveting.

Another feature of construction gradually adopted was the placing of the cylinders horizontally. This was first done in the case of an outside-connected engine, the "Ocmulgee," which was sent to the Southwestern Railroad Company, of Georgia, in January, 1858. This engine had a square smokebox, and the cylinders were bolted horizontally to its sides. The plan of casting the cylinder and half-saddle in one piece and fitting it to the round smokebox was introduced by Mr. Baldwin, and grew naturally out of his original method of construction. Mr. Baldwin was the first American builder to use an outside cylinder, and he made it for his early engines with a circular flange cast to it, by which it could be bolted to the boiler. The cylinders were gradually brought lower, and at a less angle, and the flanges prolonged and enlarged. In 1852, three six-wheels-connected engines, for the Mine Hill Railroad Company, were built with the cylinder flanges brought around under the smoke-box until they nearly met, the space between them being filled with a spark-box. This was practically equivalent to making the cylinder and half-saddle in one casting. Subsequently, on other engines on which the spark-box was not used, the half-saddles were cast so as almost to meet under the smokebox, and, after the cylinders were adjusted in position, wedges were fitted in the interstices and the saddles bolted together. It was finally discovered that the faces of the two half-saddles might be planed and finished so that they could be bolted together and bring

INTENDED as a sort of Jack of all trades, Baldwin demonstrator No. 13361 was locomotive, fire engine and winch all in one. Built in 1894. (Collection of C. A. Brown)

the cylinders accurately in position, thus avoiding the troublesome and tedious job of adjusting them by chipping and fitting to the boiler and frames. With this method of construction, the cylinders were placed at a less and less angle, until at length the truck wheels were spread sufficiently, on all new or modified classes of locomotives in the Baldwin list, to admit of the cylinders being hung horizontally, as is the present almost universal American practice. By the year 1865, horizontal cylinders were made in all cases where the patterns would allow it. The advantages of this arrangement are manifestly in the interest of simplicity and economy, as the cylinders are thus rights or lefts, indiscriminately, and a single pattern answers for either side.

In July, 1866, the engine "Consolidation" was built for the Lehigh Valley Railroad, on the plan and specification furnished by Mr. Alexander Mitchell, Master Mechanic of the Mahanoy Division of that Railroad. This engine was intended for working the Mahanoy plane, which rises at the rate of 133 feet per mile.

LOCOMOTIVE "CONSOLIDATION"
Lehigh Valley R. R.

The "Consolidation" had cylinders 20 by 24 inches, four pairs of drivers connected, 48 inches in diameter, and a Bissell pony truck in front, equalized with the front drivers. The weight of the engine, in working order, was 90,000 pounds, of which all but about 10,000 pounds were on the drivers. This engine constituted the first of a class to which it gave its name, and Consolidation engines have since been constructed for a large number of railways, not only in the United States, but also in many foreign countries. The heaviest of these locomotives weigh over three times as much as the original "Consolidation."

It has already been noted, that as early as 1839 Mr. Baldwin felt the importance of making all like parts of similar engines absolutely uniform and interchangeable. It was not attempted to accomplish this object, however, by means of a complete system of standard gauges, until many years later. In 1861 a beginning was made of organizing all the departments of

manufacture upon this basis, and from it grew an elaborate and perfected system, embracing all the essential details of construction. An independent department of the Works, having a separate foreman and an adequate force of skilled workmen with special tools adapted to the purpose, is organized as the Department of Standard Gauges. A system of standard gauges and templets for every description of work to be done is made and kept by this department. The original templets are kept as "standards," and are never used on the work itself, but from them exact duplicates are made, which are issued to the foremen of the various departments, and to which all work is required to conform. The working gauges are compared with the standards at regular intervals, and absolute uniformity is thus maintained. The result of this system is interchangeableness of like parts in engines of the same class, insuring to the purchaser the minimum cost of repairs, and rendering possible, by the application of this method, the large production which these Works have accomplished.

Thus had been developed and perfected the various essential details of existing locomotive practice when Mr. Baldwin died, September 7, 1866. He had been permitted, in a life of unusual activity and energy, to witness the rise and wonderful increase of a material interest which had become the distinguishing feature of the century. He had done much, by his own mechanical skill and inventive genius, to contribute to the development of that interest. His name was as "familiar as household words" wherever on the American continent the locomotive had penetrated. An ordinary ambition might well have been satisfied with this achievement. But Mr. Baldwin's claim to the remembrance of his fellow-men rests not alone on the results of his mechanical labors. A merely technical history, such as this, is not the place to do justice to his memory as a man, as a Christian, and as a philanthropist; yet the record would be manifestly imperfect, and would fail properly to reflect the sentiments of his business associates who so long knew him in all relations of life, were no reference made to his many virtues and noble traits of character. Mr. Baldwin was a man of sterling integrity and singular conscientiousness. To do right, absolutely and unre-

TOO BAD we don't have a color photograph of this paint job, but we can surely pause in admiration of the striper's artistic touch, which adorns the B&O's classic American Standard Locomotive "Director General" as originally built at Eddystone in 1894. This high stepping machine was preserved long after the fast trains were too heavy for her to manage. After appearances at Fairs of 1927 at Halethorpe and 1939 at New York, she was cut up during World War II. (Collection of C. A. Brown)

servedly, in all his relations with men, was an instinctive rule of his nature. His heroic struggle to meet every dollar of his liabilities, principal and interest, after his failure, consequent upon the general financial crash in 1837, constitutes a chapter of personal self-denial and determined effort which is seldom paralleled in the annals of commercial experience. When most men would have felt that an equitable compromise with creditors was all that could be demanded in view of the general financial embarrassment, Mr. Baldwin insisted upon paying all claims in full, and succeeded in doing so only after nearly five years of unremitting industry, close economy, and absolute personal sacrifices. As a philanthropist and a sincere and earnest Christian, zealous in every good work, his memory is cherished by many to whom his contributions to locomotive improvement are comparatively unknown. From the earliest years of his business life the practice of systematic benevolence was made a duty and a pleasure. His liberality constantly increased with his means. Indeed, he would unhesitatingly give his notes, in large sums, for charitable purposes, when money was absolutely wanted to carry on his business. Apart from the thousands which he expended in private charities, and of which, of course, little can be known, Philadelphia contains many monuments of his munificence. Early taking a deep interest in all Christian effort, his contributions to missionary enterprise and church extension were on the grandest scale, and grew with increasing wealth. Numerous church edifices in this city, of the denomination to which he belonged, owe their existence largely to his liberality, and two at least were projected and built by him entirely at his own cost. In his mental character, Mr. Baldwin was a man of remarkable firmness of purpose. This trait was strongly shown during his mechanical career, in the persistency with which he would work at a new improvement or resist an innovation. If he were led sometimes to assume an attitude of antagonism to features of locomotive construction which after-experience showed to be valuable, (and a desire for historical accuracy has required the mention, in previous pages, of several instances of this kind) it is at least certain that his opposition was based upon a conscientious belief in the mechanical impolicy of the proposed changes.

After the death of Mr. Baldwin the business was reorganized, in 1867, under the title of "The Baldwin Locomotive Works," M. Baird & Co., proprietors. Messrs. George Burnham and Charles T. Parry, who had been connected with the establishment from an early period, the former in charge of the finances, and the latter as General Superintendent, were associated with Mr. Baird in the copartnership. Three years later Messrs. Edward H. Williams, William P. Henszey and Edward Longstreth became members of the firm. Mr. Williams had been connected with railway management on various lines since 1850. Mr. Henszey had been Mechanical Engineer, and Mr. Longstreth the General Superintendent of the Works for several years previously.

A class of engines known as Moguls, with three pairs of drivers connected, and a swinging pony truck in front equalized with the forward drivers, took its rise in the practice of this establishment from the "E. A. Douglas," built for the Thomas Iron Company in 1867. Mogul locomotives were soon extensively employed in heavy freight service on American railways, and their use continued for many years after

MOGUL LOCOMOTIVE
Thomas Iron Company

the building of the "Douglas." They have now, however, been generally replaced, in main line work, by locomotives of more powerful types. Large numbers of Mogul locomotives have been built for export, and in plantation and other forms of special service, this type is deservedly popular.

In 1867, on a number of eight-wheeled four-coupled engines for the Pennsylvania Railroad, the four-wheeled swing bolster truck was first applied, and thereafter a large number of engines have been so constructed. The two-wheeled or "pony truck" has been built both on the Bissell plan, with double inclined slides, and with the ordinary swing bolster, and in both cases with the radius bar pivoting from a point about four feet back from the center of the truck. In the case of both the two-wheeled and the four-wheeled truck, however, the swing bolster is now the rule; the four-wheeled truck being made without a radius bar.

SPIT AND POLISH on the Central RR of New Jersey. This high wheeled compound 4-4-0 must have burned up the rails between Elizabeth and Somerville. (Collection of C. A. Brown)

PHILADELPHIA & READING 4-2-2 camelback No. 385, later re-numbered No. 316. Built in 1895. (Collection of C. A. Brown)

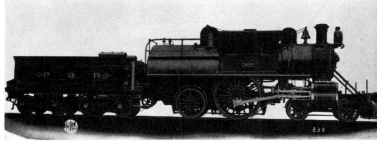

Of the engines above referred to as the first on which the swing bolster truck was applied, four were for express passenger service, with drivers 66 inches in diameter, and cylinders 17 by 24 inches. One of them, placed on the road September 9, 1867, was in constant service until May 14, 1871, without ever being off its wheels for repairs, making a total mileage of 153,280 miles. All of these engines had their driving wheels spread 8 feet 6 inches between centers.

THE LOCOMOTIVE THAT MADE 153,280 MILES BEFORE BEING SHOPPED
FOR GENERAL REPAIRS

Steel tubes were first used in three ten-wheeled freight engines, numbers 211, 338 and 368, completed for the Pennsylvania Railroad in August, 1868. Steel boilers were first made in 1868 for locomotives for the Pennsylvania Railroad Company, and the use of this material for the barrels of boilers as well as for the fireboxes subsequently became universal in American practice.

In 1866, the straight boiler with two domes, first used in 1856, was again introduced; and until about 1880 the practice of the establishment included both the wagon-top boiler with single dome, and the straight boiler with one or two domes. Since 1880, the use of two domes has been exceptional, both wagon-top and straight boilers being constructed with one dome.

In 1868, a locomotive of three and one-half feet gauge was constructed for the Averill Coal and Oil Company, of West Virginia. This was the first narrow gauge locomotive in the

practice of the Works. In 1869, three locomotives of the same gauge were constructed for the União Valenciana Railway of Brazil and were the first narrow gauge locomotives constructed at these Works for general passenger and freight traffic. In the following year the Denver and Rio Grande Railway, of Colorado, was projected on the three-feet gauge, and the first locomotives for the line were designed and built in 1871. Two classes, for passenger and freight, respectively, were constructed. The former were six-wheeled with four wheels coupled 40 inches in diameter, and 9 by 16-inch cylinders. They weighed each, loaded, about 25,000 pounds. The latter were eight-wheeled, with six wheels coupled, 36 inches in diameter, and 11 by 16-inch cylinders. These locomotives weighed each, loaded, about 35,000 pounds. Both types had a swinging truck with a single pair of wheels in front of the cylinders. The six-coupled design was for freight service, and was subsequently built in larger sizes. The four-coupled type for passenger service was found to be too small and to be unsteady on the track, owing to its comparatively short wheel base. It was therefore abandoned, and the ordinary American pattern, eight-wheeled, four-coupled, substituted. Following the engines for the Denver and Rio Grande Railway, others for other narrow gauge lines were called for, and the manufacture of this description of rolling stock soon assumed importance.

The Consolidation type, as first introduced for standard gauge in 1866, was adapted to the three feet gauge in 1873. In 1877, a locomotive on this plan, weighing in working order about 60,000 pounds, with cylinders 15 by 20 inches, was built for working the Garland extension of the Denver and Rio Grande Railway, which crossed the Rocky Mountains with maximum grades of 211 feet per mile, and minimum curves of 30 degrees. The performance of this locomotive, the "Alamosa," is given in the following extract from a letter from the then General Superintendent of that railway:

DENVER, COL., August 31, 1877

"On the 29th inst. I telegraphed you from Veta Pass—Sangre de Cristo Mountains—that engine 'Alamosa' had just hauled from Garland to the Summit one baggage car and seven coaches, containing 160 passengers.

HEAVY BALANCED compound Atlantic for the New York Central & Harlem River. (Collection of C. A. Brown)

NOTE: *Yes, the New York Central occasionally purchased a locomotive from Baldwin, and No. 3804 is visible proof of this fact.* (Frederick Westing)

CHICAGO, MILWAUKEE & ST. PAUL No. 838, was a handsome 4-4-2 compound built in 1896. (Collection of C. A. Brown)

NOTE: *A neat Vauclain compound Atlantic. High-pressure cylinders rest atop the large low-pressure cylinders as was normal practice whenever possible.* (Frederick Westing)

Yesterday I received your reply asking for particulars, etc.

"My estimate of the weight was 85 net tons, stretched over a distance of 360 feet, or including the engine of 405 feet.

"The occasion of this sized train was an excursion from Denver to Garland and return. The night before, in going over from La Veta, we had over 200 passengers, but it was but 8 P. M., and fearing a slippery rail, I put on engine No. 19 as a pusher, although the engineer of the 'Alamosa' said he could haul the train, and I believe he could have done so. The engine and train took up a few feet more than the half circle at 'Mule Shoe,' where the radius is 193 feet. The engine worked splendidly, and moved up the 211 feet grades and around the 30-degree curves seemingly with as much ease as our passenger engines on 75 feet grades with three coaches and baggage cars.

"The 'Alamosa' hauls regularly eight loaded cars and caboose, about 100 net tons; length of train about 230 feet.

"The distance from Garland to Veta Pass is 14¼ miles, and the time is one hour and twenty minutes.

"Respectfully yours,

(Signed)   W. W. BORST, *Supt.*"

In addition to narrow gauge locomotives for the United States, this branch of the product has included a large number of three feet, meter, and three and one-half feet gauge locomotives, which have been shipped to various parts of the world.

Locomotives for single-rail railroads were built in 1878 and early in 1879, adapted respectively to the systems of General Roy Stone and Mr. W. W. Riley.

Mine locomotives, generally of narrow gauge, for underground work, and not over 5½ feet in height, were first built in 1870. These machines were generally four-wheels-connected, with inside cylinders and a crank axle. The width over all of this plan was only 16 inches greater than the gauge of the track. A number of outside-connected mine locomotives were also constructed, the width being 32 inches greater than the gauge of the track. A locomotive of 20 inches gauge for a gold mine in California was built in 1876, and was found entirely practicable and efficient.

In 1870, in some locomotives for the Kansas Pacific Railway, the steel tires were shrunk on without being secured by bolts or rivets in any form, and since that time this method of putting on tires has been usually employed.

In 1871, 40 locomotives were constructed for the Ohio and Mississippi Railway, the gauge of which was changed from six feet to four feet nine inches. The entire lot of 40 locomotives was completed and delivered in about twelve weeks. The gauge of the road was changed on July 4, and the new locomotives went at once into service in operating the line on the standard gauge.

During the same year two "double-ender" tank locomotives of the 2-4-4 type were constructed for the Central Railroad of New Jersey, and were the first of this pattern at these Works.

The product of the Works, which had been steadily increasing for some years in sympathy with the requirements of the numerous new railroads which were constructing, reached 331 locomotives in 1871, and 422 in 1872. Orders for 90 locomotives for the Northern Pacific Railroad were entered during 1870-71, and for 124 for the Pennsylvania Railroad during 1872-73, and mostly executed during those years. A contract was also made during 1872 with the Veronej-Rostoff Railway of Russia for ten locomotives to burn Russian anthracite coal. Six were Moguls, with cylinders 19 by 24 inches and driving wheels 54 inches in diameter; and four were passenger locomotives, American pattern, with cylinders 17 by 24 inches, and driving wheels 66 inches in diameter. Nine American pattern locomotives, with 15 by 24-inch cylinders, and 60-inch driving wheels, were also constructed in 1872-73 for the Hango-Hyvinge Railway of Finland.

Early in 1873, Mr. Baird retired from the business, having sold his interest in the Works to his five partners. Mr. Baird died May 19, 1877. A new firm was formed under the style of Burnham, Parry, Williams & Co., dating from January 1, 1873, and Mr. John H. Converse, who had been connected with the Works since 1870, became a partner. The product of this year was 437 locomotives, the greatest in the history of the business up to that time. During a part of the year ten locomotives per week were turned out, and nearly 3,000 men were employed. Forty-five locomotives for the Grand Trunk Railway of Canada were built in August, September and October, 1873, and all were delivered in five weeks after shipment of the first.

2-FOOT GAUGE SOUTH AMERICAN beauty built by Baldwin in 1897. (Collection of C. A. Brown)

GALVESTON, HOUSTON & HENDERSON No. 82 was the first factory built engine to burn oil. Built in 1902, this one of a class lived out a useful career on its owners short piece of Texas real estate. The GH&H main line is the shortest of the four railroads serving Galveston and Houston.

It is interesting to note that during World War I before the coming of the interurban electric line between these two cities that the GH&H ran eight (8) round trip passenger trains between Galveston & Houston and the Sunday schedule was supplemented by a "Sea Wall Special."

The Sea Wall special was operated also by the other railroads serving the two cities and they were operated on a handicap basis. The GH&H line being the shortest between these two cities, therefore, placed the departure from Houston a few minutes after the other trains leaving for Galveston on the Sunday morning excursion trains known as the "Sea Wall Specials." Approaching Galveston all railroads are required to cross Galveston Bay on a trestle (now a causeway) two miles long. The Sunday Specials were all scheduled to arrive at the north end of the trestle at the same time, but the agreement was that the handicapped train arriving at the trestle earliest was allowed on the trestle ahead of the other trains. These Sea Wall Specials apparently became a tradition in the area and the Monday morning papers always carried the performance of the participating trains.

It was in this service that GH&H locomotive No. 82 became famous in the Texas railroad world. The typical train leaving Houston was made up of fifteen to eighteen open platform wooden coaches with No. 82 at the head end and a low drivered 0-6-0 switcher on the rear end as helper to assist the train out of the station. The helper stayed with the last car of the train as long as it could, but as soon as the train was approaching road speed, the switcher came to a stop and returned to Houston. Once rolling at road speed No. 82 had no difficulty in reaching speeds between 70 & 80 miles an hour even with eighteen coaches behind her. The level tangent track between Galveston and Houston on the GH&H route made this performance possible.

During the week No. 82 was regularly assigned to the Galveston News Special which was an early morning train consisting of baggage cars loaded with newspapers published by the Galveston Daily News, then the best known and most widely circulated newspaper in the state of Texas. This with usually four or five baggage cars regularly made the run between Galveston and Houston of fifty miles in fifty minutes including five stops within the city of Houston for unprotected railroad grade crossings. The train also observed a slow down crossing Galveston Bay on the two mile long trestle, which required five minutes for the crossing. According to the general yardmaster at Galveston, No. 82 was the best known locomotive on the railroad and was the pet of Mr. Jim Hill who was general manager of the railroad during the period of its greatest performances. Mr. Hill was no relation to the famous empire builder of Great Northern fame.

The locomotive saw some service during World War II and was finally scrapped in Galveston in 1949. (Collection of C. A. Brown)

"NYDIA" WAS THE NAME of this inspection car built for the Susquehanna Coal Co. in 1889. (Collection of C. A. Brown)

PHILADELPHIA & READING inspection engine No. 1—Baldwin product of 1898. (Collection of C. A. Brown)

These locomotives were built to meet the requirements of a change of gauge from 5 feet 6 inches to 4 feet 8½ inches. In November, 1873, under circumstances of special urgency, a small locomotive for the Meier Iron Company of St. Louis, was wholly made from the raw material in sixteen working days.

The financial difficulties which prevailed throughout the United States, beginning in September, 1873, and affecting chiefly the railroad interests and all branches of manufacture connected therewith, operated, of course, to curtail the production of locomotives for quite a period. Hence, only 205 locomotives were built in 1874, and 130 in 1875. Among these may be enumerated two sample locomotives for burning anthracite coal (one passenger, 16 by 24-inch cylinders, and one Mogul freight, 18 by 24-inch cylinders) for the Technical Department of the Russian Government; also twelve Mogul freight locomotives, 19 by 24-inch cylinders, for the Charkoff Nicolaieff Railroad of Russia. A small locomotive to work by compressed air, for drawing street cars, was constructed during 1874 for the Compressed Air Locomotive and Street Car Company, of Louisville, Ky. It had cylinders 7 by 12 inches, and four wheels coupled, 30 inches in diameter, and was the first Baldwin locomotive to have plate frames. Another and smaller locomotive, to work by compressed air, was constructed three years later for the Plymouth Cordage Company, of Massachusetts, for service on a track in and about their works. It had cylinders 5 by 10 inches, four wheels coupled, 24 inches diameter, and weighed 7,000 pounds; and was successfully employed for the work required.

In 1875 the Baldwin Locomotive Works acquired a controlling interest in the Standard Steel Works, located at Burnham, Pennsylvania.

The year 1876, noted as the year of the Centennial International Exhibition, in Philadelphia, brought some increase of business, and 232 locomotives were constructed. An exhibit consisting of eight locomotives was prepared for this occasion. With the view of illustrating not only the different types of American locomotives, but the practice of different railroads, the exhibit consisted chiefly of locomotives constructed to fill

orders from various railroad companies of the United States and from the Imperial Government of Brazil. A Consolidation locomotive for burning anthracite coal, for the Lehigh Valley Railroad, for which line the first locomotive of this type was designed and built in 1866; a similar locomotive, to burn bituminous coal, and a passenger locomotive for the same fuel for the Pennsylvania Railroad; a Mogul freight locomotive, the "Principe do Grão Pará," for the Dom Pedro Segundo Railway of Brazil, and a passenger locomotive (anthracite burner) for the Central Railroad of New Jersey, comprised the larger locomotives contributed by these Works to the Exhibition of 1876. To these were added a mine locomotive and two narrow (three feet) gauge locomotives, which were among those used in working the Centennial Narrow Gauge Railway. As this line was in many respects unique, we subjoin the following extracts from an account by its General Manager of the performance of the two three-feet gauge locomotives:

"The gauge of the line was three feet, with double track three and a half miles long, or seven miles in all. For its length, it was probably the most crooked road in the world, being made up almost wholly of curves, in order to run near all the principal buildings on the Exhibition grounds. Many of these curves were on our heaviest grades, some having a radius of 215, 230 and 250 feet on grades of 140 and 155 feet per mile. These are unusually heavy grades and curves, and when *combined* as we had them, with only a 35-pound iron rail, made the task for our engines exceedingly difficult.

"Your locomotive 'Schuylkill,' Class 8-18-C (eight-wheeled, four wheels coupled three and a half feet diameter; cylinders, 12 by 16; weight, 42,650 pounds), began service May 13th, and made 156 days to the close of the Exhibition. The locomotive 'Delaware, Class 8-18-D (eight-wheeled, six wheels coupled three feet diameter; cylinders, 12 by 16; weight, 39,000 pounds), came into service June 9th, and made 131 days to the close of the Exhibition. The usual load of each engine was five eight-wheeled passenger cars, frequently carrying over 100 passengers per car. On special occasions, as many as six and seven loaded cars have been drawn by one of these engines.

"Each engine averaged fully 16 trips daily, equal to 56 miles, and as the stations were but a short distance apart, the Westinghouse air brake was applied in making 160 daily stops, or a total of 25,000 for each engine. Neither engine was out of service an hour, unless from accidents for which they were in no way responsible."

[NOTE.—Average weight of each loaded car about 12 gross tons.]

"EMILIA" had lots of class and may have been the world's first locomotive with a sleeper cab. (Collection of C. A. Brown)

LIGHT ELECTRIC locomotive for the Metropolitan Railway, built in 1899. (Collection of C. A. Brown)

The year 1876 was also marked by an extension of locomotive engineering to a new field in the practice of these Works. In the latter part of the previous year an experimental steam street car was constructed for the purpose of testing the applicability of steam to street railways. This car was completed in November, 1875, and was tried for a few days on a street railway in Philadelphia. It was then sent to Brooklyn, December 25, 1875, where it ran from that time until June, 1876. One engineer ran the car and kept it in working order. Its consumption of fuel was between seven and eight pounds of coal per mile run. It drew regularly, night and morning, an additional car, with passengers going into New York in the morning, and returning at night. On several occasions, where speed was practicable, the car was run at the rate of 16 to 18 miles per hour.

In June, 1876, this car was withdrawn from the Atlantic Avenue Railway of Brooklyn, and placed on the Market Street Railway of Philadelphia. It worked on that line with fair success, and very acceptably to the public, from June till nearly the close of the Centennial Exhibition.

This original steam car was built with cylinders under the body of the car, the connecting rods taking hold of a crank axle, to which the front wheels were attached. The rear wheels of the car were independent, and not coupled with the front wheels.

The machinery of the car was attached to an iron bed-plate bolted directly to the wooden framework of the car body. The experiment with this car demonstrated to the satisfaction of its builders the mechanical practicability of the use of steam on street railways, but the defects developed by this experimental car were: first, that it was difficult, or impossible, to make a crank axle which would not break, the same experience being reached in this respect which had already presented itself in locomotive construction; second, it was found that great objection existed to attaching the machinery to the wooden car body, which was not sufficiently rigid for the purpose, and which suffered by being racked and strained by the working of the machinery.

For these reasons this original steam car was reconstructed, in accordance with the experience which nearly a year's service

had suggested. The machinery was made outside-connected, the same as an ordinary locomotive, and a strong iron framework was designed entirely independent of the car body, and supporting the boiler and all the machinery.

The car as thus reconstructed was named the "Baldwin," and is shown by the accompanying illustration.

STEAM STREET CAR

The next step in this direction was the construction of a separate motor, to which one or more cars could be attached. Such a machine, weighing about 16,000 pounds, was constructed in the fall of 1876, and sent to the Citizen's Railway of Baltimore, which had a maximum grade of seven feet per hundred, or 369.6 feet per mile. It ascended this grade drawing one loaded car, when the tracks were covered with mixed snow and dirt to a depth of eight to ten inches in places. Another and smaller motor, weighing only 13,000 pounds, was constructed about the same time for the Urbano Railway, of Havana, Cuba. Orders for other similar machines followed, and during the ensuing years, 1877-80, 107 separate motors and 12 steam cars were included in the product. Various city and suburban railways were constructed with the especial view of employing steam power, and were equipped with these machines. One line, the Hill and West Dubuque Street Railway, of Dubuque, Iowa, was constructed early in 1877, of three and one-half feet gauge with a maximum gradient of nine in 100, and was worked exclusively by two of these motors. The details and

"F. C. LATROBE" must have been an inspection vehicle for her owner, Citizen's Railway Company. With no couplers, it is hard to visualize what other work could have been assigned to it. (Collection of C. A. Brown)

MISSOURI KANSAS & TEXAS bought this sporty inspection car in 1894. (Collection of C. A. Brown)

character of construction of these machines were essentially the same as locomotive work, but they were made so as to be substantially noiseless, and to show little or no smoke and steam in operation.

Steel fireboxes with vertical corrugations in the side sheets were first made by these Works early in 1876, in locomotives for the Central Railroad of New Jersey, and for the Delaware, Lackawanna and Western Railroad.

STEAM MOTOR AND STREET CAR

The first American locomotives for New South Wales and Queensland were constructed by the Baldwin Locomotive Works in 1877, and have since been succeeded by additional orders. Six locomotives of the Consolidation type for three and one-half feet gauge were also constructed in the latter year for the Government Railways of New Zealand, and two freight locomotives, six-wheels-connected, with forward truck, for the Government of Victoria. Four similar locomotives (ten-wheeled, six coupled, with 16 by 24-inch cylinders) were also built during the same year for the Norwegian State Railways.

Forty heavy Mogul locomotives (19 by 24-inch cylinders, driving wheels 54 inches in diameter) were constructed early in 1878 for two Russian Railways (the Koursk Charkoff Azof, and the Orel Griazi). The definite order for these locomotives was received on the sixteenth of December, 1877, and as all were required to be delivered in Russia by the following May, especial despatch was necessary. The working force was increased from 1,100 to 2,300 men in about two weeks. The first of the forty engines was erected and tried under steam on January 5th, three weeks after receipt of order, and was finished, ready to dismantle and pack for shipment, one week later. The last engine of this

order was completed February 13th. The 40 engines were thus constructed in about eight weeks, besides 28 additional engines on other orders, which were constructed, wholly or partially, and shipped during the same period.

Four tramway motors of 12 tons weight were built early in 1879, on the order of the New South Wales Government, for a tramway having grades of six per cent, and running from the railway terminus to the Sydney Exhibition Grounds. Subsequent orders followed for additional motors for other tramways in Sydney.

FOR THE INDIAN HEAD Naval Proving Ground, the Baldwin Locomotive works built this trolley motor in 1898, and made sure the sandbox covers stayed in place by weighting them down with builder's plates. (Collection of C. A. Brown)

4-WHEEL ELECTRIC LOCOMOTIVE built in 1901 for the Atlantic Coast Lumber Co. (Collection of C. A. Brown)

EARLY BALDWIN-WESTINGHOUSE electric locomotive was this 25 ton switcher built in 1902. (Collection of C. A. Brown)

CHAPTER VI.

LOCOMOTIVE DEVELOPMENT DURING THE YEARS 1880-1900

The five-thousandth locomotive, finished in April, 1880, presented some novel features. It was designed for fast passenger service on the Bound Brook line between Philadelphia and New York, and to run with a light train at a speed of 60 miles per hour, using anthracite coal as fuel. It had cylinders 18 by 24 inches, one pair of driving wheels 78 inches in diameter, and a pair of trailing wheels 45 inches in diameter, and equalized with the driving wheels. Back of the driving wheels and over the trailing wheels space was given for a wide firebox (eight feet long by seven feet wide inside) as required for anthracite coal. By an auxiliary steam cylinder placed under the waist of the boiler, just in front of the firebox, the bearings on the equalizing beams between trailing and driving wheels could be changed to a point forward of their normal position, so as to increase the weight on the driving wheels when required. The adhesion could thus be varied between the limits of 35,000 and 45,000 pounds on the single pair of driving wheels. This feature of the locomotive was made the subject of a patent.

In 1881, a compressed air locomotive was constructed for the Pneumatic Tramway Engine Company, of New York, on plans prepared by Mr. Robert Hardie. Air tanks of steel, one-half inch thick, with a capacity of 465 cubic feet, were combined with an upright cylindrical heater, 32⅝ inches in diameter. The weight of the machine was 35,000 pounds, of which 28,000 pounds were on four driving wheels, 42 inches in diameter. The cylinders were 12½ inches diameter by 18 inches stroke.

STEAM INSPECTION CAR

Another novelty of the year was a steam car to take the place of a hand car. The accompanying illustration shows the design. Its cylinders were four

by ten inches, and wheels 24 inches diameter. Built for standard gauge track, its weight in working order was 5,110 pounds. Similar cars have since been constructed.

During this year the largest single order placed on the books to that date was entered for the Mexican National Construction Company. It was for 150 locomotives, but only a portion of them were ever built.

The year 1882 was marked by a demand for locomotives greater than could be met by the capacity of existing locomotive works. Orders for 1,321 locomotives were entered on the books during the year, deliveries of the greater part being promised only in the following year.

Early in 1882 an inquiry was received from the Brazilian Government for locomotives for the Cantagallo Railway, which were required to meet the following conditions: to haul a train of 40 gross tons of cars and lading up a grade of 8.3 per cent (438 feet per mile), occurring in combination with curves of 40 metres radius (131 feet radius, or 43.8 degrees). The line was laid with heavy steel rails, to a gauge of 1.100 metres, or 3 feet 7⅛ inches. The track upon which it was proposed to run these locomotives was a constant succession of reverse curves, it being stated that 91 curves of the radius named occurred within a distance of 3,429 metres, or about two miles. The line had previously been operated on the "Fell" system, with central rack-rail, and it was proposed to introduce locomotives working by ordinary adhesion, utilizing the central rail for the application of brake power. An order was eventually received to proceed with the construction of three locomotives to do this work. The engines built were of the following general dimensions, viz.: cylinders, 18 by 20 inches; six driving wheels, connected, 39 inches in diameter; wheel base, 9 feet 6 inches; boiler, 54 inches in diameter, with 190 tubes 2 inches diameter, 10 feet 9 inches long; and with side tanks, carried on the locomotive. In March, 1883, they were shipped from Philadelphia, and on a trial made October 17, in the presence of the officials of the road and other prominent railway officers, the guaranteed performance was accomplished. One of the engines pulled a train weighing 40 tons, composed of three freight cars loaded

STEAM DUMMIES were a frequent item delivered to urban and suburban railways throughout the world. This 0-4-2 hauled a trailer in the suburbs of Minneapolis. (Collection of C. A. Brown)

FOR THE NEW YORK ELEVATED, Baldwin built much steam power—this little teakettle in 1876. (Collection of C. A. Brown)

with sleepers, and one passenger car, and made the first distance of eight kilometres to Boca do Mato with a speed of 24 kilometres per hour; from there it started, making easily an acclivity of 8.5 per cent in grade, and against a curve of 40 metres in radius. Eight additional locomotives for this line were constructed at intervals during the following ten years, and the road has been worked by adhesion locomotives since their adoption as above described.

In 1885 a locomotive was built for the Dom Pedro Segundo Railway of Brazil, having five pairs of driving wheels connected, and a leading two-wheeled truck. From this has arisen the title "Decapod" (having ten feet) as applied to subsequent locomotives of this type. The driving wheel base of this loco-

DECAPOD TYPE LOCOMOTIVE
Dom Pedro Segundo Railway, Brazil
Cylinders, 22" x 26"   Drivers, Diam., 45"   Weight, Total Engine, 141,000 lb

motive was 17 feet. The rear flanged driving wheels, however, were given one-quarter inch more total play on the rails than the next adjacent pair; the second and third pairs were without flanges, and the front pair was flanged. The locomotive could therefore pass a curve of a radius as short as 500 feet, the rails being spread one-half inch wider than the gauge of track, as is usual on curves. The flanges of the first and fourth pairs of driving wheels making practically a rigid wheel base of 12 feet 8 inches, determined the friction on a curve. During this year the first rack-rail locomotive to be exported by these Works was constructed for the Ferro Principe do Grão Pará Railroad of Brazil. Its general dimensions were: cylinders, 12 by 20 inches; pitch line of cog-wheel, 41.35 inches; weight, 15.74 tons. Several additional similar locomotives, but of different weights, have since been constructed for the same line.

At the close of this year Mr. Edward Longstreth withdrew from the firm on account of ill health, and a new partnership was formed, adding Messrs. William C. Stroud, William H. Morrow, and William L. Austin. Mr. Stroud had been connected with the business since 1867, first as bookkeeper, and subsequently as Financial Manager. Mr. Morrow, since entering the service in 1871, had acquired a varied and valuable experience, first in the accounts, then in the department of Extra Work, and subsequently as Assistant Superintendent, becoming General Manager on Mr. Longstreth's retirement. Mr. Austin, who entered the Works in 1870, had for several years been assistant to Mr. Henszey in all matters connected with the designing of locomotives.

LOCOMOTIVE WITH OUTSIDE FRAMES
Antofogasta Railway, Chile

On February 11, 1886, Mr. S. M. Vauclain, who had been connected with the Works since July 1, 1883, was appointed General Superintendent. The retirement of Mr. Longstreth was necessarily followed by a number of changes in the organization. Mr. Edwin W. Heald, who had been assisting Mr. Longstreth and was in line for promotion to the position of General Superintendent, was unable to assume the duties of the office on account of poor health, hence Mr. Vauclain's appointment.

A locomotive for the Antofogasta Railway (30 inches gauge) of Chile, constructed with outside frames, was completed in November, 1886, and is shown by the illustration herewith. The advantages of this method of construction of narrow gauge locomotives in certain cases were evidenced in the working of this machine, in giving a greater width of firebox between the

BET YOU NEVER KNEW there were five Smith Brothers. Built in 1881 for the Santiago de Cuba R.R. (Collection of C. A. Brown)

CAMOUFLAGED TO LOOK like a horse car, this 3'6" gauge mogul was intended to avoid frightening the horses as it crossed the Willamette Bridge. (Collection of C. A. Brown)

frames, and a greater stability of the engine due to the outside journal bearings.

In 1887, a new form of boiler was brought out in some ten-wheeled locomotives constructed for the Denver and Rio Grande Railroad. A long wagon-top was used, extending sufficiently forward of the crown sheet to allow the dome to be placed in front of the firebox and near the center of the boiler, and the crown sheet was supported by radial stays from the outside shell. Many boilers of this type have since been constructed.

Mr. Charles T. Parry, who had been connected with the Works almost from their beginning, and a partner since 1867, died on July 18, 1887, after an illness of several months.

The first locomotives for Japan were shipped in June, 1887. These were two six-wheeled engines of three feet six inches gauge for the Mie Kie mines.

Mr. William H. Morrow, a partner since January 1, 1886, and who had been previously associated with the business since 1871, died February 19, 1888.

The demand for steam motors for street railway service attained large proportions at this period, and 95 were built during the years 1888 and 1889. Two rack-rail locomotives on the Riggenbach system, one with a single cog-wheel and four carrying wheels, and weighing in working order 32,000 pounds, for the Corcovado Railway of Brazil, and the other having two cog-wheels and eight carrying wheels, and weighing in working order 79,000 pounds, for the Estrada de Ferro Principe do Grão Pará of Brazil, were constructed during this year. Illustrations of these locomotives are presented herewith.

RACK LOCOMOTIVE, RIGGENBACH SYSTEM

The ten-thousandth locomotive was built in June, 1889, for the Northern Pacific Railroad. This locomotive had 22 by 28-inch cylinders, and weighed 147,500 pounds in working

order. It was representative of the heaviest class of Consolidation locomotive built at that time.

RACK LOCOMOTIVE WITH TWO COG WHEELS

In October, 1889, the first compound locomotive in the practice of the Works was completed and placed on the Baltimore and Ohio Railroad. It was of the four-cylinder type, as designed and patented by Mr. S. M. Vauclain. The economy in fuel and water and the efficiency of this design in both passenger and freight service led to its introduction on many leading railroads, and Vauclain compound locomotives were built in large numbers during the fifteen years following the construction of the first one.

In 1889 a test case was made to see in how short a time a locomotive could be built. On June 22d, Mr. Robert Coleman ordered a narrow gauge locomotive of the American type, which was to be ready for service on his railroad in Lebanon County, Pa., by July 4th following. The locomotive was actually completed on July 2d, having been built from the raw material in eight working days.

The manufacture of wrought iron wheel centers for both truck and driving wheels was begun at this time under patents of Mr. S. M. Vauclain, Nos. 462,605, 462,606 and 531,487.

During the year 1890, the Erecting Shop, which fronted on Broad Street, adjoining the main office, was entirely reconstructed. The new shop was a single-story building, 42 feet high to the eaves, and measuring 160 feet wide by 337 feet long. It contained nineteen tracks, each capable of accommodating four locomotives. All the machinery in the shop was driven by electric motors, and material was handled by two electric traveling cranes of 100 tons capacity each. This is the first instance on record of a shop being electrically equipped throughout.

In 1890 the first rack-rail locomotive on the Abt system was constructed for the Pike's Peak Railroad, and during this year and 1893 four locomotives were built for working the grades of that line, which vary from 8 to 25 per cent. One of these

FAIRFIELD TRACTION CO. No. 1, built in 1901 was later sold to the Lancaster Traction Co. (Collection of C. A. Brown)

BUFFALO & SUSQUEHANNA No. 14 had an unusual cab roof—1901. (Collection of C. A. Brown)

locomotives, weighing in working order 52,680 pounds, pushes 25,000 pounds up the maximum grades of one in four. An illustration is here given of one of these locomotives, which is a four-cylinder compound.

RACK LOCOMOTIVE, ABT SYSTEM

Three Mogul locomotives, of one metre gauge, 15 by 18-inch cylinders, driving wheels 41 inches diameter, were completed and shipped in July, 1890, for working the Jaffa and Jerusalem Railway in Palestine; and two additional locomotives for the same line were constructed in 1892.

In 1891 the name of the firm was changed to Burnham, Williams & Co., the partners being George Burnham, Edward H. Williams, William P. Henszey, John H. Converse, William C. Stroud, and William L. Austin.

In 1891 the largest locomotives in the practice of the Works, to that date, were designed and constructed for the St. Clair Tunnel of the Grand Trunk Railway, under the St. Clair River.

TEN-COUPLED TANK LOCOMOTIVE
Cylinders, 22″ x 28″   Drivers, Diam., 50″
Weight, Total, 186,800 lb.

Four tank locomotives were supplied, as shown in the accompanying illustration. The tunnel is 6,000 feet long, with grades of two per cent at each entrance, 2,500 and 1,950 feet long respectively. Each locomotive was required to take a train load of 760 tons exclusive of its own weight, and in actual operation each of these locomotives has hauled from 25 to 33 loaded cars in one train through the tunnel. This tunnel was subsequently electrified, and since 1908 trains have been hauled through it by Baldwin-Westinghouse electric locomotives.

For the New York, Lake Erie and Western Railroad, five compound locomotives of the Decapod type were completed in December, 1891. Their general dimensions were as follows: cylinders, high-pressure 16 inches, low-pressure 27 inches diameter, stroke 28 inches; five pairs of driving wheels coupled, 50 inches diameter, in a wheel base of 18 feet 10 inches; boiler, 76 inches diameter, of the Wootten type; weight in working order, 195,000 pounds; and weight on driving wheels, 172,000 pounds. The first, fourth and fifth pairs of driving wheels were flanged, but the fifth pair had one-fourth inch additional play on the track. These locomotives were used as pushers on the Susquehanna Hill, where curves of five degrees are combined with grades of 60 feet per mile, doing the work of two ordinary Consolidation locomotives. From 1,250 to 1,300 net tons of cars and lading, making a train of 45 loaded cars, were hauled by one of these locomotives in connection with a Consolidation type locomotive having 20 by 24-inch cylinders.

Mr. William C. Stroud, who had been a partner since 1886, died on September 21, 1891.

The first locomotives for Africa were constructed during this year. They were of the Mogul type, with cylinders 18 by 22 inches, driving wheels 48 inches diameter, and of three feet six inches gauge.

The product of 1892 and 1893 included, as novelties, two rack-rail locomotives for a mountain railway near Florence, Italy, and 25 compound Forney type locomotives for the South Side Elevated Railroad of Chicago.

At the World's Columbian Exposition in Chicago, May to October, 1893, inclusive, an exhibit was made, consisting of seventeen locomotives, as follows:

STANDARD GAUGE.—A Decapod locomotive, similar to those previously described, built in 1891 for the New York, Lake Erie and Western Railroad.

A high-speed locomotive of new type, with Vauclain compound cylinders, a two-wheeled leading truck, two pairs of driving wheels, and a pair of trailing wheels under the firebox. This locomotive was named "Columbia," and the same name has been applied to the type.

DETROIT AND LIMA NORTHERN No. 100 had an almost interurban car appearance—1898. (Collection of C. A. Brown)

An express passenger locomotive of the pattern used by the Central Railroad of New Jersey; one of the pattern used by the Philadelphia and Reading Railroad, and one of the pattern used by the Baltimore and Ohio Railroad. The three roads mentioned together operated the "Royal Blue Line" between New York and Washington.

A saddle tank double-ender type locomotive, with steam windlass, illustrating typical logging locomotive practice.

A single expansion American type locomotive with cylinders 18 by 24 inches.

A single expansion Mogul locomotive with cylinders 19 by 24 inches.

A single expansion ten-wheeled freight locomotive with cylinders 20 by 24 inches, for the Baltimore and Ohio Southwestern Railroad.

A compound ten-wheeled passenger locomotive shown in connection with a train exhibited by the Pullman Car Company.

A compound Consolidation locomotive for the Norfolk and Western Railroad.

Three locomotives were shown in connection with the special exhibit of the Baltimore and Ohio Railroad, *viz.:* one compound, one single-expansion, and one ten-wheeled passenger locomotive.

NARROW GAUGE.—A metre gauge compound American type locomotive.

A three feet gauge ten-wheeled compound locomotive with outside frames, for the Mexican National Railroad.

A 30-inch gauge saddle tank locomotive for mill or furnace work.

The depression of business which began in the summer of 1893, reduced the output of the Works for that year to 772, and in 1894 to 313 locomotives.

Early in 1895, a new type of passenger locomotive, illustrated herewith, was brought out for the Atlantic Coast Line. To this the name "Atlantic" type was given. The advantages of this design are a large boiler, fitting the engine for high speed; a firebox of liberal proportions and of desirable form placed over the rear frames, and having ample depth and width; and the location of the driving wheels in front of the firebox, allowing the boiler to be placed lower than in the ordinary American or ten-wheeled type. For the enginemen,

ATLANTIC TYPE LOCOMOTIVE

who, in this class of locomotive, ride behind, instead of over the driving wheels, greater ease in riding, and greater safety in case of the breakage of a side-rod, are important advantages.

The first electric locomotive was constructed in 1895, and was intended for experimental work for account of the North American Company. The electrical parts were designed by Messrs. Sprague, Duncan & Hutchison, Electrical Engineers, New York. Two other electric locomotives for use in connection with mining operations were built in 1896, in co-operation with the Westinghouse Electric and Manufacturing Company, which supplied the electrical parts.

ELECTRIC LOCOMOTIVE, 1895

A high speed passenger locomotive, having a single pair of driving wheels, and embracing other novel features, was built in 1895, for service on the New York division of the Philadelphia and Reading Railroad. The boiler was of the Wootten type, and the cylinders were compound. The cut on page 87 shows the general design. This locomotive and a duplicate built in the

BALDWIN DEMONSTRATOR 14420 was built for display at the Southern States & International Exhibition held in Atlanta in 1895. Later sold to the Intercolonial Rwy. of Canada. (Collection of C. A. Brown)

following year were regularly used in passenger service, hauling five cars and making the distance between Jersey City and Philadelphia, 90 miles, in 105 minutes, including six stops.

HIGH SPEED LOCOMOTIVE, PHILADELPHIA & READING RY.
Cylinders, 13" and 22" x 26"   Drivers, Diam., 84¼"
Weight, Total Engine, 115,000 lb.

In July, 1895, a combination rack and adhesion locomotive was constructed for the San Domingo Improvement Company. This locomotive was designed by Messrs. Wm. P. Henszey and S. M. Vauclain, and was made the subject of a patent. It had compound cylinders 8 inches and 13 inches diameter by 18 inches stroke to operate two pairs of coupled adhesion wheels, and a pair of single expansion cylinders, 11 inches by 18 inches, to operate a single rack wheel constructed upon the Abt system. It was furnished with two complete sets of machinery, entirely independent of each other, and was built with the view

COMBINATION RACK AND ADHESION LOCOMOTIVE
San Domingo Improvement Co.

eventually to remove the rack attachments and operate by adhesion alone.

During the years 1895 and 1896 contracts were executed for several railroads in Russia, aggregating 138 locomotives of the four-cylinder compound type.

On January 1, 1896, Messrs. Samuel M. Vauclain, Alba B. Johnson, and George Burnham, Jr., were admitted to partnership.

Two combination rack and adhesion locomotives, for the Peñoles Mining Company of Mexico, were built in 1896, having compound cylinders 9½ and 15 inches diameter by 22 inches stroke, connected to the driving wheels through walking beams.

Each locomotive had three coupled axles, which carried rack pinions of the Abt system. When operating on the rack section of the line, all the wheels ran loose on the axles, and acted as carrying wheels only. When, however, it was necessary to propel the locomotive by adhesion alone, two pairs of wheels could be secured to their respective axles, and thus made to turn with them, by means of clutches. These clutches were controlled by a hand lever placed in the cab. This device was made the subject of a patent,

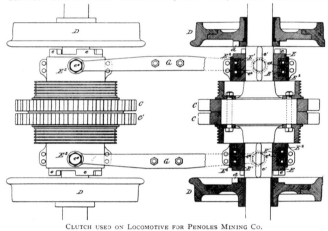

COMBINATION RACK AND ADHESION LOCOMOTIVE
For the Peñoles Mining Co.

which was granted to Messrs. S. M. Vauclain and J. Y. McConnell. The drawing of the clutch mechanism below is reproduced from the patent specification.

In the latter part of the year 1896, six locomotives were built for the Baltimore and Ohio Railroad, for express passenger service. One of these locomotives, No. 1312, is here illustrated.

CLUTCH USED ON LOCOMOTIVE FOR PEÑOLES MINING CO.

CAMELBACK 0-8-0 for a Mexican Coal Company—1901. (Collection of C. A. Brown)

They were of the ten-wheeled type, and handled the fast passenger trains on the Baltimore and Ohio Railroad running between Philadelphia, Baltimore and Washington with great efficiency for about fifteen years, when they were replaced by heavier power.

TEN-WHEELED LOCOMOTIVE
Baltimore and Ohio Railroad
Cylinders, 21″ x 26″   Drivers, Diam., 78″   Weight, Total Engine, 145,000 lb.

Early in 1897, a group of unusually interesting locomotives were shipped to the Nippon Railway (Japan). These locomotives were all designed to burn a most inferior quality of coal, requiring large grate area and a firebox of ample depth and volume. They were of two types—the Atlantic, for passenger service, and a modified design of Consolidation for freight

THE FIRST MIKADO TYPE LOCOMOTIVE
Nippon Railway
Cylinders, 18½″x24″   Drivers, Diam., 44″   Weight, Total Engine, 119,600 lb.

service. The latter had a wide, deep firebox, which was placed entirely back of the driving wheels and over a rear truck. The accompanying illustration represents the design. All these locomotives proved highly successful. Freight locomotives of a design similar to those built for the Nippon Railway, were subsequently introduced in the United States, and were appropriately designated the "Mikado" type.

In the summer of 1897, the Reading Railway placed a fast train on its Atlantic City Division, allowing 52 minutes for running time from Camden to Atlantic City, a distance of 55½ miles, making the average rate of speed 64 miles per hour. The train averaged five and six cars, having a total weight of about 200 tons, not including the engine and tender. This train was hauled by a locomotive of the Atlantic type, having Vauclain compound cylinders, and shown in the accompanying illustration. The records show that for fifty-two days from July 2d to August 31, 1897, the average time consumed on the run was 48 minutes, equivalent to a uniform rate of speed from start to stop of 69 miles per hour. On one occasion the

ATLANTIC TYPE LOCOMOTIVE
Philadelphia and Reading Railway
Cylinders, 13″ and 22″ x 26″   Drivers, Diam., 84¼″
Weight, Total Engine, 142,900 lb.

distance was covered in 46½ minutes, an average of 71.6 miles per hour. The Railway Company's official record of the train for the season is reproduced on the following page. The service proved so popular that additional trains, making equally high speed, were subsequently established.

In 1898, the first cast steel frames used by the Baldwin Locomotive Works were applied to a consignment of Consolidation locomotives built for the Atchison, Topeka and Santa Fe Railway Company.

In November, 1898, a locomotive was built for the Lehigh Valley Railroad for use on the mountain cut-off between Coxton and Fairview, near Wilkesbarre. This locomotive was of the Consolidation type, with Vauclain compound cylinders, and was guaranteed to haul a load of 1,000 net tons exclusive of the weight of the engine and tender, on a grade of 66 feet per mile, at an average speed of 17 miles per hour. It fulfilled this guar-

LONG ISLAND No. 1, a classy 4-4-2 camelback, built in 1901. (Collection of C. A. Brown)

Copy of Train Despatcher's sheet, showing exact running time of train, to which is added a statement showing number of cars in train, number of passengers carried and average number of miles per hour for each trip

LOCOMOTIVE 1027

JULY

AUGUST

antee and fourteen similar locomotives were subsequently ordered by this Company.

Dr. Edward H. Williams, who had been connected with the Works as a partner since 1870, died December 21, 1899, at Santa Barbara, California.

CONSOLIDATION TYPE LOCOMOTIVE, LEHIGH VALLEY RAILROAD
Cylinders, 18″ and 30″ x 30″   Drivers, Diam., 55″
Weight, Total Engine, 226,000 lb.

The year 1899 was marked by a large increase in foreign business, notably in England and France. Contracts were made in England covering thirty locomotives for the Midland Railway, twenty locomotives for the Great Northern Railway, and twenty locomotives for the Great Central Railway. Ten locomotives were also ordered by the French State Railways, and ten by the Bone-Guelma Railway, in the French colonies of Algiers.

COMPOUND ATLANTIC TYPE LOCOMOTIVE
For the Bavarian State Railways

In the fall of this year two Vauclain compound Consolidation freight locomotives were built for the Bavarian State Railways. These were ordered as samples, the Company practically announcing its intention of modeling future locomotives for their freight traffic after these engines. So well did these sample locomotives perform, that in the following year, the management decided to order two passenger engines of the compound Atlantic type, and also embody in their passenger motive power the new features contained in these machines.

PENNSYLVANIA RAILROAD No. 1486, a Vauclain Compound 2-8-0 of 1891. (Collection of C. A. Brown)

The Baldwin Locomotive Works exhibited two locomotives at the Paris Exposition of 1900— a "goods" locomotive of the Mogul type for the Great Northern Railway, of England, and an Atlantic type passenger locomotive for the French State Railways. The exhibit of the French State Railways also included a compound American type passenger locomotive built by the Baldwin Locomotive Works. These engines were built in the regular course of business for the companies whose names they bore, and went into service on these roads immediately after the Exposition was over. In this year also large orders were filled for the Chinese Eastern Railroad, the Paris-Orleans Railway, the Finland State, the Egyptian State and the Belgian State Railways.

CHAPTER VII.

THE INTRODUCTION OF THE MODERN, HIGH-POWER LOCOMOTIVE, AND THE CONSEQUENT ENLARGEMENT OF THE BALDWIN PLANT

The beginning of the twentieth century witnessed great industrial prosperity in America and large demands for railway freight transportation. The introduction of cars of large capacity became general on American railroads, a tendency which had been gradually developing for some years. This involved increased train tonnage, improved road beds, heavier rails, stronger bridges and more powerful locomotives. The

COMPOUND PRAIRIE TYPE LOCOMOTIVE
Atchison, Topeka and Santa Fe Railway

locomotive has always reflected the changes in railroad practice. Just as the demand for increased horse power, involving greater steaming capacity and a larger grate area, evolved the Atlantic type engine from the American or eight-wheeled passenger engine; so, in order to secure a locomotive with ample heating surface and suitable firebox to handle heavy trains at high speed, the Prairie type was designed, being a logical development of the Mogul type. The Prairie type had a leading pony truck, three pairs of driving wheels, and a wide firebox extending over the frames and placed back of the driving wheels. To support this overhanging weight, a pair of trailing wheels was placed underneath the firebox. Fifty locomotives of this type were built for the Chicago, Burlington and Quincy Railroad, and forty-five for the Atchison, Topeka and Santa Fe Railway, in 1901; and other roads adopted the design to a limited extent. The Prairie type, however, is no longer being built for main line service.

THE BIG AND LITTLE of it in 1898. A rather large (for the time) freight engine poses with an industrial switcher in the Philadelphia back shop. (Collection of C. A. Brown)

At the Pan-American Exposition, held at Buffalo, N. Y., during 1901, a new departure in locomotive practice was exhibited by the Baldwin Locomotive Works. This was a ten-wheeled locomotive, built for the Illinois Central Railroad, the firebox and tender of which were of special construction, embodying the inventions of Mr. Cornelius Vanderbilt, M. E. The firebox was cylindrical in form, with annular corrugations, its axis eccentric to that of the boiler. It was riveted to the back head of the boiler, and was supported at the bottom by the mud

TEN-WHEELED LOCOMOTIVE
With Vanderbilt Boiler and Tender

rings; but otherwise was entirely disconnected from the outer shell, thus eliminating stay bolts and crown bars, necessary to flat surfaces in usual construction. It was supposed that the ease with which the firebox could be removed, and the absence of the usual repairs incidental to the renewal of stay bolts, would commend it. Defects developed, however, which caused this type of boiler to be abandoned after a few years' trial. The feature of the tender was a cylindrical instead of the ordinary U-shaped tank placed back of the coal space, the advantage being a better distribution of weight, and a smaller proportion of dead weight to carrying capacity. These tenders are still being built when specified by railroad companies.

The year 1901 was especially noticeable for the large volume of domestic business handled, there being great demand for motive power from the railroads of the West and Southwest. Large orders were placed with the Baldwin Locomotive Works in this year by the Union Pacific; Chicago, Burlington and Quincy; Choctaw, Oklahoma and Gulf; Toledo, St. Louis and Western; Atchison, Topeka and Santa Fe; Chicago and Alton;

Missouri, Kansas and Texas; Chicago, Milwaukee and St. Paul, and Southern Pacific Railroads. The Pennsylvania Railroad in this year, ordered over 150 locomotives of various types from the Baldwin Locomotive Works, and the Baltimore and Ohio Railroad also placed an order for over 100 locomotives.

The locomotives built for export during 1901, included thirteen for the New Zealand Government Railways, which were designed to use lignite as fuel. They had three pairs of coupled driving wheels, a four-wheeled leading truck, and a two-wheeled

FIRST PACIFIC TYPE LOCOMOTIVE
Built for the New Zealand Railways

trailing truck, over which was placed a deep, wide firebox. This type subsequently became known as the "Pacific," and because of its high steaming capacity and adhesion, was built in large numbers for heavy passenger service in the United States.

The month of February, 1902, witnessed the completion of the twenty-thousandth locomotive built by the Baldwin Locomotive Works. This engine embodied several interesting features, including a new arrangement of Vauclain compound cylinders. In the compound locomotives previously constructed, a high and a low pressure cylinder had been used on each side of the locomotive, the two cylinders on the same side being placed one above the other. In locomotive No. 20,000 the axes of the four cylinders were placed in the same horizontal plane, the two high pressure

THE RIGGENBACH system of cog rack was used for this incline locomotive built in 1885 for the Leopoldina Rwy. of Peru. (Collection of C. A. Brown)

cylinders being between the frames and the two low pressure outside. The high pressure pistons were connected to cranks, placed on the axle of the first pair of driving wheels; while the low pressure pistons were connected to crank pins outside the wheels, in the usual manner. With this construction there were of course four sets of guides, as well as four crossheads and main rods. The two cranks on the axle were placed 90 degrees apart, and each of them was 180 degrees from the corresponding crank pin on the outside of the wheel. The two pistons on the same side of the locomotive thus opposed one another in movement, starting their strokes simultaneously from opposite ends of

BALANCED COMPOUND LOCOMOTIVE
Baldwin Engine No. 20,000

their respective cylinders. With this construction, the disturbing effects of the reciprocating weights are partially neutralized; and no excess weight need be used in counterbalancing the driving wheels. This obviates the so-called "hammer blow," which is always present in locomotives having outside cylinders only. Balanced compound locomotives, as described above, can carry a maximum load on driving wheels without detriment to the track, as the greatest pressure on the rail is that due to the static wheel load.

In balanced compound locomotives of the Vauclain type, the steam distribution to each pair of cylinders is controlled by a single piston valve, so that the valve gear is no more complicated than that of a single expansion locomotive. Upward of 500 of these locomotives had been built up to the close of 1912, the majority of them for fast passenger service. With the advent of high temperature superheating, however, the building of this type of locomotive for American railroads practically ceased.

The construction of locomotive No. 20,000 and the completion of 70 years of continuous operation were celebrated on the evening of February 27, 1902, at the Union League, of Philadelphia, by a banquet at which 250 guests, including many of the most representative men in the United States, were present.

In May, 1902, a Decapod locomotive was built for the Atchison, Topeka and Santa Fe Railway. This was the first tandem compound in the experience of the Works and the heaviest locomotive built up to that time. The total weight of the engine alone was 267,800 pounds, of which 237,800 pounds were on the five pairs of driving wheels. It was designed for heavy freight hauling on the steep grades encountered on one section of this road.

MIKADO TYPE LOCOMOTIVE
Bismarck, Washburn and Great Falls Railway

The first locomotive built to burn lignite fuel in the United States was constructed in this year for the Bismarck, Washburn and Great Falls Railway. The Mikado type was selected in order to secure sufficient grate area and firebox volume. The design is illustrated above. Mikado type locomotives were subsequently built in large numbers for heavy freight service in the United States.

The discovery of large quantities of crude petroleum in gushers located in the Beaumont oil fields, of Texas, caused the railroads tapping this field to adopt, to some extent, this fuel on their locomotives. Oil-burning locomotives were built for the Atchison, Topeka and Santa Fe, the Southern Pacific, and the Galveston, Houston and Henderson Railroads, in 1902. Since that date, oil has practically replaced coal as a locomotive fuel in the Southwest, and is extensively used in certain sections of

RALEIGH AND GASTON No. 9 posed in an angle not usually seen in builder's photos. Class of 1883. (Collection of C. A. Brown)

the middle West. Oil-burning locomotives have also been introduced in the Pacific Coast District and the far Northwest.

With the increased use of electrically driven trains for interurban, elevated and subway traffic, many orders were received for electric motor trucks in this year. Electrical locomotives, both for surface and mine haulage, showed a marked increase in this year also, both in variety of design and the number constructed.

In the year 1903 the Baldwin Locomotive Works completed 2,022 locomotives, its largest annual output up to that time. Among these were four four-cylinder balanced compound At-

TANDEM COMPOUND SANTA FE TYPE LOCOMOTIVE
Atchison, Topeka and Santa Fe Railway
Cylinders, 19″ and 32″ x 32″   Drivers, Diam., 57″
Weight, Total Engine, 287,240 lb.

lantic type locomotives for the Atchison, Topeka and Santa Fe Railway, which proved highly successful. The same road received 26 single-expansion Pacific type locomotives for heavy passenger service, and also a consignment of tandem compound locomotives for freight service. These engines were similar to the Decapod locomotive previously described, except that a trailing truck was added. This improved the curving qualities of the engines when running backward. To this type the name Santa Fe was given.

During the year 1903, standard locomotive designs were prepared at these Works for the Associated Lines, which at that time comprised the Southern Pacific Company, Union Pacific Railroad, Oregon Short Line Railroad, Oregon Railroad and Navigation Company, and the Chicago and Alton Railway. As the various lines were already equipped with sufficient light power, only heavy designs for common standards were adopted.

namely: an Atlantic and a Pacific type locomotive for passenger service, two sizes of Consolidation engines for freight service, a Mogul locomotive for fast freight, and a six-wheeled switcher. These designs were prepared under the supervision of William A. Austin, Assistant Mechanical Engineer of the Baldwin Locomotive Works, and F. W. Mahl, Mechanical Engineer of the Southern Pacific, who represented the Associated Lines.

Owing to the rapid increase in the production of the Works, additional erecting facilities were required; and in 1903 a new erecting shop, arranged on a novel plan, was completed at Twenty-sixth Street· and Pennsylvania Avenue. This shop was built in the form of a round house, having 27 stalls, with an 80-foot turntable in the center. It was used principally for finishing and testing purposes.

In 1904 there was a temporary falling off in production, 1,485 locomotives being completed during that year. At the Louisiana Purchase Exposition, held at St. Louis, from May to November of the same year, the Baldwin Locomotive Works exhibited the following locomotives:

STANDARD GAUGE.—A balanced compound Atlantic type locomotive, for the Atchison, Topeka and Santa Fe Railway.

A four-cylinder compound Atlantic type locomotive for the Chicago, Burlington and Quincy Railroad. (This engine had been built two years previously, and was withdrawn from service to be placed on exhibition.)

A tandem compound Santa Fe type locomotive for the Atchison, Topeka and Santa Fe Railway.

An Atlantic type locomotive for the Chicago and Alton Railway.

A Pacific type locomotive for the Union Pacific Railroad.

A Consolidation type locomotive for the Southern Pacific Company.

A Pacific type locomotive for the St. Louis and San Francisco Railroad.

A two-cylinder compound Consolidation type locomotive for the Norfolk and Western Railway.

A single-expansion Consolidation type locomotive for the Norfolk and Western Railway.

FOR THE LINE OF THE FAMOUS "SKUNK", Baldwin built this 2-4-4 tank engine in 1887. The Fort Bragg RR later became the California Western Rwy. & Navigation Co. (Collection of C. A. Brown)

A ten-wheeled locomotive for the Norfolk and Western Railway.

An Atlantic type locomotive for the Norfolk and Western Railway.

A Consolidation type locomotive with Wootten firebox, for the Delaware, Lackawanna and Western Railroad.

A Mogul type locomotive for the Missouri, Kansas and Texas Railway.

There were also shown four electric trucks, designed for standard gauge track.

NARROW GAUGE.—An electric mining locomotive for the Norfolk Coal and Coke Company. (Gauge, three feet six inches.)

An electric mining locomotive for the Berwind-White Coal Mining Company. (Gauge, three feet.)

MALLET COMPOUND ARTICULATED LOCOMOTIVE
American Railroad of Porto Rico
Cylinders, 12½″ and 19″ x 20″   Drivers, Diam., 37″
Weight, Total Engine, 106,650 lb.

An electric locomotive for industrial haulage. (Gauge, two feet.)

The electric locomotives and trucks were exhibited in the Palace of Electricity in conjunction with the Westinghouse Electric and Manufacturing Company, which furnished the electrical equipment.

During this year three Mallet compound articulated locomotives, designed for meter gauge, were built for the American Railroad of Porto Rico. One of these engines is illustrated above. These locomotives had three pairs of driving wheels, 37 inches in diameter, in each group. The total weight was 106,650 pounds, and the tractive force 20,200 pounds working compound. These were the first Mallet articulated locomotives built in the experience of the Works.

Among other interesting locomotives exported during 1904, may be mentioned 16 tank engines for the Imperial Government Railways of Japan. These locomotives had three pairs of driving wheels and a two-wheeled rear truck. They were constructed with plate frames, in accordance with specifications furnished by the railway company. In addition, 150 locomotives of the same type were built during the following year.

Toward the close of the year 1904 the output began to increase, and in 1905, 2,250 locomotives were turned out. Among these were 572 engines for the Pennsylvania Railroad System, including the lines east and west of Pittsburgh; and 160 of

SIX-COUPLED TANK LOCOMOTIVE
For the Imperial Government Railways of Japan

these locomotives, all of the Consolidation type, were completed between October 10th and November 22d. This year witnessed the introduction of the Walschaerts valve motion on several American railroads. It was applied to a large number of the Pennsylvania Railroad engines above referred to, and also to 38 ten-wheeled locomotives for the Chicago, Rock Island and Pacific Railway.

Among the locomotives exported during the year 1905, may be mentioned 20 of the ten-wheeled type, built for the New South Wales Government Railways. These engines were built to the railway company's drawings and specifications. A large number of special features, including plate frames and the Allen valve motion, entered into their construction.

During the year 1906 a number of large electric locomotives were furnished to the New York, New Haven and Hartford

THIS ODD 2-8-0 TENDER *and* tank engine was built for the 2'6″ Antofogasta Railway in 1889. (Collection of C. A. Brown)

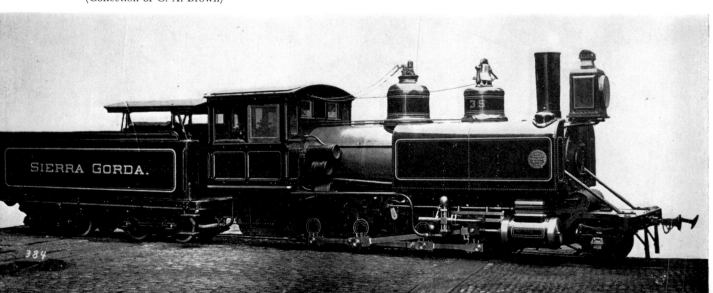

Railroad Company, for the purpose of replacing steam locomotives in the vicinity of New York City. Each of these locomotives was mounted on two four-wheeled trucks, and equipped with four single phase alternating current motors, which rotated the axles without intermediate gearing. The nominal capacity of each unit was 1,000 horsepower.

MALLET COMPOUND ARTICULATED LOCOMOTIVE
Great Northern Railway
Cylinders, 21½" and 33" x 32"   Drivers, Diam., 55"
Weight, Total Engine, 355,000 lb.

In 1906, the Great Northern Railway received five Mallet compound articulated locomotives, which were the heaviest, at that time, in the experience of the Works. These locomotives were carried on six pairs of driving wheels divided into two groups, and a two-wheeled truck front and back. They weighed 355,000 pounds, of which 316,000 pounds were carried on the driving wheels. One of these locomotives is illustrated above.

BALANCED COMPOUND PRAIRIE TYPE LOCOMOTIVE
Atchison, Topeka and Santa Fe Railway
Cylinders, 17½" and 29"x28". Drivers, Diam., 69". Weight, Total Engine, 248,200 lb.

During this year an order was also received for 57 balanced compound Prairie type locomotives for the Atchison, Topeka and Santa Fe Railway. These locomotives were designed for

fast freight service, and had inside high-pressure cylinders, inclined at an angle of seven degrees, in order that their main rods could clear the first driving axle. The total weight in working order was 248,200 pounds, of which the driving wheels carried 174,700 pounds. One of them is illustrated on the previous page.   Thirty-one similar locomotives were built in 1907.

Among the important foreign orders filled during the year 1906, may be mentioned one from the Italian Government Railways for 20 locomotives. The number was equally divided between balanced compound ten-wheeled locomotives for passenger service, and single-expansion Consolidation locomotives for freight service. One of the passenger locomotives is illustrated below.

BALANCED COMPOUND TEN-WHEELED LOCOMOTIVE
For the Italian Government Railways

Owing to the increasing demand for electric trucks, a new shop equipped with the most approved machinery for turning out this class of work, was built early in 1906. This shop had a capacity of 100 trucks per week.

During the same year, a tract of 184 acres was purchased at Eddystone, Pa., about twelve miles from the city, where extensive foundries and blacksmith shops were erected. The removal of these shops from the Philadelphia plant, allowed room for additional machine and erecting shops.

A life size bronze statue of Matthias W. Baldwin was unveiled on June 2, 1906, and presented by the Baldwin Locomotive Works to the Park Commission of the City of Philadelphia. This statue was first placed in a prominent position in front of the Main Office, and subsequently moved to the City Hall Plaza.

PHILADELPHIA & READING No. 547 with an 1890 model U-Haul trailer. (Collection of C. A. Brown)

On December 31, 1906, Mr. George Burnham, Jr., who had been a member of the Firm since 1896, retired from the partnership.

On January 29, 1907, fire partially destroyed the shop building located at the southeast corner of Fifteenth and Spring Garden Streets. The several departments affected were at once moved into other quarters, and work was continued with but little delay.

THE BALDWIN STATUE AS LOCATED
OPPOSITE THE MAIN OFFICE

In February, 1907, the thirty-thousandth locomotive was completed. This engine was of the Santa Fe type, having single-expansion cylinders and a smokebox superheater. It was built for the Pittsburg, Shawmut and Northern Railroad Company.

In May and June, 1907, 20 balanced compound locomotives of the ten-wheeled type were completed for the Paris-Orleans Railway of France. The compound features were ar-

ranged on the deGlehn system, and the engines were built throughout to drawings and specifications furnished by the Railway Company. All measurements were made on the metric system, this being the first instance in the experience of the Works where metric standards were used exclusively in the construction of a locomotive. An illustration of one of these engines is presented herewith.

At the Jamestown Ter-Centennial Exposition, held at Norfolk, Va., in 1907, the Works exhibited five steam locomotives, three Baldwin-Westinghouse electric locomotives, and three electric trucks.

BALANCED COMPOUND LOCOMOTIVE
For the Paris-Orleans Railway of France

During this same year (1907), 20 Consolidation type locomotives and two inspection cars were built for the South Manchuria Railways. All these locomotives were of standard gauge.

The financial depression, which began during the fall of 1907, resulted in a greatly decreased demand for railway supplies of all kinds, and the year 1908 witnessed the completion of only 617 locomotives, of which 174 were exported. Among the latter may be mentioned a Mallet articulated compound locomotive of the 2-6-6-2 type, which was built for plantation service in San Domingo. This locomotive developed a tractive force of 10,500 pounds, which was remarkable in consideration of the fact that it was of only two feet six inches gauge, and was suitable for use on 25-pound rails.

Mr. William P. Henszey, who had been identified with the Works since March 7, 1859, and a member of the Firm since 1870, died on March 23, 1909. Mr. Henszey had had an unusually wide experience in all branches of locomotive engineering, and even after his retirement as Chief Mechanical Engineer, he spent

IN 1891 BALDWIN built this ten-wheeler compound camelback for the Lehigh Valley. (Collection of C. A. Brown)

much time in the draughting room at the Works, and his advice was constantly sought. He was largely responsible for the standardization of locomotive details and for the per.ecting of a system of manufacture, whereby like parts of engines of the same class were made interchangeable. Many successful locomotives of unusual types, which were built to meet difficult service requirements, were the direct result of his ingenuity and skill as a designer.

WILLIAM P. HENSZEY

At the Alaska-Yukon-Pacific Exposition held at Seattle Washington, in 1909, two locomotives were exhibited: a Mallet articulated compound for the Great Northern Railway, and a balanced compound Atlantic type for the Spokane, Portland and Seattle Railway.

During this year, an important change in organization was effected. On July 1, 1909, the partnership of Burnham, Williams & Co. was dissolved, and a stock company under the name of Baldwin Locomotive Works was incorporated under the laws of the State of Pennsylvania with the following officers:

John H. Converse, President
Alba B. Johnson, Vice-President and Treasurer
William L. Austin, Vice-President and Engineer
Samuel M. Vauclain, General Superintendent
William de Krafft, Secretary and Assistant Treasurer

The above officers constituted the Board of Directors.

The great growth of the business and its need for a larger working capital, led to the issue on April 1, 1910, of $10,000,000 first mortgage five per cent bonds.

JOHN H. CONVERSE

John H. Converse, who had been connected with the Works since 1870 and a partner since 1873, died at his home in Philadelphia on May 3, 1910. Throughout the 40 years of his connection with the Works, while Mr. Converse was occupied primarily with the general financial and commercial administration of the business, he was also deeply interested in every improvement in locomotive engineering. He took an active part in civic, philanthropic and religious interests. He was succeeded as President of the Company by William L. Austin.

THIS ODD 0-6-6-0 double compound was built for the Sinnemehoning Valley in 1892. She later became the property of the Buffalo & Susquehanna RR. (Collection of C. A. Brown)

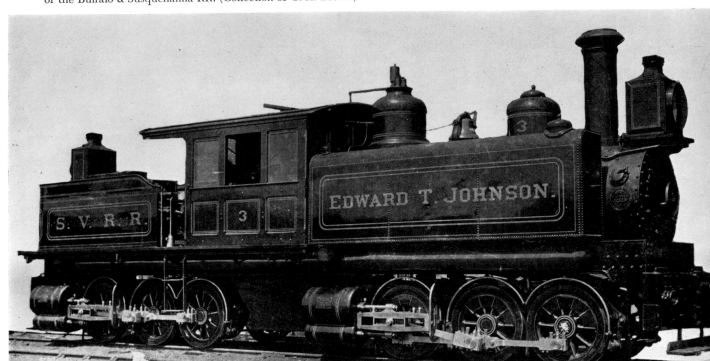

WILLIAM L. AUSTIN

ALBA B. JOHNSON

On July 1, 1911, the entire property owned by Baldwin Locomotive Works was sold to a new corporation known as the Philadelphia Locomotive Works. This was immediately reorganized as The Baldwin Locomotive Works. This is a public joint stock company, organized under the laws of Pennsylvania, and capitalized subject to the mortgage bonds above mentioned at $40,000,000 ($20,000,000 cumulative preferred stock and $20,000,000 common stock). The stock is listed on the Philadelphia and New York Exchanges.

The first Board of Directors of the new company was composed as follows:

William L. Austin, Chairman; Roland L. Taylor, Alba B. Johnson, Samuel MacRoberts, Samuel M. Vauclain, Charles D. Norton, Edward T. Stotesbury, Otis H. Cutler, Edmund C. Converse, Francis M. Weld, T. deWitt Cuyler, William Burnham.

The officers of the new company were as follows:

William L. Austin, Chairman of the Board
Alba B. Johnson, President
Samuel M. Vauclain, Vice President
William de Krafft, Secretary and Treasurer

In 1910, the first Baldwin internal combustion locomotives, built in accordance with patents granted to A. H. Ehle, were constructed; and thereafter these machines assumed a permanent place among the products of the Works. These locomotives are distinctive, principally in that they employ no chains whatever; the final drive being through specially designed side-rods. This allows freedom of the driving-wheels and spring suspension of all the principal parts, including the motor, frames and transmission. There are no sliding gears in the transmission, the different gear ratios being obtained by the engagement of positive jaw clutches; while the gears remain constantly in mesh. These locomotives are specially suitable for industrial, contractors' and light switching service. They were first built in four standard sizes, weighing respectively three and one-half, five, seven and nine tons. Subsequently a larger size, weighing 23 tons, and suitable for standard gauge only, was added. In 1919, the designs were revised to include five sizes, weighing from five to 25 tons.

BOOMER TWO-FOOTER. Built in 1892 for the Laurel River and Hot Springs, this engine ended up as No. 16 on the Sandy River line in Maine. (Collection of C. A. Brown)

Illustrations of Baldwin internal combustion locomotives are presented on pages 122 and 158.

In 1911, the Board of Directors authorized the purchase of a tract of 370 acres at East Chicago, Indiana. Plans were subsequently developed for the construction of works for the manufacture of tires and wheels, as part of the business of the Standard Steel Works Co., and for the building of locomotives, as part of the business of The Baldwin Locomotive Works. Up to the close of 1923, however, these shops had not been constructed.

The subject of superheating was receiving much attention at this time, and a large number of superheaters were applied to locomotives built during 1911 and 1912. In the majority of cases superheaters of the fire-tube type were used, in accordance with patents controlled by the Locomotive Superheater Co. The Vauclain type of smokebox superheater, originally designed

BALANCED COMPOUND PACIFIC TYPE LOCOMOTIVE
Atchison, Topeka and Santa Fe Railway
Cylinders, 17½" and 29" x 28"   Drivers, Diam., 73"
Weight, Total Engine, 268,800 lb.

in 1905, was also used to some extent, but service tests firmly established the economies due to high superheat, and the use of the fire-tube superheater, on large locomotives, is now practically universal. Superheaters in conjunction with compound cylinders are employed on Mallet locomotives; and they have also been used, to a limited extent, on balanced compound locomotives built for the Atchison, Topeka & Santa Fe Ry. An illustration of a Pacific type locomotive, so equipped, is shown above.

The successful introduction of the superheater in American locomotive practice, was followed by the construction of locomo-

tives for all classes of service, of materially greater capacity than those previously built. This increase in capacity was accompanied by the extensive use of such labor-saving devices as mechanical stokers, coal pushers on tenders, and power operated fire-doors and grate shakers. In fact, without the use of these devices it would be difficult to operate, at full capacity, the largest locomotives now in service.

Reference has been made to a design of heavy freight locomotive known as the Mikado, which has four pairs of coupled driving wheels with a two-wheeled leading and two-wheeled trailing truck. Since 1909, this type has come into extensive use on American railroads, and, because of its increased steaming capacity, has largely replaced the Consolidation type for mainline service. A development of the Mikado type is found in the

SANTA FE TYPE LOCOMOTIVE
Chicago, Burlington and Quincy Railroad
Cylinders, 30" x 32"   Drivers, Diam., 60"
Weight, Total Engine, 378,700 lb.

Santa Fe, with five pairs of coupled driving wheels. Locomotives of the Santa Fe type, as has been mentioned, were built for the Atchison, Topeka & Santa Fe Ry. in 1903; but it was about ten years later before this type began to be used, to any considerable extent, on other roads. In the spring of 1912, the Chicago, Burlington & Quincy R. R. placed in service five locomotives of the Santa Fe type, one of which is illustrated above. These locomotives were followed by a large number of others of similar type, which were built not only for the Burlington System, but also for various other roads throughout the country.

In 1910, a Mikado type locomotive, designed to burn lignite fuel, was built for the Oregon Railroad and Navigation Com-

PROBABLY ONE OF THE LAST STEAM ENGINES built for rapid transit elevated service, No. 46 of the South Side (Chicago) Rapid Transit was built in 1893. (Collection of C. A. Brown)

pany. This locomotive was constructed in accordance with specifications prepared by Mr. J. F. Graham, Superintendent of Motive Power, and the design was based on that of the standard Consolidation type locomotives for the Associated Lines. It

LIGNITE-BURNING MIKADO TYPE LOCOMOTIVE
For the Oregon Railroad and Navigation Co.
Cylinders, 23½″ x 30″   Drivers, Diam., 57″
Weight, Total Engine, 263,000 lb.

proved highly successful, and the Mikado type locomotives subsequently built for the Union and Southern Pacific Systems and their associated lines, were directly based upon it.

A large number of Mallet locomotives were built during this period, for pushing and heavy road service on steep grades. Among the most interesting of these were two groups of locomotives, one of the 2-8-8-2 type and the other of the 2-6-6-2 type, constructed for the Southern Pacific Co. and used in freight and passenger service respectively. In order to give the enginemen a better view when running through tunnels and snow-sheds,

MALLET ARTICULATED FREIGHT LOCOMOTIVE
For the Southern Pacific Company
Cylinders, 26″ and 40″ x 30″   Drivers, Diam., 57″
Weight, Total Engine, 436,200 lb.

these locomotives were operated with the cab end leading, the tender being coupled to the smoke-box end. As oil was used

for fuel, this arrangement was entirely practicable. An illustration of one of the freight locomotives is presented herewith.

In the years 1910 and 1911, six locomotives of the 2-6-6-2 type, which were included in a large number built for the Atchison, Topeka & Santa Fe Ry., were fitted with articulated boilers. The front boiler section, instead of being supported on sliding

ARTICULATED LOCOMOTIVE WITH FLEXIBLE BOILER
For the Atchison, Topeka and Santa Fe Railway
Cylinders, 24″ and 38″ x 28″   Drivers, Diam., 69″
Weight, Total Engine, 381,800 lb.

bearings, was rigidly mounted on the frames, and was attached to the rear boiler section by a flexible connection. The illustration shows one of these locomotives, in which the flexible connection consisted of a series of rings, fastened together to form a bellows-shaped structure. This arrangement was built in accordance with patents granted to Samuel M. Vauclain.

It is worthy of historical record that in 1912 an old locomotive, built by the Baldwin Locomotive Works in 1878 for the Madeira Mamoré Railway, Brazil, was resurrected from the jungle where it had lain for 35 years upon the abandonment of the original project. This locomotive, known as the "Colonel Church," was found to be for the most part in excellent condition, and after replacement of missing parts and a few repairs was put into service. Although more than 45 years old it was still operating on this railway in 1923. It is illustrated on pages 115 and 116.

An interesting group of 18 Mallet locomotives was completed in 1912 for the Imperial Government Rys. of Japan. These locomotives were of the 0-6-6-0 type, and had a gauge of three feet six inches. They were equipped with superheaters,

THIS 2-4-2 T was a New England boomer, built in 1893 for the Concord & Montreal, it later became No. 725 of the Boston & Maine, was then sold to the Groveton Paper Co. (Collection of C. A. Brown)

and weighed, exclusive of tenders, 142,650 pounds each. An illustration on page 117 shows the design.

Baldwin electric trucks were first purchased by Japan in 1912, when the Imperial Government Railways ordered five for interurban service.

THE ORIGINAL "COLONEL CHURCH" ON
THE MADEIRA MAMORÉ RY., BRAZIL

Locomotive number 40,000 was completed in June, 1913. It was of the Pacific (4-6-2) type, and was built for the Pennsylvania Lines West of Pittsburgh, to drawings and specifications furnished by the Railway Company. Since 1903, Pacific type locomotives had been built to a constantly increasing extent, for heavy passenger service; and locomotive number 40,000 was, at the time of its construction, among the largest in service. It was equipped with a superheater and was fired by a mechanical stoker of the Crawford under-feed type. An illustration of the locomotive is presented on page 117.

In September, 1913, the Erie Railroad ordered a locomotive of the triple articulated type, which was designed and built in accordance with patents granted to George R. Henderson, who at that time was Consulting Engineer of The Baldwin Locomotive Works. This locomotive had the 2-8-8-8-2 wheel arrangement, and was practically a Mallet, with a steam driven tender. It had six cylinders, all of which were of the same size and cast from the same pattern. The two cylinders which drove the middle group of wheels received superheated steam direct from the boiler, and thus acted as the high pressure cylinders; and they

THE "COLONEL CHURCH" RESTORED TO ACTIVE SERVICE

exhausted into the front and rear cylinders, which acted as the low pressure. The exhaust from the front cylinders was discharged up the stack to create a draught for the fire, while that from the rear cylinders, after passing through a feed-water heater, escaped up a pipe at the rear of the tank. Pumps were used to force the heated feed-water into the boiler.

The first locomotive of this type was completed in April, 1914, and was placed in pushing service on a heavy grade near Susquehanna, Penna. It was named "Matt H. Shay," after the oldest living engineer then in the service of the Erie. On a

NOTE the odd spacing between the 3rd and 4th pairs of drivers on this little plantation engine of 1894. (Collection of C. A. Brown)

test run to determine its hauling capacity on practically level track, this locomotive has hauled a train of 250 loaded cars having a length of 1.6 miles and weighing 17,912 tons. This load was hauled up a maximum grade of 0.09 per cent., combined with a curve of five degrees.

MALLET ARTICULATED LOCOMOTIVE
Imperial Government Railways of Japan
Cylinders, 16″ and 25″ x 24″   Drivers, Diam., 49″
Weight, Total Engine, 142,650 lb.

After this locomotive had been fully tried out, two more of similar dimensions were built for the Erie R. R., and completed in 1916. These locomotives are in regular service on the Susquehanna Hill. One of them is illustrated on page 118.

While these developments were taking place in the field of steam locomotive engineering, Baldwin-Westinghouse electric locomotives were becoming increasingly prominent in the prod-

PACIFIC TYPE LOCOMOTIVE, PENNSYLVANIA LINES
Baldwin Locomotive No. 40,000
Cylinders, 26″ x 26″   Drivers, Diam., 80″
Weight, Total Engine, 302,000 lb.

uct of the Works. Among these locomotives may be mentioned five, which were built in 1910 for service in the Hoosac Tunnel, Mass., on the line of the Boston & Maine R. R. This tunnel is 4¾ miles long, and its operation with steam locomotives

had become difficult because of the accumulation of smoke and gas, which made it impossible to fully utilize the track capacity of the tunnel. The results obtained with electric traction have been most satisfactory, and the capacity of the tunnel has been greatly increased.

TRIPLE ARTICULATED LOCOMOTIVE
Erie Railroad
Cylinders, (6) 36″ x 32″   Drivers, Diam., 63″
Weight, Total, 860,350 lb.   Tractive Force, 160,000 lb.

Up to the close of 1912, 100 Baldwin-Westinghouse single-phase locomotives had been built for the New York, New Haven & Hartford R. R., for service on the electrified section of the line between New York and Stamford, Conn. The electrification was subsequently extended to New Haven. The electric locomotives built for this road are of various types, and are used in passenger, freight and switching service. The illustration on

ELECTRIC LOCOMOTIVES
New York, New Haven and Hartford Railroad

ERIE RR RECEIVED this 4-4-0 compound camelback in 1897. (Collection of C. A. Brown)

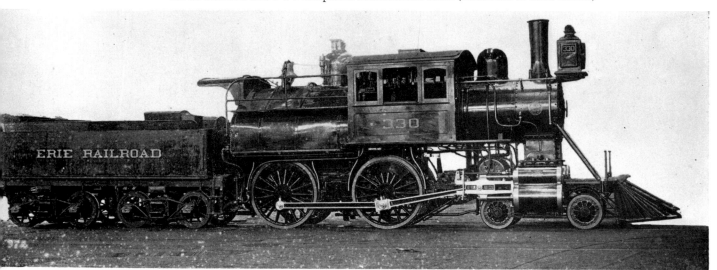

the previous page represents ten large New Haven electric locomotives of the articulated type, ready for shipment from The Baldwin Locomotive Works to Pittsburgh, to receive their electrical equipment at the Westinghouse plant.

Another interesting group of electric locomotives were those built for the Norfolk & Western Ry. for service between Bluefield and East Vivian, West Virginia, a distance of 30 miles. This line handles a heavy coal traffic, and its capacity, under steam operation, was limited by the number of trains which could be moved through Elkhorn Tunnel, where the line is single tracked. The tunnel has a length of 3,100 feet, and is approached from the West by a 2 per cent grade, and from the East by a grade of 2.36 per cent. When the road was electrified, 20 steam locomotives of the Mallet type were replaced by 12 electric locomotives, and the capacity of the line was greatly increased because of the higher speed at which the trains could be handled. Each electric locomotive consists of two units having a combined weight of 270 tons, each unit being of the 2-4-4-2 type. Two of these locomotives handle a train weighing 3,250 tons through the tunnel in three minutes; while with steam operation, on account of slow speeds and frequent stalling, it was necessary to allow 20 minutes for three Mallet locomotives to take a train through the tunnel.

The development of electric mine and industrial locomotives, during this period, was characterized by refinement in general design and detailed construction. These Works were pioneers in developing and standardizing plate steel and cast steel bar frames for mine locomotives. The accompanying illustration shows one of these locomotives, equipped with a cast steel frame of the bar type. Greater strength and accessibility were secured with this construction, and also, in many cases, lighter mechanical parts, thus allowing the use

ELECTRIC MINING LOCOMOTIVE
With Cast Steel Bar Frames

of heavier and more powerful electrical equipment for a given total weight of locomotive.

During the past few years a large number of storage battery locomotives have been built for mine and industrial service. The Edison storage battery, because of its light weight and durability, has proved particularly well suited for this kind of work.

The completion at Eddystone, in 1912, of a large erecting shop, provided additional erecting facilities much needed to relieve congestion at the Philadelphia Plant. This shop was specially designed for the construction of locomotives of the largest size; it covers 7½ acres of ground, and has over-all

Eddystone Erecting Shop

dimensions of 480 by 880 feet. The building has a steel framework, with concrete foundations and side walls of hollow tile. The roof is laid with reinforced cement tile and the floor is of wooden blocks laid on concrete. An illustration of this shop is presented above.

George Burnham, Sr., who entered the Works in 1836, died at his home in West Philadelphia on December 10, 1912, in the ninety-sixth year of his age. Mr. Burnham had been a member of the Firm since 1867, and had been identified with the Company for an unbroken period of 76 years.

BALDWIN BUILT this oddity in 1897 for the Holman Locomotive Speeding Truck Company. The locomotive was later converted to a conventional 4-4-0 and sold to the Kansas City & Northern Connecting RR. (Collection of C. A. Brown)

CHAPTER VIII.

THE PERIOD OF THE WORLD WAR

Since the financial panic of 1907, the volume of business handled by the Works had been exceedingly fluctuating; and when the European War broke out in August, 1914, the Baldwin Plants were operating at only about one-third of their full capacity. The significance of the conflict was at once perceived by the officials of The Baldwin Locomotive Works, and the manufacturing facilities of the Company were promptly placed at the disposal of the Allied Governments.

The pressing needs for ordnance, ammunition and other supplies by France and Great Britain, were such that all efforts in these early days of the War were directed towards the development of armaments and munitions. In Russia, however, greater distances and a desperate shortage of motive power and equipment necessitated the purchase of locomotives. Mr. S. M.

MALLET ARTICULATED LOCOMOTIVE
Vologda-Archangel Railway, Russia

Vauclain, then Vice-President of The Baldwin Locomotive Works, visited Russia in the fall of 1914 and also early in 1915, and was instrumental in securing a large part of this business. The first order thus obtained called for 30 Mallet locomotives of the 0-6-6-0 type, for the Vologda-Archangel Railway. These locomotives were of three feet six inches gauge, and they were successfully and rapidly completed and shipped. One of them is illustrated above. This order was followed by others, placed later by the Russian Government, and covering large numbers of heavy Decapod locomotives of five feet gauge, gasoline locomotives of 75 centimetres (2' 5½") gauge, gasoline trucks and gasoline tractors. The locomotives are illustrated on this page. One hundred of the Decapod locomotives, which could not be delivered in Russia because of the Bolshevik revolution, were subsequently purchased by the United States Government and so modified that they could be used temporarily on the railroads of the United States.

DECAPOD TYPE LOCOMOTIVE
For the Russian Government
Cylinders, 25"x28"   Drivers, Diam., 52"   Weight, Total Engine, 200,000 lb.

The gasoline locomotives were intended for trench service, a class of work for which they were well fitted, since as they emit no smoke they were comparatively inconspicuous.

The French Government, late in the summer of 1914, sent a mission to the United States to make certain purchases. Early in November, 1914, the mission received cable instructions from France to purchase 20 tank locomotives of a gauge of 60 centimetres (1' 11⅝"), which were to be built to American designs and shipped as promptly as possible. The Baldwin Locomotive Works took this order on November 3rd, and the 20 loco-

GASOLINE LOCOMOTIVE
For the Russian Government

WOOD RACK ON TENDER of this 2-6-2 for the Polson Logging Co. No. 45 marks this engine as a wood burner. (Collection of C. A. Brown)

motives, boxed and ready for shipment overseas, left the Works on November 21st. This was the beginning of a series of orders from the French Government which included both steam and gasoline locomotives totalling over 1,000 in number. Among these were 280 locomotives of the "Pechot" type, designed for service on the narrow (60 centimetres) gauge lines in the advanced areas. These locomotives were built throughout to the metric system of measurement, in accordance with designs furnished by the French Government. They were carried on two steam driven trucks or bogies, thus providing unusual

PECHOT TYPE LOCOMOTIVE
For the French Government

flexibility and excellent tracking and riding qualities. The boiler had two fireboxes, placed in the middle between the bogies; and there was a separate boiler barrel, smokebox and stack at each end of the locomotive. The total weight in working order, with water-tanks and coal-boxes filled, was 28,100 pounds. These locomotives were built during the years 1915 and 1916. The illustration above represents the design.

The locomotives built for the British Government, for service similar to that performed by the Pechot locomotives, were of the ten-wheeled (4-6-0) type with side tanks. A total of 495 of these were built during the latter part of 1916 and the Spring of 1917. The design generally followed American practice, as shown in the illustration on page 124; and the locomotives weighed, in working order, 32,500 pounds each.

The British Government also received 465 standard gauge locomotives of various types. Conspicuous among these were

150 locomotives of the Consolidation (2-8-0) type, which were built in 1917. These locomotives had cylinders 21 inches in diameter by 28 inches stroke, and the weight in working order was 162,500 pounds.

The remainder of the standard gauge locomotives built for the British Government were of the 0-4-0, 0-6-0, 2-6-2 and 4-6-0 types. The last named had separate tenders, while the others were tank engines.

In addition to the locomotives built for strictly military purposes, large orders for Mikado (2-8-2) type freight locomotives were also received, during the war period, from two prominent

TEN-WHEELED LOCOMOTIVE
For the British Government

French railways—the Paris, Lyons and Mediterranean, and the Nord. These locomotives were built throughout to the metric system, in accordance with specifications furnished by the purchasing companies. They used superheated steam and were of the balanced compound type, with inside high-pressure cylinders driving the second pair of coupled wheels and outside low-pressure cylinders driving the third pair. The total weight of one of these locomotives, exclusive of tender, was 202,000 pounds, of which the driving wheels carried 149,400 pounds.

The construction of all of these locomotives for military service abroad, together with those ordered by domestic railways, soon placed the Works on a full capacity basis. Moreover, during this period orders were received from the British and French Governments for the machining of a large number of shells, varying in calibre from 4.7 inches to 12 inches. These shells were manufactured in such of the locomotive shops as

BY 1881, when Central R.R. of N.J. No. 162 was delivered, the peaked roof cabs had given away to the curved roof. But the round top windows and cab panels were to continue for many years. (Collection of C. A. Brown)

were available for the purpose, and also in new shops, specially built and equipped for this kind of work. The principal additions made to the Philadelphia plant were a four-story extension of the truck shop, measuring 90 by 97 feet, and an eight-story building of re-inforced concrete, measuring 98 feet 6 inches by 396 feet. A group of large shops one story in height, was also built at the Eddystone Plant and utilized for the completion of the shell order from the French Government.

With the entrance of the United States into the War, in April, 1917, all industries manufacturing war supplies of any kind received a great stimulus. The presence of the American Army in France required the immediate construction of a great amount of motive power and rolling stock; and to meet the de-

CONSOLIDATION TYPE LOCOMOTIVE FOR THE UNITED STATES GOVERNMENT
The first "Pershing Locomotive" built
Cylinders, 21" x 28"   Drivers, Diam., 56"
Weight, Total Engine, 166,400 lb.

mand for locomotives, The Baldwin Locomotive Works were entrusted with what were probably the largest and most urgent orders ever placed in the history of locomotive building. The first of these orders was placed on July 17, 1917, and called for 150 locomotives of the Consolidation (2-8-0) type. These locomotives, in general design, were similar to the Consolidation engines built for the British Government, the principal difference being that they were equipped with superheaters, whereas the British locomotives used saturated steam. The first of the locomotives for the United States Government was completed on August 10th, less than a month after the receipt of the order, and the last of the 150 on October 1st. These "Pershing Engines," as they became known, were subsequently ordered in large numbers; and when hostilities closed they were being shipped from the Works at the rate of 300 per month.

Additional erecting capacity was required in order to handle all this work, and a second erecting shop, generally similar to that constructed in 1912, was built at Eddystone during the winter of 1917-1918.

"PERSHING LOCOMOTIVES" LOADED FOR SHIPMENT

Through the initiative of Mr. S. M. Felton, Director of Military Railways, and his mechanical aide, Colonel Milliken, an interesting method was developed of shipping the Pershing locomotives to France, erected complete with the exception of the headlight, smokestack and cab. The locomotives and tenders were placed in the holds of the vessels on their own wheels, and after unloading them at St. Nazaire, France, comparatively little work was required before they were ready for service. Much time and trouble were saved in this way.

In addition to the Pershing locomotives, narrow gauge steam locomotives of the 2-6-2 type, and gasoline locomotives of the 5, 7½, and 25-ton sizes, were also built for the United States Government.

NO CAB OR SHELTER for the fireboy on this fast stepping camelback—only a steam pressure gauge. "Never mind the cinders, just keep shovelling." (Collection of C. A. Brown)

On September 6, 1917, Mr. S. M. Vauclain was appointed Senior Vice-President of The Baldwin Locomotive Works, Mr. Grafton Greenough Vice-President in Charge of Sales, and Mr. John P. Sykes Vice-President in Charge of Manufacture.

Mr. Vauclain, as has been mentioned in these pages, had been connected with the Works since 1883. The great increase in the size and capacity of the Plant which occurred during his term of service was due, to a large extent, to his untiring energy and to his exceptional ability as an organizer and executive. He also took an active interest in the development of the locomotive, and became recognized the world over as a locomotive expert and designer. It is safe to say that the production record made by the Works during the period of the War would not have been attained had it not been for his courage, energy and ability.

Mr. Greenough entered the service of the Company on December 28, 1885, as an employee of the Engineering Department. In August, 1899, he was transferred to the Operating Department in the capacity of Assistant Superintendent. At the time of the Louisiana Purchase Exposition in 1904 he was placed in charge of the St. Louis Office, later assuming charge of the sales organization in Philadelphia as General Sales Manager.

Mr. Sykes was apprenticed to The Baldwin Locomotive Works, entering service in 1879. He served in the capacities of Contractor, Assistant Foreman and General Foreman until 1905 when he was appointed Superintendent of the (then new) Eddystone Shops. In 1907 he left the parent company to become General Superintendent of the Standard Steel Works Company at Burnham, Pa., later returning to The Baldwin Locomotive Works as Assistant General Superintendent. In July, 1911, he was appointed General Superintendent, which position he held until his selection as Vice-President in Charge of Manufacture.

One of the most notable achievements of The Baldwin Locomotive Works during the War, was the building of a group of railway gun mounts for the United States Navy. These mounts carried 14-inch naval guns, which were available for shore service; and the original idea was to use them against a number of long-range German guns which were mounted near Ostend and firing into Dunkirk. The designs for the mounts were prepared at the Naval Gun Factory, Washington, under the direction of Captain A. L. Willard, Superintendent; Commander Harvey Delano, U. S. N., and George A. Chadwick, Chief Draftsman. When the designs were submitted to the bidders on January 25, 1918, Mr. S. M. Vauclain, who was then Chairman of the Munitions Committee of the War Industries Board, agreed that The Baldwin Locomotive Works would build the mounts, with the assistance of the American Bridge Company, in from 100 to 120 days. Five mounts were thereupon ordered; the first one, scheduled for delivery on May 15, 1918, was completed on April 25, while the last, which was scheduled for June 15, was completed May 25. Considering the fact that the design was new

FOURTEEN-INCH RAILWAY GUN MOUNT

throughout, that there was a shortage of labor, and that many serious obstacles had to be overcome, this was an exceptionally creditable piece of work.

Each of these mounts was carried on 24 wheels, grouped in four trucks of six wheels each. The maximum firing elevation of the guns was 43 degrees; but when firing at angles of fifteen degrees and upward, a structural steel foundation, surrounding a pit, was necessary, for the purpose of absorbing a portion of the shock and providing room for the recoil of the gun. These foundations were also supplied by The Baldwin Locomotive Works.

By the time the mounts were completed, conditions in Europe had changed to such an extent that it was impossible to send them to the Belgian Coast as first intended; hence they

McCLOUD RIVER RR wanted a double ender, so this was the result. No. 6 was actually two separate locomotives run from a common cab. One can imagine the difficulties trying to synchronize both engines as time began to wear the linkage in the control mechanisms. She later became two separate units; one of them having been used by the contractor who constructed "Treasure Island" in San Francisco Bay in 1939. (Collection of C. A. Brown)

were shipped to the West Front, and were in service several weeks prior to the signing of the armistice. In all, the five batteries were fired 782 times on 25 different days, at ranges which averaged from 30,000 to 40,000 yards; and while it was not possible, in the majority of cases, to make observations, it is known that severe damage was done.

These first five mounts were followed by six others, of similar construction; and after the signing of the armistice, the Works completed two additional mounts of an improved type, so designed that the gun could be fired at all angles without transferring the weight to a separate foundation. The new mounts were given thorough tests and proved highly satisfactory.

The Works also built 38 caterpillar mounts, designed to carry 7-inch rifles. These were also constructed for the Navy, having been designed at the Naval Gun Factory. This type of mount had broad caterpillar treads, and could be run over rough roads and soft soil. In the field, these mounts were hauled about by tractors of 120 horsepower.

In addition to building complete mounts, The Baldwin Locomotive Works constructed several styles of railway trucks for gun and howitzer mounts. At the time hostilities closed, preparations were being made for the manufacture, on a large scale, of heavy tanks equipped with Liberty motors. These were intended to destroy the wire defenses and machine gun nests put up by the Germans in their retreat. After the signing of the armistice, however, the order for these tanks was cancelled.

The war activities of The Baldwin Locomotive Works also included the construction of two large plants on their property at Eddystone for the manufacture of rifles and ammunition, and accomplishments in this connection constitute a series of achievements worthy of record.

On April 30, 1915, the British Government placed a contract with the Remington Arms Company of Delaware for 1,500,000 rifles to be manufactured in one of the plants mentioned above, under the general direction of Mr. S. M. Vauclain. The work of constructing, equipping and organizing this enormous plant was fully accomplished, and production established by December 31, 1915, continuing until the close of 1918.

Mr. Charles H. Schlacks was engaged as General Manager on May 1, 1915, and to him great credit is due for the completion of the organization and the remarkable manufacturing results obtained:

The main building of the Rifle Plant covered 14 acres of ground, and had a length of 1,040 feet and a maximum width of 816 feet. Great difficulty was experienced in obtaining delivery of equipment and machinery in time to meet the terms of the British contract, and some idea of the extent of the installation may be had from the fact that 10,000 machines, 40,200 feet of shafting, and 424,000 feet of belting were required.

The first British contract, mentioned above, was followed by another, signed August 2, 1915, calling for 500,000 rifles, and necessitating additional equipment. Because of the complexity of rifle manufacture, it was impossible to obtain experienced workmen; hence it was some time after the completion of the Plant before it could be operated at capacity. In consequence, an extension of time was granted for the completion of these contracts.

Soon after the United States entered the war, April 6, 1917, and in view of its prospective rifle requirements, cancellation of the British contracts, after the completion of 600,000 rifles, was arranged. Later, the British-owned machinery and equipment passed by agreement to the United States Government who continued the British arrangement with the Remington Arms Company for its operation in the manufacture of rifles for the United States Army.

The first contract for rifles for the United States Government was signed on July 12, 1917; and during the twelve months beginning September, 1917, 1,000,000 rifles were completed, the greatest known achievement in rifle production. These rifles differed slightly from those manufactured for the British Government, in that they fired a .300 calibre rimless cartridge; whereas the British rifle, which was an Enfield (model of 1914) fired a .303 calibre rim cartridge.

On January 2, 1918, the Remington Arms Company of Delaware was absorbed by the Midvale Steel and Ordnance Company

EARLY SOUTHERN PACIFIC CAB in front Mallet poses with the C. P. Huntington at Sacramento. S.P. cab forward steamers were delivered by Baldwin from the 20's up to World War II. (Collection of C. A. Brown)

EDDYSTONE RIFLE PLANT, MIDVALE STEEL AND ORDNANCE CO.

PLANT OF EDDYSTONE MUNITIONS CO.

(Eddystone Rifle Plant). The latter Company operated the Plant until after the close of the war.

The completion of rifle number 1,000,000 for the United States Government was celebrated by a mass meeting held on September 23, 1918. The meeting was attended by a number of notable army, navy and industrial officials, and by more than 14,000 employees of the Plant.

Operations at the Plant ceased on January 11, 1919, at which time nearly 300,000 rifles were in process of manufacture. The Government then leased the premises for a storage plant.

The total number of rifles manufactured in this Plant was 1,959,954, in addition to spare parts equivalent to 200,000 rifles. The greatest production exceeded 6,000 rifles per day, and the maximum number of employees was 15,294. When it is remembered that nearly two-thirds of all the rifles used in combat by the American Army in France were manufactured at Eddystone, the value of the work done can, to some extent, be appreciated; and the achievement was the more remarkable in view of the exceptional difficulties encountered in equipping the Plant and securing labor and material.

The second Plant referred to was built primarily for the production of Russian ammunition ordered by the British Government. Early in 1915, Messrs. J. P. Morgan and Company, representing His Britannic Majesty's Government, were requested to negotiate with American manufacturers for the production of 3-inch Russian shrapnel, and Mr. S. M. Vauclain made a tentative agreement for the manufacture of 2,500,000 of such shells. As the Charter of The Baldwin Locomotive Works did not permit it to handle explosives, the Eddystone Ammunition Corporation was formed on June 10, 1915, for the purpose of carrying out the contract.

The new Company was organized with S. M. Vauclain as Managing Director, Andrew Fletcher as President, Captain Walter M. Wilhelm as Vice-President and General Manager, and John P. Sykes as Consulting Manager. The stock of the Company was held and owned outside of The Baldwin Locomotive Works because of provisions in the Charter to which previous reference has been made.

THE LOS ANGELES TERMINAL RR apparently had passenger service at one time as evidenced by the trim 4-4-0 built by Baldwin in 1890. (Collection of C. A. Brown)

THIS CAN BE DESCRIBED as a ten-wheeler. No. 50 of the 2'8" Antofogasta Rwy. was built in 1890 (Collection of C. A. Brown)

A BIG PASSENGER ENGINE in its day, New York Pennsylvania & Ohio No. 317 was delivered in 1890. (Collection of C. A. Brown)

CINCINNATI, Jackson & Mackinac No. 30, class of 1890. (Collection of C. A. Brown)

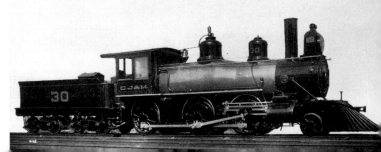

A contract, calling for 2,500,000 rounds of 3-inch Russian artillery ammunition with shrapnel shells, was executed on July 23, 1915, for completion by December 31, 1916. Work was immediately started on the construction of the Plant, which was located along the river front on what was originally swamp lands. The main buildings consisted of two shops, each 450 by 750 feet, connected to an office building 50 by 450 feet, which was placed between them. These buildings were of steel and tile construction, two stories high; the upper floors of the shop buildings being removable, so that cranes could be subsequently installed for after-war production. A large number of smaller structures, which were used for powder-loading buildings, store-houses, magazines, etc., were also erected. The office building was completed and occupied November first.

In connection with this Plant, a modern wharf was built along the Delaware River front. This wharf was equipped with a 50-ton gantry crane, and had a minimum depth of 30 feet of water alongside, so that large cargo steamers could dock and load.

Some difficulty was experienced in equipping the Plant, and much of the heavy machinery was manufactured by The Baldwin Locomotive Works since it could not be obtained elsewhere. In addition to this, The Baldwin Locomotive Works installed the heat-treating plant and supervised its operation.

Additional time was allowed on the contracts, and the order was finally completed on August 10, 1917.

In connection with this work the Eddystone Ammunition Corporation secured the contract for proving Russian ammunition of their own and other makes, and a proving ground for this purpose was established at Lakehurst, New Jersey, with Captain C. K. Rockwell in charge, who distinguished himself in overcoming what appeared to be insurmountable difficulties in record time.

By this arrangement the Eddystone Ammunition Corporation were required to test ammunition for other manufacturers, and lots representing some 7,600,000 of 3-inch Russian shrapnel and high explosive shells with their component parts were tested.

The work done at the proving ground was of the greatest value, and was an unqualified success. The last shot was fired December 24, 1917.

The work done in the plant of the Eddystone Ammunition Corporation was necessarily of a dangerous character, and while every precaution was taken to safeguard the workers, there was one serious disaster. On April 10, 1917, four days after the United States declared war on Germany, an explosion occurred in "F" building, a loading shop isolated from the main building on account of the large amount of powder used. The building was completely demolished, and 128 people were killed, while a large number of others were injured. Heroic work was done at the rescue, both by employees and also by outsiders who happened to be in the vicinity and who could reach the spot. The cause of the explosion has never been determined.

In May, 1917, the United States Government requested the Eddystone Ammunition Corporation to submit a proposition covering the manufacture of a large amount of 3-inch shrapnel. Because of British and Russian interests represented, however, the proposed program could not be accepted by the Directors of the Corporation. After some negotiation, the United States Government agreed to purchase the machinery and equipment of the Eddystone Ammunition Corporation; and The Baldwin Locomotive Works, the owners of the buildings, organized a subsidiary company to manufacture the shrapnel. This subsidiary was organized on September 27, 1917, as the Eddystone Munitions Company.

The officers of the Company were as follows:

Charles H. Schlacks, Chairman of the Board
James McNaughton, President
Captain Walter M. Wilhelm, Vice-President
J. L. Tate, Secretary and Treasurer
W. C. Stagg, Assistant Secretary and Treasurer

For nearly a year previous to the organization of the Eddystone Munitions Company, Mr. McNaughton had been directing the affairs of the Eddystone Ammunition Corporation as personal representative of Mr. Vauclain. He was thus peculiarly well qualified to assume the presidency of the new Company. On

A TANK-BACK TYPE 2-6-6 locomotive built for the Central Mexicano RR in 1890. (Collection of C. A. Brown)

THE WADLEY & MT. VERNON RR received this diamond stacked 4-4-0 in 1890 and later sold it to the E. P. Rentz Lumber Co. (Collection of C. A. Brown)

October 1, 1917, he was also appointed Consulting Vice-President of The Baldwin Locomotive Works.

The original order, placed by the United States Government, called for 750,000 complete rounds of 3-inch shrapnel. After the work had been started, the size of the shells was changed to 75 millimetres, which materially retarded delivery. Difficulty was experienced in maintaining the output of these shells, on account of failure to receive the component parts promptly.

On April 1, 1918, a contract was signed for 1,000,000 75-millimetre high explosive shells. The cartridge case shop, in the meantime, was manufacturing cartridge cases of high quality at the rate of 60,000 per week. In addition there were loaded, assembled and packed over 1,600,000 rounds of 75-millimetre shrapnel, the component parts of which were furnished by the Government.

During the early months of 1918, the Government also ordered large quantities of various kinds of fuses, boosters and adapters, necessitating a number of changes in the shop layout and the installation of new machinery. This was accomplished, however, in an incredibly short space of time.

In addition to the work for the United States Government, a contract was made with the British Government for 500,000 6-inch high explosive shells. The armistice was signed before this contract was finished, but 475,000 of the shells were actually completed, the maximum production reaching 4,200 per day.

The epidemic of influenza, which swept the country early in the fall of 1918, seriously affected the work of the Company on account of the great amount of illness among the employees. Among the first to succumb was Captain Walter M. Wilhelm, Vice-President, who died on October third. This was a severe loss, as owing to his wide experience in the manufacture of munitions, his services were of exceptional value.

The maximum number of employees of the Eddystone Munitions Company was 6,583, and the average number 4,213. The labor situation presented many problems, due to the heavy labor turn-over and the difficulty of securing skilled workers. Excellent wages, backed by a bonus system and considerate tactful management, did much to hold employees who would otherwise have sought employment elsewhere.

After the signing of the Armistice, on November 11, 1918, production rapidly slackened, and on December 31st of that year manufacturing ceased. The machinery and equipment were sold, and the buildings turned over to The Baldwin Locomotive Works, to be subsequently re-equipped as locomotive shops.

An idea of the extent of the War activities of The Baldwin Locomotive Works and its associated companies, may be obtained from the following summary of material supplied to the Allied Nations and the United States:

Locomotives built........................5551
Gun mounts (7 and 14-inch)............51
Foundations for 14-inch mounts.........20
Trucks for gun and howitzer mounts......5 sets
Total number of shells (including those manufactured by Eddystone Ammunition Corporation and Eddystone Munitions Company).............................6,565,355
Cartridge cases........................1,863,900
Miscellaneous ammunition items.........1,905,213

The aggregate value of the War contracts executed and delivered by The Baldwin Locomotive Works, the Standard Steel Works Company, the Eddystone Ammunition Corporation, and the Eddystone Munitions Company, was approximately $250,000,000.

In connection with the War activities of The Baldwin Locomotive Works, it should be recorded, as a matter of historical interest, that among those lost on board the Cunard steamer "Lusitania," when that vessel was torpedoed by a German submarine on May 7, 1915, were W. Sterling Hodges and his family. Mr. Hodges, at the time, was en route for Paris, where he was to act as one of the representatives of The Baldwin Locomotive Works.

While the greater part of the product of the Works, during the War, was for military purposes, a record should also be made of a number of interesting locomotives for railway service. At the Panama-Pacific International Exposition, held in San Fran-

INTO THE BOOMING SOUTHWEST, Baldwin sent this handsome 4-4-0 for the Missouri, Kansas & Texas in 1890. (Collection of C. A. Brown)

LOS ANGELES TERMINAL RR No. 7, Vauclain compound 4-6-0 of 1891. (Collection of C. A. Brown)

cisco during 1915, an exhibit of five steam locomotives was presented as follows:

A Mikado type locomotive for the Southern Pacific Co.

A locomotive of similar construction for the San Pedro, Los Angeles and Salt Lake R. R.

A Pacific type locomotive for the Atchison, Topeka & Santa Fe Ry.

A Santa Fe type locomotive for the Chicago, Burlington & Quincy R. R.

A stock locomotive of the Mikado type designed for logging service.

MOUNTAIN TYPE LOCOMOTIVE
Jamaica Government Railways
Cylinders, 19″ x 26″   Drivers, Diam., 46″
Weight, Total Engine, 157,400 lb.

Two electric trucks were also exhibited; and an exhibit made by the McCloud River R. R., included a Baldwin locomotive built for that line. The Works received the Grand Prize for locomotives and electric trucks.

In July, 1916, the first locomotives of the Mountain (4-8-2) type to be built by The Baldwin Locomotive Works, were completed. They were of standard gauge, for the Jamaica Government Rys. The illustration above shows the general design. This type of locomotive was subsequently built in considerable numbers, for heavy passenger service in the United States.

In 1916 two Baldwin-Westinghouse locomotives were put into operation in freight service on the lines of the Buenos Aires Western Railway in Argentina, hauling 600-ton trains from the docks of Buenos Aires to the terminal through a 2½-mile tunnel.

The Government assumed control of all the trunk line railways of the United States, December 28, 1917, at a time when the various lines were taxed to their capacity. The operation of the railways was intrusted to the United States Railroad Administration, which body immediately assumed the right to centralize the purchases of all railroad equipment, including locomotives. The Director General of the Railroad Administration immediately appointed a committee to standardize the specifications for

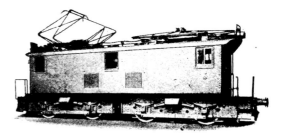

BALDWIN-WESTINGHOUSE LOCOMOTIVE
On the Buenos Aires Western Ry., Argentina

locomotives; and in accordance with his ruling, that committee and a committee of railway officials collaborated with the representatives of the locomotive builders in preparing twelve specifications and designs of locomotives comprising twelve sizes of engines divided among eight types. The locomotive builders sharing in this work were The Baldwin Locomotive Works, the American Locomotive Company and the Lima Locomotive Works, Incorporated. The first conference was held at the office of The Baldwin Locomotive Works, March 13, 14 and 15, 1918, and subsequent meetings were held in the Interstate Commerce Building, Washington, with the result that an order for standard locomotives was placed and divided among the three builders April 30, 1918, and subsequent orders were placed with the last two companies named. Some locomotives of each of the twelve standard specifications were built by both The Baldwin Locomotive Works and the American Locomotive Company,

CENTRAL NEW ENGLAND & Western bought this ten-wheeler from Baldwin in 1892. (Collection of C. A. Brown)

NO. 1502 of the Pennsylvania RR was a handsome compound 4-6-0, built in 1892. (Collection of C. A. Brown)

whereas the activities of the Lima Locomotive Works were confined to two types of engines.

The standard locomotives were distributed to the various railroads of the country as directed by the Railroad Administration. Although these locomotives have been used as bases for the specifications of many locomotives built since the railroads

ONE OF THE UNITED STATES GOVERNMENT STANDARD LOCOMOTIVES
Heavy Mikado Type
Cylinders, 27″ x 32″   Drivers, Diam., 63″
Weight, Total Engine, 320,000 lb.

were returned to their owners, the details and equipment of subsequent locomotives have been arranged to suit the standards of the individual roads for which they were built.

Only one order for standard locomotives was placed with these Works, because the capacity of the plant was practically absorbed by the Government's demand for Military Railway locomotives and for military and naval equipment.

MALLET ARTICULATED LOCOMOTIVE, SOUTHERN RAILWAY
Baldwin Locomotive No. 50,000
Cylinders, 25″ and 39″ x 30″   Drivers, Diam., 56″
Weight, Total Engine, 427,000 lb.

On May first, 1918, Mr. A. B. Ehst, who had been connected with the Works since February 16, 1887, was appointed Comptroller. Mr. Ehst was in charge of the Accounting Department at the time of his appointment.

Locomotive number 50,000 was completed in September, 1918. This engine was of the Mallet type, with 2-8-8-2 wheel arrangement, and was one of a group of twelve, specially designed for service on the Appalachia Division of the Southern Ry. System. These locomotives had been ordered before the standardization program was decided upon. Locomotive number 50,000 was equipped with a superheater and mechanical stoker, and weighed, in working order, 427,000 pounds, exclusive of tender. The illustration on the previous page represents the design.

During the year 1918, work was started on the construction of ten Baldwin-Westinghouse electric locomotives for the Chicago, Milwaukee and St. Paul Railway. These locomotives were of the 4-6-2+2-6-4 type, and of sufficient capacity to handle unassisted, a 12-car passenger train weighing 950 tons over grades of two per cent. They were placed in service be-

A BALDWIN-WESTINGHOUSE LOCOMOTIVE ON THE CHICAGO, MILWAUKEE
AND ST. PAUL RAILWAY

tween Harlowton, Montana, and Avery, Idaho, a distance of 440 miles. This run is regularly made without changing locomotives, although crews are changed approximately half-way between terminals. The monthly mileage per locomotive frequently exceeds 11,000, and the work done is of special interest in view of the difficult operating and climatic conditions encountered on this section of the line.

BUFFALO, Rochester & Pittsburgh No. 53 with Vauclain Compound cylinders, built in 1891. (Collection of C. A. Brown)

CHICAGO & NORTH WESTERN No. 820—class of 1892.
(Collection of C. A. Brown)

CHAPTER IX.

EVENTS SUBSEQUENT TO THE WORLD WAR

When the Armistice was signed and it became necessary to turn attention to the problems of peace, it was found that the removal of war business, however gradually accomplished, would reveal a lack of balance in the general organization of the Works. As a consequence of this business being obtained direct from the United States and Allied Governments, the Commercial and Financial Departments remained undeveloped, while the Industrial Department had been enormously increased to take care of the emergencies of war. This lack of balance was particularly noticeable in the Sales Department, as war work had been obtained with practically no solicitation.

In adjusting to meet the new conditions, it was obviously necessary to expand the Commercial Organization so as to be able to obtain the business necessary for greatly enlarged shops and manufacturing facilities. The opportunity for sales was especially attractive in foreign countries where Germany, formerly the most active competitor, had lost ground.

In order to inaugurate a more vigorous selling campaign, the Sales Department, in March, 1919, was reorganized, and two distinct departments were created—a Domestic Sales Department and a Foreign Sales Department. The long established Extra Work Department, with its record of past successes, was abolished; and the work formerly committed to its care was divided between the two Sales Departments. Mr. Grafton Greenough, formerly Vice-President in Charge of Sales, was made Vice-President in Charge of Domestic Sales. Mr. Francois de St. Phalle, who had been connected with the Works since 1903, and who during the War had acted as Manager of Munitions, was appointed Vice-President in Charge of Foreign Sales. Both departments were organized on the basis of zone management, with sections especially devoted to sales in certain determined districts and countries. Twelve direct Baldwin offices were opened in foreign countries, and men of the highest capacity selected and equipped to act as Baldwin Managers in those countries.

On May 19, 1919, Mr. Alba B. Johnson resigned from the presidency. Mr. Johnson first entered the service of the Works as junior clerk on May 14, 1877. He left the following year to enter the employment of the Edge Moor Iron Works of Wilmington, Delaware, returning to The Baldwin Locomotive Works on September 1, 1879. From that time until his resignation, he served the Works continuously; first as assistant to Mr. John H. Converse; as a member of the firm of Burnham, Williams and Company from January 1, 1896; as Vice-President and Treasurer from July 1, 1909, and finally as President from July 1, 1911. Mr. Johnson's contribution to the success of The Baldwin Locomotive Works was steady and important throughout these many years. His efforts to develop the foreign business of the Company were untiring, and his abilities in the executive capacities in which he was engaged were strengthened by an exceptional memory for the facts of important transactions throughout the period of his long service.

Mr. Johnson was succeeded as President by Mr. S. M. Vauclain. He continued to serve, however, as a member of the Board of Directors.

On May 19, 1919, Mr. William de Krafft was appointed Vice-President in Charge of Finance, and Treasurer. Mr. de Krafft had been connected with the Works since March 29, 1895. After serving in a number of the shop offices, he was transferred to the Purchasing Department, and subsequently to the Financial Department in the Main Office. When the Company was first incorporated, on July 1, 1909, Mr. de Krafft was appointed Secretary and Assistant Treasurer. At the time of the second incorporation, July 1, 1911, he was appointed Secretary and Treasurer, which position he held until his appointment as Vice-President.

Upon the appointment of Mr. de Krafft as Vice-President, Mr. Arthur L. Church, who had been connected with the Works since March, 1886, was appointed Secretary and Assistant Treasurer.

Two orders of special interest, which were filled for export during the winter of 1919-1920, called respectively for 150 locomotives for the Polish Government and 30 for the South African

MISSOURI, Kansas & Texas No. 294, compound 4-6-0 of 1892. (Collection of C. A. Brown)

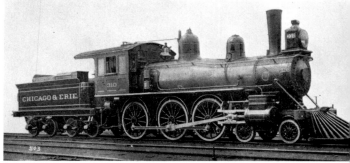

CHICAGO & ERIE No. 310 was a handsome ten-wheeler assigned to the heavy passenger trains of the early 1890's. (Collection of C. A. Brown)

Railways. The Polish locomotives were of standard gauge, and practically duplicates of the "Pershing" Consolidation engines previously described. The South African locomotives were of three feet six inches gauge, and of the Mountain (4-8-2) type. They had a total weight, exclusive of tender, of 205,100

MOUNTAIN TYPE LOCOMOTIVE
For the South African Rys.
Cylinders, 22½" x 26"   Driving Wheels, Diam., 51"   Weight, Total Engine, 205,100 lb.

pounds, and were of exceptional capacity in view of the narrow gauge and the restricted clearance limits imposed. They were built in accordance with drawings and specifications furnished by the railway, and the design incorporated plate frames and various other special features. One of these locomotives is illustrated herewith.

CONSOLIDATION TYPE LOCOMOTIVE
For the Roumania State Rys.
Cylinders, 21" x 28"   Driving Wheels, Diam., 56"   Weight, Total Engine, 167,000 lb.

The year 1920 is further notable for an important European contract covering 25 Consolidation type locomotives for the Roumanian Government. Negotiations for this order were personally carried on by President Vauclain, who made a special trip to Europe to confer with the King of Roumania and high Government officials interested in their country's reconstruction. These locomotives were contracted for on a credit basis, the security being the oil owned by Roumania. Partial payments were made, in fact, in oil itself, The Baldwin Locomotive Works nego-

tiating the sale of this oil for cash. Because of its unique character the negotiations attracted considerable attention all over the world, many considering it a reversion to the ancient system of trade by barter.

Most of these locomotives were designed to burn a combination of inferior coal and fuel oil, but one was built to use fuel oil exclusively in accordance with the system in vogue in the United States.

CONSOLIDATION TYPE LOCOMOTIVE
For the Andaluces Ry., Spain
Cylinders, 19" x 26"   Driving Wheels, Diam., 55½"   Weight, Total Engine, 135,000 lb.

CONSOLIDATION TYPE LOCOMOTIVE IN SERVICE ON THE ANDALUCES RY., SPAIN

Another European order of importance covered 15 Consolidation type locomotives for the Andaluces Railway of Spain, the first order in several years from that country. The locomotives were designed to burn low grade coal. The report of the

BRAINERD & NORTHERN MINNESOTA RAILWAY No. 2, the James B. Ransom. 1892. (Collection of C. A. Brown)

railway covering the actual operation of these locomotives was very favorable. They showed a notable fuel economy over any other locomotives of equal power in the same class of service on the line.

Ten Mallet tank locomotives of special design were constructed for the Bone-Guelma Railway of the French North African Province of Tunis.

MALLET LOCOMOTIVE
For the Bone-Guelma Ry., Tunis
Cylinders, H. P., 13½" x 22", L. P., 21" x 22"
Driving Wheels, Diam., 43¼"   Weight, Total Engine, 140,900 lb.

SIX-WHEELED LOCOMOTIVE
For the Federated Malay States Ry.
Cylinders, 16" x 20"   Driving Wheels, Diam., 42"   Weight, Total Engine, 78,000 lb.

MOGUL TYPE LOCOMOTIVE
For the Federated Malay States Ry.
Cylinders, 14" x 18"   Driving Wheels, Diam., 37"   Weight, Total Engine, 62,000 lb.

Twenty locomotives were built for the Federated Malay States in the Far East, based upon the very satisfactory results given by the Pacific type locomotives previously constructed for these railways.

PACIFIC TYPE LOCOMOTIVE
For the Federated Malay States Ry.
Cylinders, 17" x 24"   Driving Wheels, Diam., 54"   Weight, Total Engine, 114,800 lb.

During 1920, ten switching locomotives were completed for the Pekin-Suiyuan Railway in China. The first train over the new line was hauled by a Baldwin locomotive.

WAITING FOR THE FIRST TRAIN ON THE PEKIN-SUIYUAN RAILWAY

Another important order from the Far East called for 12 locomotives for the South Manchuria Railways. These locomotives were equipped with superheaters, mechanical stokers and other labor-saving devices, and were thoroughly modern in every respect.

THIS LOW DRIVERED 4-4-0 was built as No. 107 for the Louisville New Albany and Chicago in 1892. The engine later bore the markings of the Chicago, Indianapolis and Louisville. (Collection of C. A. Brown)

Twenty-five Mikado type locomotives were built according to the special design and specifications of the Argentine State Railways. The order specified quick delivery, a stipulation which

PACIFIC TYPE LOCOMOTIVE
For the South Manchuria Rys.
Cylinders, 24″ x 26″   Driving Wheels, Diam., 69″   Weight, Total Engine, 190,000 lb.

the post-war conditions of transport in the United States made difficult of fulfillment. However, The Baldwin Locomotive Works proved equal to the emergency by pressing into service its fleet of motor trucks in the transportation of materials from distant points. In certain instances material was brought across the entire State of Pennsylvania, from Pittsburgh to Philadelphia, a distance of 357 miles.

BALDWIN TRUCKS TRANSPORTING MATERIAL

These locomotives proved most satisfactory in service and created much comment favorable to locomotives built in the United States.   One of them is illustrated below.

MIKADO TYPE LOCOMOTIVE
For the Argentine State Rys.
Cylinders, 18″ x 22″   Driving Wheels, Diam., 42″   Weight, Total Engine, 131,300 lb.

SANTA FE TYPE LOCOMOTIVE
For the Paulista Ry., Brazil
Cylinders, 20″ x 22″   Driving Wheels, Diam., 42″   Weight, Total Engine, 159,600 lb.

PACIFIC TYPE LOCOMOTIVE
For the Noroeste Ry. of Brazil
Cylinders, 15″ x 20″   Driving Wheels, Diam., 44″   Weight, Total Engine, 92,500 lb.

The Paulista Railway of Brazil ordered six Santa Fe (2-10-2) type locomotives for the meter gauge lines, the first locomotives of this type built for South America. They were equipped with superheaters and adhered closely to the best principles of modern design and construction.

The Noroeste of Brazil ordered 10 Pacific type locomotives and 10 Consolidation type locomotives during the year 1920. Al-

PENNSYLVANIA RR No. 1510, compound 4-4-0 of 1892. (Collection of C. A. Brown)

though light, these locomotives were modern in every respect and entirely adequate to meet the constantly increasing traffic requirements on the meter gauge lines of Brazil.

CONSOLIDATION TYPE LOCOMOTIVE
For the United Rys. of Havana, Cuba
Cylinders, 21" x 28"   Driving Wheels, Diam., 56"   Weight, Total Engine, 169,200 lb.

PACIFIC TYPE LOCOMOTIVE
Atchison, Topeka and Santa Fe Railway
Cylinders, 25" x 28"   Drivers, Diam., 73"
Weight, Total Engine, 298,170 lb.

MIKADO TYPE LOCOMOTIVE
Atchison, Topeka and Santa Fe Railway
Cylinders, 27" x 32"   Drivers, Diam., 63"
Weight, Total Engine, 317,350 lb.

The falling sugar prices brought about a downward trend in the volume of business in the West Indies. In Cuba, in spite of this fact, considerable business developed in plantation locomotives and in spare parts. Seventeen Consolidation type locomotives were built for the United Railways of Havana, during 1920.

The year 1921 witnessed a severe business depression practically all over the world, and in the United States the railroads purchased only such equipment as was absolutely required. The volume of domestic business therefore was comparatively

MOUNTAIN TYPE LOCOMOTIVE
Atchison, Topeka and Santa Fe Railway
Cylinders, 28" x 28"   Drivers, Diam., 69"
Weight, Total Engine, 355,760 lb.

SANTA FE TYPE LOCOMOTIVE
Atchison, Topeka and Santa Fe Railway
Cylinders, 30" x 32"   Drivers, Diam., 63"
Weight, Total Engine, 379,160 lb.

PACIFIC TYPE LOCOMOTIVE
National Railways of Mexico
Cylinders, 25" x 28"   Drivers, Diam., 67"
Weight, Total Engine, 250,870 lb.

small, and embraced for the entire year only 339 new locomotives and 91 repaired locomotives. The largest of these domestic orders was from the Atchison, Topeka and Santa Fe Railway and covered 50 locomotives divided into four classes—10 each of the Pacific and Santa Fe types, and 15 each of the Mikado

2-6-6 tank engine for the Reading suburban service was built by Baldwin in 1892. (Collection of C. A. Brown)

and Mountain types. One of the Santa Fe type locomotives bore the construction number 55,000.

The most interesting development during 1921 was the renewal of business on a reasonably large scale with the railways of Mexico. Early in the year, after an investigation of conditions in that country, it was determined to establish a Baldwin branch office in Mexico City, which was placed in charge of Mr. Paul G. Cheatham.

MIKADO TYPE LOCOMOTIVE
National Railways of Mexico
Cylinders, 25" x 30"   Drivers, Diam., 57"
Weight, Total Engine, 270,000 lb.

CONSOLIDATION TYPE LOCOMOTIVE
National Railways of Mexico
Cylinders, 21" x 28"   Drivers, Diam., 55"
Weight, Total Engine, 174,960 lb.

President S. M. Vauclain made a trip to Mexico City early in the month of August, accompanied by Mr. Grafton Greenough, Vice-President in Charge of Domestic Sales, and Mr. Morris Bockius, Chief Counsel. The party was cordially received by President Obregon, who encouraged our negotiations with the National Railways of Mexico. The total number of locomotives ordered by these railways during the year was 83, divided as fol-

lows: 20 Pacific type for passenger service, 23 Mikado type for heavy freight service and 20 standard gauge and 20 narrow gauge Consolidation type, also for freight service.

CONSOLIDATION TYPE LOCOMOTIVE
Mexican Railway
Cylinders, 22" x 28"   Drivers, Diam., 51"
Weight, Total Engine, 191,700 lb.

CYLINDER SHOP, EDDYSTONE

In addition to the locomotives for the National Railways of Mexico, 11 of the Consolidation type were ordered by the Mexican Railway and seven by various industrial concerns,

GREAT NORTHERN No. 600 was a well proportioned compound 4-6-0 of 1892. (Collection of C. A. Brown)

JIG FOR THE ERECTION OF PLATE FRAMES

making a total of 103 ordered for service in Mexico during the year. The locomotives for the Mexican Railway were built in a remarkably short space of time, as the order was received on May 23rd, and the last engine was shipped on July 1st. These engines were of special interest, and are illustrated on page 152.

Electric locomotives built during the year 1921 were confined to the small mining and industrial types.

In the Manufacturing Department the outstanding features of 1921 were the installation of a new cylinder shop at the Eddystone Plant and the perfecting of a device for speed and accuracy in erecting locomotives. Under the supervision of Mr. J. P. Sykes, Senior Vice-President in Charge of Manufacture, the new cylinder shop was located in the buildings originally belonging to the Eddystone Ammunition Corporation. Building No. 1 was admirably suited for the purpose, its dimensions of 750 by 425 feet not only insuring ample cylinder-storage space, but also allowing room for the machining of the various cylinder components. The arrangement of shop machinery allows room for a system of railway tracks and motor truck roads inside the buildings. All machines are of modern design, driven by electric motors, while overhead cranes serve all parts of the shop, and make possible the most scientific system of routing the work through the various machine operations.

The erecting shop facilities were greatly improved by the installation of a device to simplify the assembling of locomotives. This device consists of an adjustable form, or "jig," which can be set for the correct alinement of frames for any size or type of locomotive, and for any gauge of track. Where previously the correct lining up of frames called for a large measure of personal skill, the new system makes the operation mechanically exact without special knowledge on the part of the workman. It thus economizes time and insures accuracy. The importance of this system can be appreciated when it is remembered that the correct alinement of locomotive frames also means the correct alinement of the entire machine.

Under the able leadership of Mr. Sykes, improvements similar to those effected in the erecting shop were carried into the other departments of the Plant. While The Baldwin Loco-

BALTIMORE & Ohio South Western received this 4-6-0 with extended smoke box in 1893. (Collection of C. A. Brown)

motive Works had always excelled in speed of production, this speed was materially increased by reason of the improvements noted above, and greater accuracy was at the same time assured. The year 1921 therefore showed a marked advance in the mechanical departments of the Works, this advance logically following the world-wide sales policy of close attention to the individual requirements of all customers.

WEIGHING A LOCOMOTIVE

Another important addition to the equipment of the Eddystone Plant during this year, was a scale for weighing locomotives, which was completed on February 8, and which unquestionably has yet to be surpassed in size and novelty of construction. It comprises a platform track scale of immense proportions, 24 individual wheel scales, concrete scale foundations of massive construction, and a suitable building which covers and protects the scale and its mechanism. The large scale is composed of six sections, each designed to carry a theoretical concentrated load of 150 tons, making a total capacity of 900 tons with a working capacity of 450 tons. With this equipment, accurate total and distributed weights of the largest locomotives can be obtained.

The "Rushton Radial Driving Wheel," designed by Mr. Kenneth Rushton, then Vice-President in Charge of Engineering, was applied to several Consolidation type locomotives built for the Guayaquil & Quito Ry. of Ecuador, in 1921. This device is so arranged as to hold the driving axles in rigid alinement, while at the same time it allows a radial deflection of the front and back pairs of driving wheels, so that sharp curves can be easily traversed. This construction is applicable to outside-frame locomotives only.

Mr. Kenneth Rushton died suddenly on September second, 1921, after a short illness, and at the age of 60 years. His service with The Baldwin Locomotive Works dated from 1883, and during this term of nearly 40 years he inaugurated many improvements in locomotive design and patented various useful devices. The best known of these is the Rushton Trailing Truck, designed for use under a deep, wide firebox, placed back of the driving

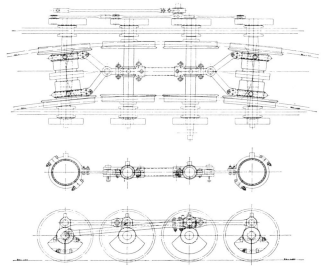

RUSHTON RADIAL DRIVING WHEEL

CAMELBACK Columbia No. 694 for the Philadelphia & Reading, 1894. (Collection of C. A. Brown)

wheels. With this construction increased steaming capacity, so essential in a high-power locomotive, was obtained.

In order to analyze the business situation in the foreign field, several of the Foreign Sales officers were sent personally to investigate conditions. Mr. F. de St. Phalle, Vice-President in Charge of Foreign Sales, made two comprehensive trips, one covering South America, and the other Europe. On this latter

KENNETH RUSHTON

trip he was accompanied by Mr. A. W. Hinger, Sales Manager for the European District. Mr. N. W. Sample, Jr., Sales Manager for the Far East Section, made a tour covering the principal countries of the Far East.

European business in 1921 was practically at a standstill, owing to unsettled political and financial conditions. In the Far East, China labored under famine and civil strife, conditions which accentuated the needs of her transportation system. The Pekin-Hankow Railway purchased from The Baldwin Locomotive Works 30 Prairie (2-6-2) type locomotives, this type

PRAIRIE TYPE LOCOMOTIVE FOR THE PEKIN-HANKOW RY., CHINA
Cylinders, 20″ x 26″ Driving Wheels, Diam., 59″ Weight, Total Engine, 154,600 lb.

GASOLINE LOCOMOTIVE FOR DINGER SUGAR MILL CO., JAVA

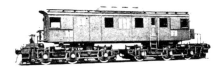

BALDWIN-WESTINGHOUSE LOCOMOTIVE
For the Chilean State Ry.

BALDWIN-WESTINGHOUSE EXPRESS LOCOMOTIVE ON THE CHILEAN STATE RAILWAYS

FOR THE BLUE ISLAND suburban district in Chicago-Rock Island 2-6-6-T was built in 1893. (Collection of C. A. Brown)

MORE THAN HALF A CENTURY after this photo was taken in 1893, five engines of this class were still on the active roster of the B & O, their class E-8 sub 60: 1212, 1214, 1216, 1224, 1228. (Collection of C. A. Brown)

TEN-WHEELED LOCOMOTIVE
For the Federaux de l'Est Bresilien, Brazil
Cylinders, 16″ x 20″   Driving Wheels, Diam., 45″   Weight, Total Engine, 84,700 lb.

TEN-WHEELED LOCOMOTIVE
For the Great Western Railway, Brazil
Cylinders, 16½″ x 20″   Driving Wheels, Diam., 42″   Weight, Total Engine, 82,200 lb.

being especially adapted to the prompt movement of the miscellaneous traffic on its lines. It has been demonstrated that locomotives of Baldwin design are particularly adapted to service on Chinese railways, because of the similarity of topography and the great distances in China and the United States.

Transportation activities in Japan were centered on street railways and interurban projects, Baldwin electric motor trucks being in steady demand.

Business in the East Indies consisted principally of engineering specialties and a Baldwin internal combustion locomotive for a sugar mill in Java.

The record of orders for 1921 indicated that the countries of South America were recovering from the abnormal business conditions more quickly than those of the Eastern Hemisphere.

In Chile, a step forward in the electrification project was

MIKADO TYPE LOCOMOTIVE
For the Sorocabana Ry., Brazil
Cylinders, 19″ x 20″   Driving Wheels, Diam., 41¾″   Weight, Total Engine, 127,000 lb.

made by placing an order for 39 Baldwin-Westinghouse locomotives, and awarding a contract for the electrification of 144 miles of main line track. This operation was intended to relieve the heavy pressure of traffic, and to help solve the fuel and freight problems which were becoming most difficult. No doubt in the near future the electrification will be extended to other lines of the State system.

Brazil, always in the fore in railroad affairs, added to the equipment of its railways certain fine examples of Baldwin locomotives. Seventeen ten-wheeled type locomotives were constructed for the Cie. de F. Federaux de l'Est Bresilien, and four of the same type for the Great Western Railway.

The Sorocabana Railway ordered 10 Mikado type locomotives to augment its unusually fine equipment of modern power.

BALDWIN-WESTINGHOUSE FREIGHT LOCOMOTIVE
Chilean State Rys.

DEMONSTRATOR No. 13400 eventually became No. 431 of the Choctaw, Oklahoma & Gulf. 1894. (Collection of C. A. Brown)

BALDWIN DEMONSTRATOR No. 13405 was a straight forward 2-6-0 of 1894. Sold to the Lima Northern, and later showed up on the roster of the Detroit & Lima Northern. (Collection of C. A. Brown)

During the year the Paulista Railway placed in service the first electric locomotives of large size in Brazil, when it opened to traffic the line between Jundiahy and Louveria upon the completion of electrification between these two points.

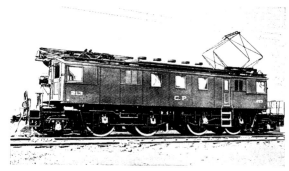

BALDWIN-WESTINGHOUSE ELECTRIC PASSENGER LOCOMOTIVE
For the Paulista Ry., Brazil

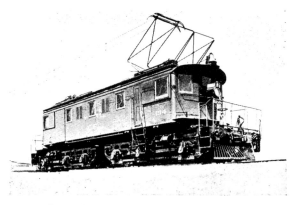

BALDWIN-WESTINGHOUSE ELECTRIC FREIGHT LOCOMOTIVE
For the Paulista Ry., Brazil

This electrification project calls for the use of electric power between Jundiahy and Campinas, a distance of 28 miles, and the extension of the system to Sao Carlos, a distance of 100 miles, the terminus of the meter gauge lines.

SANTA FE TYPE LOCOMOTIVE
For the Argentine State Rys.
Cylinders, 22″ x 24″   Driving Wheels, Diam., 48″   Weight, Total Engine, 195,800 lb.

MOUNTAIN TYPE LOCOMOTIVE
For the Argentine State Rys.
Cylinders, 19″ x 24″   Driving Wheels, Diam., 50″   Weight, Total Engine, 170,850 lb.

PACIFIC TYPE LOCOMOTIVE
For the Argentine State Rys.
Cylinders, 20″ x 26″   Driving Wheels, Diam., 60″   Weight, Total Engine, 170,000 lb.

The first Baldwin-Westinghouse electric locomotives ordered by this railway comprised two of the 2-4-0+0-4-2 type, weighing 140 tons, for passenger service, and two of the 0-6-0+0-6-0 type, weighing 117 tons, for freight service.

PENNSYLVANIA RR class F-3, 2-6-0 No. 839 was built by Baldwin in 1901. (Collection of C. A. Brown)

SANTA FE tandem 2-10-0 compound, built in 1902. Cylinders 19″ and 32″ × 32″. (Collection of C. A. Brown)

CENTRAL RR OF N.J. No. 453, 1894. (Collection of C. A. Brown)

FOR THE COMPETITIVE Chicago-West Coast mail trains whose contracts were awarded by the P.O. Dept. on the basis of competition timing, Baldwin built this high stepping 2-4-2 compound in 1895. (Collection of C. A. Brown)

The largest foreign order for the year was received from the Argentine State Railways and covered 10 Santa Fe type; 50 Mountain type; and 25 Pacific type locomotives, together with a large quantity of spare parts and miscellaneous engineering specialties. The locomotives are illustrated on page 162.

This business was negotiated on an unusual credit basis whereby the State Railways were loaned 30% in cash on the total value of the order. This method of financing met with considerable criticism in the United States, but its wisdom has been amply demonstrated. Through this order The Baldwin Locomotive Works received business approximating $4,000,000, and has firmly established itself with a customer of the highest standing.

MALLET TANK LOCOMOTIVE
For the Ferrocarril del Sur, Colombia

The Republic of Colombia received a credit of $2,000,000, and from this fund were purchased the first Mallet locomotives in service in that country. These were of the 2-6-6-2 type, illustrated above.

In the Fall of 1921, the Southern Pacific Company ordered 50 heavy freight locomotives of the 2-10-2 type. These locomotives were finished in the Spring of the following year, but as the Railroad Company was not in immediate need of addi-

2-10-2 TYPE LOCOMOTIVE, SOUTHERN PACIFIC COMPANY
Cylinders, 29½" x 32"
Drivers, Diam., 63½"   Weight, Total Engine, 398,000 lb.

tional power, they were held at the Works until the entire 50 had been completed. Mr. Vauclain saw in this an opportunity to create a demonstration by shipping a group of these locomotives across the Continent in a single train. This train, consisting of 20 of the new engines in addition to the necessary propelling locomotives, was known as the "Prosperity Special." It left the Eddystone Plant on May 26th, 1922, and was moved

THE "PROSPERITY SPECIAL" LEAVING EDDYSTONE

over the Pennsylvania System to East St. Louis and thence over the St. Louis-Southwestern to Corsicana, Texas, where it was delivered to the Southern Pacific. The train was then hauled to Los Angeles, California, reaching its destination on July 4, after covering 3743 miles. It was given widespread publicity by the press and was viewed, while en route, by many thousands of people.

On July 1, 1922, Mr. John P. Sykes was appointed Senior Vice-President in Charge of Plants and Manufacture, and five new Vice-Presidents were appointed as follows:

BRITISH INFLUENCE shows up on the 6-wheel tender truck of this otherwise lack-lustre 2-6-0 for the Delaware, Susquehanna & Schuylkill. 1894. (Collection of C. A. Brown)

FITCHBURG RR NO. 5—A high wheeled 4-6-0 of 1898. (Collection of C. A. Brown)

SANTA FE TEN-WHEELER outshopped by Baldwin in 1899. (Collection of C. A. Brown)

NORFOLK & WESTERN No. 62—1898. (Collection of C. A. Brown)

Mr. Chas. A. Bourgeois, in Charge of Manufacture. Mr. Bourgeois had entered the service of the Works in 1887 and was holding the position of Works Manager at the time of his appointment as Vice-President.

Mr. Jacques L. Vauclain, in Charge of Equipment. Mr. Vauclain had entered the service of the Company on December 10, 1906, serving in various shop departments. He was assistant to Mr. Sykes at the time of his appointment.

MIKADO TYPE LOCOMOTIVE FOR THE PATAGONIA RAILWAYS, ARGENTINA

Mr. Harry Glaenzer, in Charge of Engineering. Mr. Glaenzer had been connected with the Engineering Department since January, 1905, and was in charge of locomotive design when appointed Vice-President.

Mr. William A. Russell, in Charge of Purchasing. Mr. Russell had been connected with the Works since September, 1897, and was Purchasing Agent at the time of his appointment.

Mr. Henry V. Wille, Consulting Vice-President Concerning Engineering and Metallurgy. Mr. Wille entered the service of the Company in 1893, and was in general charge of Tests and Inspection at the time of his appointment.

During the visit made by Mr. St. Phalle to Argentina in 1921, negotiations were begun looking to the development of the National Railways in Patagonia. Although the order for the first locomotives was given to foreign competitors, the Government gave a supplementary order in May, 1922, for 25 locomotives of the Mikado type, 75 cm. gauge, to The Baldwin Locomotive Works, in order that the line could be put in operation before the close of the then existing administration. The completed locomotives were shipped in forty days from the receipt of the official order.

SHOPS OF THE CUBA NORTHERN RY.

In addition to large orders for spare parts and materials, eight Mountain type locomotives and one Pacific type locomotive were built for the Argentine State Railways.

Early in 1922 The Baldwin Locomotive Works received a contract from the Cuba Northern Railway for the construction of a railway repair shop and roundhouse at Moron, Cuba. This project included a locomotive repair shop, a coach and car repair shop, power plant, foundry, smith shop, flue shop and roundhouse. The Baldwin Locomotive Works prepared plans for these shops, placed all orders for materials and supervised their construction.

Two Mikado type locomotives, the first Baldwin locomotives sold in Siam, were constructed during 1922 for the Siam State Railways.

CALUMET & BLUE ISLAND RR No. 47, a staunch 2-8-0 of 1895. (Collection of C. A. Brown)

CLERESTORY CABS became popular on some roads in the mid 90's, as represented by No. 106 of the Buffalo & Susquehanna RR. (Collection of C. A. Brown)

The sale of electric trucks to Japan during the first six months of 1922, gave promise of satisfactory business with the Orient. During that period orders were received for approximately 150 electric trucks.

MIKADO TYPE LOCOMOTIVE
For the Siam State Rys.
Cylinders, 17" x 24"   Driving Wheels, Diam., 43.6"   Weight, Total Engine, 118,600 lb.

ONE OF 30 CARS EQUIPPED WITH BALDWIN TRUCKS
On the Tokio Municipal Electric Ry., Japan

The first electric locomotives of the type generally used in the United States, to operate on the Japanese trunk lines, were the Baldwin-Westinghouse locomotives on the Chichibu Railway. Five such locomotives, to handle mixed freight and passenger trains, were shipped in October, 1922.

Two Baldwin-Westinghouse locomotives were constructed during the year for the Imperial Government Railways of Japan, and are now in local freight service near Tokyo.

In July, 1922, 25 locomotives, duplicates of the Consolidations purchased in 1919, were ordered by the Polish State Railways. These were shipped to Danzig for re-erection there under the direction of the Polish Government.

A marked improvement in domestic business became noticeable during the summer of 1922, when trunk line railroads began to place motive power orders on a large scale. Conspicuous among these was an order for 100 Decapod (2-10-0) type locomotives, placed by the Pennsylvania System in August. In

BALDWIN-WESTINGHOUSE ELECTRIC LOCOMOTIVE
Operating on the Chichibu Ry., Japan

January, 1923, before all of these locomotives had been delivered, 100 duplicates were ordered, to be followed by 275 more in February, making a total of 475 locomotives, all of the same class, for this one railroad system. Delivery of all these was scheduled before the close of 1923. These locomotives were built in accordance with drawings and specifications furnished by the Railroad Company, and were equipped with superheaters, feed-water heaters and stokers. They were designed to cut off at 50 per cent of the stroke when developing full tractive force; a plan that effected considerable economy in fuel and water

LONG ISLAND RR No. 40, 1894.
(Collection of C. A. Brown)

consumption when operating at slow speeds. An illustration of one of these locomotives is presented on the next page.

Other important orders placed during the Fall of 1922 included one from the Atchison, Topeka and Santa Fe Railway for 59 locomotives of four different types, and one from the St. Louis-San Francisco Railway for 50 locomotives of the Mikado (2-8-2) and Mountain (4-8-2) types. The last named were in-

RE-ERECTING LOCOMOTIVES AT DANZIG FOR THE POLISH STATE RAILWAYS

tended for passenger service, and a number of them were placed on the run between St. Louis and Oklahoma City, covering the 542 miles each way without changing engines.

In October, 1922, the New York, New Haven and Hartford Railroad ordered 12 Baldwin-Westinghouse locomotives of the 2-6-2+2-6-2 type, for heavy fast passenger service between New York and New Haven. These locomotives were closely similar to five which had been built for the same kind of service in 1919. In the new locomotives the longitudinal frames for each group of wheels were cast in one piece with the end bumpers and transverse braces. Each casting weighed about 18,000 pounds, and the

one-piece construction avoided a large amount of machining and fitting which are necessary in a built-up frame.

Early in 1923, the Great Northern Railway ordered 58 locomotives; 28 of the Mountain type for passenger service, and 30 of the 2-10-2 type for freight service. Some of the Mountain type locomotives were equipped for burning oil and some for coal, the latter having mechanical stokers; while all of the

DECAPOD TYPE LOCOMOTIVE, PENNSYLVANIA SYSTEM
Cylinders, 30½" x 32"   Drivers, Diam., 62"
Weight, Total Engine, 386,100 lb.

MOUNTAIN TYPE LOCOMOTIVE, ST. LOUIS-SAN FRANCISCO RY.
Cylinders, 28" x 28"   Drivers, Diam., 69"
Weight, Total Engine, 339,800 lb.

2-10-2 type locomotives were oil burners. Another important order placed during this year, covered 50 locomotives of the 2-10-2 type for the Baltimore and Ohio Railroad. These locomotives were among the heaviest of their type, and had the largest tenders built up to that time by The Baldwin Locomotive Works. These tenders were carried on two six-wheeled trucks and were of the Vanderbilt type, having capacity for 23 tons of coal and 15,800 gallons of water.

Late in 1923, 25 Consolidation type locomotives for heavy freight service were built for the Philadelphia and Reading Ry. These locomotives had wide firebox boilers of the Wootten type, equipped to burn a mixture of fine anthracite and bituminous

BRIGANTINE TRANSIT CO. 2-4-2 No. 32 was later sold to the Saginaw, Tuscola & Huron RR. (Collection of C. A. Brown)

MOUNTAIN TYPE LOCOMOTIVE, GREAT NORTHERN RY.
Cylinders, 29" x 28"   Drivers, Diam., 73"
Weight, Total Engine, 357,000 lb.

2-10-2 TYPE LOCOMOTIVE, GREAT NORTHERN RY.
Cylinders, 31" x 32"   Drivers, Diam., 63"
Weight, Total Engine, 422,340 lb.

2-10-2 TYPE LOCOMOTIVE, BALTIMORE AND OHIO RAILROAD
Cylinders, 30" x 32"   Drivers, Diam., 64"
Weight, Total Engine, 436,510 lb.

CONSOLIDATION TYPE LOCOMOTIVE, PHILADELPHIA AND READING RY.
Cylinders, 27" x 32"   Drivers, Diam., 61½"
Weight, Total Engine, 314,950 lb.

coal, and were, at that time, the heaviest with this wheel arrangement built at these Works.

The Great Northern, Baltimore and Ohio, and Philadelphia and Reading locomotives, are illustrated on the previous page.

LOADING THE "PRESIDENTIAL" LOCOMOTIVE AT EDDYSTONE

TANK CARS FOR THE ARGENTINE STATE RYS.

On August 18, 1923, a Baldwin Pacific type locomotive built for the Argentine State Railways was loaded aboard steamer at the Eddystone docks. This locomotive was specially decorated, its cab fittings and jacket bands being polished and nickeled. It was said to be the most handsomely finished locomotive ever turned out by the Works. The locomotive had been selected to haul the inaugural train of the new Argentine President.

THE FIRST ATLANTIC *so named* was No. 153 of the Atlantic Coast Line, built by Baldwin in 1895. (Collection of C. A. Brown)

MALLET LOCOMOTIVE
For the Northwestern Railway of India
Cylinders, 19" and 29½" x 30"   Driving Wheels, Diam., 52"   Weight, Total Engine, 274,000 lb.

EIGHT-COUPLED SADDLE TANK LOCOMOTIVE
For the Cyprus Mines Corporation (Island of Cyprus)
Cylinders, 11" x 14"   Driving Wheels, Diam., 26"   Weight, Total Engine, 52,000 lb.

INTERIOR VIEW OF DYNAMOMETER CAR

By means of a special sling the "Presidential," weighing 75 tons, was slung on board and lashed on deck. This shipment was unique in that it was the first time that a locomotive completely assembled and ready for service had been shipped from a United States port.

INDUSTRIAL LOCOMOTIVE
For the Punjab Public Works Department, India
Cylinders, 17" x 24"   Driving Wheels, Diam., 42"   Weight, Total Engine, 153,000 lb.

STEAM CAR FOR THE AMERICAN RAILROAD OF PORTO RICO

An important engineering specialty order during the year covered 50 oil-tank cars for the Argentine State Railways.

During 1922-23, 25 Mikado type locomotives were ordered by the Chilean State Railways for service on their meter gauge lines. Following the successful shipment of the Argentine "Presidential" locomotive, a number of these locomotives were loaded on steamer at Eddystone and shipped to Valparaiso as a deck load. Others were shipped in the hold, locomotives and tenders complete, as was done during the War with the shipment of some of the Pershing locomotives to France.

An interesting engineering specialty order negotiated during the year was for a dynamometer car for the Argentine State

THE MISSOURI, KANSAS & TEXAS RR struck some anthracite coal or lignite somewhere on their line as evidenced by the wide firebox on this camelback 2-8-0 built in 1895. (Collection of C. A. Brown)

Railways. This car was built by the Middletown Car Company and the equipment was manufactured and installed by the Burr Co. In line with the growing practice of shipping railway rolling stock fully assembled, the car was boxed and shipped as a deck load. Its interior is shown on page 173.

Late in 1923 an eight-coupled saddle tank locomotive, with a rear truck, was built for the Cyprus Mines Corporation, Island of Cyprus. It is illustrated on page 173. This was the second Baldwin locomotive purchased by this company, the first having been constructed in 1921.

During 1923 a Mallet (2-6-6-2) type locomotive was constructed for service on the heavy grade section of the North Western Railway of India. It embodied the best points of Ameri-

ELECTRIC TRUCK FOR HANSHIN ELECTRIC RAILWAY, JAPAN

can design as adapted to the restrictions of the India railway system, which include a weight limitation of 18 gross tons per axle. This locomotive is illustrated on page 173.

An industrial locomotive of the 0-6-4 type, illustrated on page 174, was built for the Punjab Public Works Department, India. This locomotive was specially designed to meet exacting conditions of service.

An interesting order, completed during the latter part of 1923, comprised two steam passenger cars for the American Railroad Company of Porto Rico, and illustrated on page 174. These cars had a length of 58 feet 2 inches, weighed 87,000 pounds and had a seating capacity of 46 persons.

A summary made at the close of 1923 showed that nearly 700 electric trucks had been sold to Japan since 1912. During that period, The Baldwin Locomotive Works supplied several Japanese electric railways with Baldwin trucks exclusively, repeat orders being taken year after year.

CHAPTER X
FACILITIES AND PRODUCTION

At the present time comprehensive plans for the improvement of the Works are being carried out. The latest additions to the Eddystone Plant include a pipe and jacket shop, 200 by 350 feet in size, with 70,000 square feet of floor space, and a tank shop having over-all dimensions of 145 by 860 feet. The area covered by this building is 118,700 square feet, of which 8,500 square feet are allotted to power, leaving 110,200 square feet for shop work.

During the past two years the Baldwin field service has been particularly active in obtaining for clients engineering products not of Baldwin manufacture, and in some cases not immediately related to the locomotive business. This special service includes commodities, machinery and tools especially adapted to railway and industrial operations, general mechanical supplies, and machine and hand tools for shops. In addition sales have been consummated for cane cars, oil-tank cars, weed destroyers, cranes, tanks, track layers and miscellaneous railway and plantation material, as well as for the construction of repair shops, roundhouses, fuel supply stations and bridges. Several large orders were taken for fuel and for lubricating oil.

In this connection, special reference should be made to the shipping and receiving facilities, both domestic and foreign, which have been developed by The Baldwin Locomotive Works. The Eddystone Plant, where locomotives are erected and prepared for shipment, has track connection with three important railways. The Washington main line and a branch of the Pennsylvania Railroad System, the main line of the Baltimore & Ohio Railroad, and the Philadelphia & Reading Railway all run directly to the Plant, and connect with a system of industrial railways covering all material yards, shops and docks. The Baldwin Locomotive Works is thus not only fitted with full facilities for railway and deep water shipping, but also for the receiving of materials direct from all parts of the country or from foreign ports.

The Eddystone Plant is located on the west bank of the Delaware River about 14 miles below the City of Philadelphia, which stands second to New York only among the ports of

DOMINION ATLANTIC No. 23—1896. (Collection of C. A. Brown)

the United States, the total movement of freight through the port in 1922 amounting to 11,486,599 tons. To accommodate this traffic the Delaware has been dredged to provide a ship channel 800 feet in width and 35 feet in depth at low water. At Eddystone the channel lies about 2,000 feet off shore. In 1915, when the port facilities at Eddystone were planned, Crum Creek, about 150 feet wide and from two to six feet deep, flowed through the land selected as the development site, which was low and marshy, being under water at high tide. In general terms the project contemplated the diversion of Crum Creek to a new channel farther to the northward, the reclamation of the marshy area through which it formerly flowed, the construction upon the reclaimed land of a system of wharves with suitable storage yards and railroad connections, and the provision of a turning basin and a dredged channel affording access from the wharves to the ship channel as well as ample space for maneuvering vessels at the docks.

Reference to the plan of the Eddystone Works as thus far developed, which appears on the following page, will serve to fix in mind the features of this installation as well as the general layout of the Plant and its location with reference to the railroads running through or adjacent to it.

Mention has been made of the wharf built during the War, adjoining the plant which was leased to the Eddystone Ammunition Corporation. The northeast front of this wharf is 560 feet long, and is served by one gantry portal crane of 50 tons capacity and one of 75 tons capacity. The southeast front, 640 feet in length, is used for package freight which can be loaded by ship's tackle. Both fronts are served by adequate trackage. Sea-going steamers can thus be loaded at the Plant, for direct shipment to any foreign port.

These docking facilities, which will be increased as occasion requires, constitute the nucleus of a modern loading port at Eddystone. They have been provided in accordance with the policy of the Works to offer the most improved and complete service possible. The Branch Offices and Agencies of the Company, listed on page 185, are so located as to cover the world's territory to the best possible advantage, and are prepared to

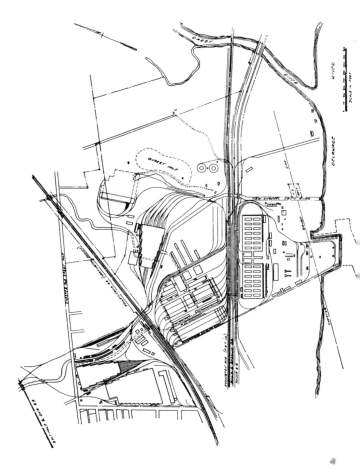

PLAN VIEW OF EDDYSTONE PLANT, 1924, SHOWING
RAILROAD CONNECTIONS AND DOCKING FACILITIES

IN 1897 BALDWIN built a number of 2-8-0 engines of B & O class E-14. On the 1947 Roster the B&O showed 3 engines, No. 1294, 1525 and 1531 in active service, attesting to the durability of the design. (Collection of C. A. Brown)

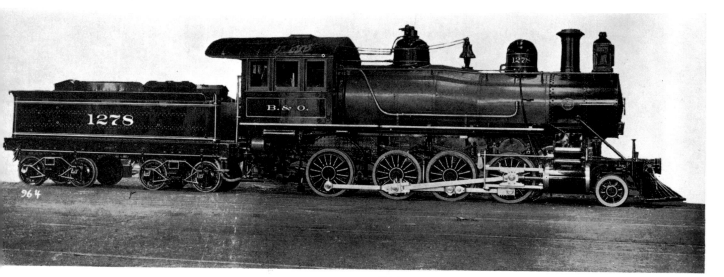

render the most prompt and efficient service. This service includes the superintendence of shipment under the expert and individual attention of a specially organized shipping department and the erection and trial of locomotives on arrival at their destination.

The illustration below shows the loading of locomotives on the steamship "Kosciuszko," and is interesting for the reason that this vessel flies the flag of the Polish Republic, and was the first steamer of Polish registry to clear from any

EDDYSTONE DOCKS. LOADING "MIKADO" LOCOMOTIVES FOR CHILE

LOADING THE "KOSCIUSZKO," THE FIRST STEAMER FLYING THE FLAG OF THE REPUBLIC OF POLAND TO VISIT ANY AMERICAN PORT

American port. She docked at Eddystone, December 1, 1919, and departed December 11, having loaded twelve locomotives for the Polish Government. Shortly thereafter she sailed direct for Danzig, the newly acquired Polish port. Two other photographs, taken on the wharf, show steamers docked for loading and illustrate the crane equipment.

Philadelphia's location is peculiarly favorable, in that it is in proximity to the principal coal mining and steel manufacturing sections of the country. The City, moreover, has a large permanent population of skilled mechanics, engaged in machine and engine building, thus giving an abundant force of expert workmen from which to draw when necessary.

LOADING ELECTRIC LOCOMOTIVES AT EDDYSTONE FOR THE CHILEAN STATE RAILWAYS

RUMFORD FALLS & RANGELY LAKES was a standard gauge line connecting the 2-foot narrow gauge lines with the outside world in 1897. The RF&RL became part of the Maine Central later including this compound mogul. (Collection of C. A. Brown)

The Works are fully equipped to build all types of locomotives and to supply locomotive duplicate and repair parts of every description. With the exception of the boiler and tank plates, chilled wheels, boiler tubes and special patented appliances, all parts of locomotives and tenders are made in the main or adjunct plants from the raw materials. The Works are also prepared to furnish such general engineering supplies and equipment as can be manufactured in a large locomotive-building plant.

Beginning with "Old Ironsides," built in 1831-32, consecutive construction numbers have been applied to the locomotives built at these Works. The growth of the business is indicated by the following statement, giving the years for the completion of locomotives numbered in even thousands:

No.	Year	No.	Year	No.	Year
1,000,	1861	20,000,	1902	39,000,	1912
2,000,	1869	21,000,	1902	40,000,	1913
3,000,	1872	22,000,	1903	41,000,	1913
4,000,	1876	23,000,	1903	42,000,	1915
5,000,	1880	24,000,	1904	43,000,	1916
6,000,	1882	25,000,	1905	44,000,	1916
7,000,	1883	26,000,	1905	45,000,	1917
8,000,	1886	27,000,	1905	46,000,	1917
9,000,	1888	28,000,	1906	47,000,	1917
10,000,	1889	29,000,	1906	48,000,	1918
11,000,	1890	30,000,	1907	49,000,	1918
12,000,	1891	31,000,	1907	50,000,	1918
13,000,	1892	32,000,	1907	51,000,	1918
14,000,	1894	33,000,	1908	52,000,	1919
15,000,	1896	34,000,	1909	53,000,	1920
16,000,	1898	35,000,	1910	54,000,	1920
17,000,	1899	36,000,	1911	55,000,	1921
18,000,	1900	37,000,	1911	56,000,	1923
19,000,	1901	38,000,	1912	57,000,	1923

The production during the years 1832-1923 was as follows:

Year	Locomotives	Year	Locomotives	Year	Locomotives
1832	1	1863	96	1894	313
1833	0	1864	130	1895	401
1834	5	1865	115	1896	547
1835	14	1866	118	1897	501
1836	40	1867	127	1898	755
1837	40	1868	124	1899	901
1838	23	1869	235	1900	1217
1839	26	1870	280	1901	1375
1840	9	1871	331	1902	1533
1841	8	1872	422	1903	2022
1842	14	1873	437	1904	1485
1843	12	1874	205	1905	2250
1844	22	1875	130	1906	2666
1845	27	1876	232	1907	2655
1846	42	1877	185	1908	617
1847	39	1878	292	1909	1024
1848	20	1879	298	1910	1675
1849	30	1880	517	1911	1606
1850	37	1881	554	1912	1618
1851	50	1882	563	1913	2061
1852	49	1883	557	1914	804
1853	60	1884	429	1915	867
1854	62	1885	242	1916	1989
1855	47	1886	550	1917	2737
1856	59	1887	653	1918	3580
1857	66	1888	737	1919	1722
1858	33	1889	827	1920	1534
1859	70	1890	946	1921	969
1860	83	1891	899	1922	684
1861	40	1892	731	1923	1696
1862	75	1893	772		

DENVER & RIO GRANDE No. 700—1896. (Collection of C. A. Brown)

The magnitude of the present organization and plant is indicated by the following figures:

Number of men employed	21,500
Hours of labor, per man, per day	10
Principal departments run continuously, hours per day	23
Horse-power employed { Steam engines	16,700
Oil engines	3,400
Electric power purchased (horse-power)	9,500
Number of buildings comprised in the Works	185
Acreage comprised in the Works { Philadelphia	19.585
Eddystone	616.186
Acreage of floor space comprised in buildings	176.9
Horse-power of electric motors employed for power transmission, aggregate	63,000
Number of incandescent electric lamps in service	15,000
Number of electric motors in service	3,560
Industrial railway, Eddystone Plant—	
Miles of standard gauge track	26
" " narrow " "	4.51
Locomotives, steam, standard gauge	9
" " narrow "	6
" gasoline " "	2
Freight cars, standard gauge	35
Dump " " "	20
Freight cars, narrow "	49
Number of locomotive cranes in service	21
" " motor trucks in service	18
Consumption of coal, in net tons, per week, about	4,200
" " iron and steel, in net tons, per week, about	6,500

With a complete organization and the most modern equipment, and with ample room for future expansion, The Baldwin Locomotive Works are fully prepared to meet any demands, either domestic or foreign, which may be made upon them.

EXPORTATION OF BALDWIN LOCOMOTIVES CHRONOLOGICALLY ARRANGED

Cuba	1838	Venezuela	1893
Austria	1841	China	1897
Germany	1845	Barbados	1898
Mexico	1856	Denmark	1898
Trinidad	1856	Soudan	1898
Brazil	1862	India	1899
Argentina	1869	France	1899
Peru	1869	Holland	1899
Nicaragua	1870	Algeria	1899
Russia	1872	British East Africa	1899
Canada	1873	Manchuria	1900
Finland	1873	Ireland	1900
Chile	1874	Belgium	1900
Spain	1874	Tunis	1900
Costa Rica	1875	Dutch Guiana	1901
New South Wales	1877	Western Australia	1901
Queensland	1877	Korea	1901
Norway	1877	Scotland	1902
New Zealand	1877	Philippines	1906
Victoria	1877	Haiti	1907
Italy	1878	Martinique	1909
Guatemala	1879	Java	1910
Hawaii	1879	Fiji Islands	1910
Jamaica	1879	Sumatra	1910
Porto Rico	1879	Honduras	1913
Ecuador	1880	Portuguese E. Africa	1914
Panama	1880	Morocco	1915
South Australia	1880	Belgian Congo	1915
San Domingo	1883	Madagascar	1916
Japan	1887	Mesopotamia	1917
San Salvador	1889	Greece	1917
Colombia	1889	Burma	1917
Newfoundland	1889	Federat'd Malay States	1918
Uruguay	1889	Poland	1919
Egypt	1890	Portuguese W. Africa	1920
Syria	1890	Celebes	1920
Sweden	1891	Roumania	1920
South Africa	1891	Cyprus	1921
Bolivia	1893	Siam	1923

THE LOCOMOTIVE that coined the type "Mikado." This was the first locomotive built with 2-8-2 wheel arrangement to be equipped with a tender. Built for the Govt. of Japan in 1897, the wheel arrangement was given the name "Mikado" in honor of the Japanese head of state. (Collection of C. A. Brown)

The Baldwin Locomotive Works

GENERAL OFFICES OF THE COMPANY, 500 NORTH BROAD STREET, PHILADELPHIA

FOREIGN OFFICES

1. *Argentine Republic*
WALLACE R. LEE, Paseo Colon 185, Buenos Aires
2. *Brazil*
C. H. CRAWFORD, Rua da Alfandega 5, Rio de Janeiro
3. *Chile*
C. R. CULLEN, Edificio Ariztia, Santiago
4. *Colombia and Panama*
A. B. HARDIE, Bogota, Colombia
5. *Cuba, Jamaica and Central America*
G. R. PEREZ, 520 National Bank of Cuba Bldg., Havana

20. *Brazil*
CORY BROS. & CO., LTD., Bahia and Pernambuco
21. *Brazil*
EDWARD C. HOLDEN, Para
22. *China*
ANDERSEN, MEYER & CO., LTD., Shanghai
23. *Hawaii*
C. BREWER & CO., LTD., Honolulu

6. *Malaysia*
J. M. WRIGHT, Nillmy Bldg., Bandoeng, Java
7. *France and Spain*
P. NEGRIER, 14 Rue Duphot, Paris
8. *Great Britain*
R. P. C. SANDERSON, 54 Victoria St., London, S. W. 1.
9. *India*
F. T. SLAYTON, Temple Chambers, Old Post Office St., Calcutta
10. *Northeastern Europe*
FRANK W. MORSE, Krolewska 1, Warsaw, Poland

FOREIGN AGENCIES

24. *Japan*
SALE & FRAZAR, LTD., Tokyo
25. *New South Wales*
R. TOWNS & CO., Sydney, Australia
26. *New Zealand*
PHILIPS & PIKE, Wellington
27. *Philippines*
PACIFIC COMMERCIAL CO., LTD., Manila
28. *Portugal*
E. PINTO BASTO & CO., LTD., Lisbon

11. *Peru*
C. R. CULLEN, Edificio Italia, Lima
12. *Porto Rico, Santo Domingo and Venezuela*
R. CARRION, Bank of Nova Scotia Bldg., San Juan
13. *Siberia*
J. W. KELKER, 21 Novotorgovaya St., Harbin Manchuria
14. *Southern Africa*
L. M. McKUNE, Loveday House, Johannesburg
15. *Southeastern Europe*
E. ST. J. GREBLE, JR., 19 Strada Brezoiano, Bucharest

29. *Portuguese East Africa*
VINES & CO., Lourenço Marques
30. *Scandinavia (Including Finland)*
OLAV BELSHEIM, Toldbogaden 8, Christiania, Norway
31. *Victoria*
NEWELL & CO., Melbourne, Australia
32. *West Australia*
LESLIE & CO., Perth

OFFICES IN THE UNITED STATES AND MEXICO

40. *New York, N. Y.*
JAMES McNAUGHTON, 120 Broadway
41. *Richmond, Va.*
GEORGE F. JONES, 512 Richmond Trust Bldg.
42. *Pittsburgh, Pa.*
CHARLES E. HALE, 375 Union Trust Building
43. *Chicago, Ill.*
CHARLES RIDDELL, 627 Railway Exchange

44. *St. Louis, Mo.*
A. S. GOBLE, 1210 Boatmen's Bank Building
45. *Boston, Mass.*
HENRY BARTLETT, 185 Devonshire St.
46. *St. Paul, Minn.*
HENRY BLANCHARD, 908 Merchants National Bank Building
47. *Houston, Texas*
RUSSELL A. HEY, 1108 Second National Bank Building

48. *Portland, Oregon*
A. J. BEUTER, 315 Northwestern Bank Building
49. *San Francisco, Cal.*
WILLIAMS, DIMOND & CO., Agents, 310 Sansome St.
50. *Los Angeles, Cal.*
C. PARRY VAUCLAIN, 702 Pacific Electric Bldg.
51. *Mexico*
P. G. CHEATHAM, 2A, Capuchinas 48, Mexico, D. F.

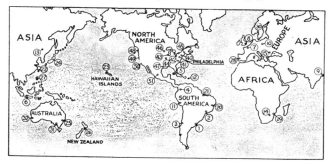

HISTORY
OF THE
Standard Steel Works Company

McCLOUD RIVER RR Prairie type No. 10 was delivered in 1901. (Collection of C. A. Brown)

Standard Steel Works Co.

OFFICES :
500 North Broad Street, Philadelphia, Pa.
WORKS : Burnham, Pa.

TRADE MARK

Organization, 1923

DIRECTORS

William L. Austin, Rosemont, Pa.
Samuel M. Vauclain, Rosemont, Pa.
Sydney E. Hutchinson, Philadelphia, Pa.
Sidney F. Tyler, Philadelphia, Pa.
B. Dawson Coleman, Lebanon, Pa.
Arthur W. Sewall, Philadelphia, Pa.
Thomas S. Gates, Philadelphia, Pa.

OFFICERS

Samuel M. Vauclain . . .	President
John P. Sykes . . .	Senior Vice-President in Charge of Plant and Manufacture
William de Krafft . . .	Vice-President in Charge of Finance, and Treasurer
A. A. Stevenson . . .	Vice-President in Charge of Manufacture
Richard Sanderson . . .	Vice-President in Charge of Sales
William A. Russell . . .	Vice-President in Charge of Purchases
Henry V. Wille . . .	Consulting Vice-President Concerning Engineering and Metallurgy
Arthur L. Church . . .	Secretary
A. B. Ehst . . .	Comptroller

North End of Plant

South End of Plant
STANDARD STEEL WORKS, BURNHAM, PA.

McCLOUD RIVER RAILROAD has been well populated by Baldwin Locomotives. No. 4, a little 2-6-2 was delivered in 1898. (Collection of C. A. Brown)

HISTORY
OF THE
Standard Steel Works Company

The executive offices of the Standard Steel Works Company are located at 500 North Broad Street, Philadelphia, Pennsylvania. The Works are situated at Burnham, on the Kishacoquillas Creek, about three miles from Lewistown, Mifflin County, Pennsylvania; a locality long identified with the iron and steel industry.

The land on which the Works are built is part of a tract originally warranted by Everhart Martin on April 2, 1755. 225 acres of the original warrant were sold to George Hanawalt on July 4, 1795, for £1000. A forge was established in 1795 by William Brown and William Maclay, who petitioned the Court in August, 1795, for "a road from Freedom Forge by the nearest and best way to the River Juniata, near to or at Mc-Clelland's Landing." In 1811 Freedom Forge was acquired by Joseph Martin, Samuel Miller and John Brown, who operated under the name of Miller, Martin and Company. In 1827 John Norris purchased the interests of William Brown, but resold it in 1833 to William Brown, Jr. The Plant was used until 1834, when it was rebuilt with "one chafery and six refinery fires" having a capacity of "800 tons of blooms per annum."

In 1847 the forge and furnace portion of the property was purchased by Archibald Wright, John Wright and John A. Wright, Philadelphia. In 1856 Messrs. Wright transferred the property to the "Freedom Iron Company" with Joseph Thomas as President. A tire mill with a capacity of 2,000 tires a year was added. In 1865 the Company installed two 5-ton Bessemer converters and rail mill, and built the Emma Furnace with the intention of using the "Stone Creek" ores to supply the Bessemer plant. The first heat was blown May 1, 1868. A tire mill and a double acting 10-ton steam hammer were imported from England. The use of the native ores proved unsuccessful,

and in 1870 the Bessemer plant was sold, some of the machinery being removed to Joliet, Illinois, some to Johnstown, Pennsylvania, and the remainder becoming the property of the Logan Iron and Steel Company.

In 1870 William Butcher leased the tire mill and hammer and the building erected for the Bessemer plant, and began the manufacture of crucible steel tires. William Butcher took with him from Philadelphia 40 men for tire rollers, hammermen and machinists. Some of these men who manufactured the first steel tires made in America remained with the Standard Steel Works for over 50 years, and one of them at the time of writing is still in the employ of the Company.

In 1871 William Butcher failed, his creditors carrying on the business until 1875, when they organized The Standard Steel Works, which was incorporated in that year. The Standard Steel Works purchased the property in 1895. The manufacture of crucible steel tires was continued for some years. With the advent of acid open-hearth steel for tires an arrangement was made with the Otis Steel Company, then the leading manu-

STEEL TIRED WHEEL WITH PLATE CENTER

facturer of steel, under which tires were produced from Otis steel ingots. This partnership continued until, realizing the necessity of producing their own steel, the Company established a complete melting plant, from which the first heat was poured March 19, 1895. This furnace, which had a capacity of 15 tons, was the first rolling open-hearth furnace to be put into operation. It was served by an electric-driven charging machine, which was the first of its kind to be used, and is still in operation.

WABASH 4-4-2 with clerestory cab roof—1898. (Collection of C. A. Brown)

TURN of the century freight power for the Buffalo, Rochester & Pittsburgh. (Collection of C. A. Brown)

The manufacture of built-up steel tired wheels for engine trucks, coaches, tenders and industrial purposes was begun in 1892. The centers were made of wrought or cast iron, and later cast steel centers were added.

In 1895 the Company designed and introduced the bolted type of steel tired wheel, which has proved to be the best type for all purposes. It has been adopted by many railroads, to the extent that other types of tire fastening have become practically obsolete. The bolted type was adopted by the Master Car Builders' Association in June, 1912, as the standard M. C. B. type of tire fastening.

In 1911 the Company introduced the rolled steel center, placing 500 such centers with bolted type tires in the Pullman service. Since then the majority of steel tired wheels have been fitted with rolled steel centers.

STEEL TIRED WHEEL WITH SPOKE CENTER

The demand for steel castings being in excess of the supply, a steel foundry was established in 1897 with two 15-ton open-hearth furnaces, which furnaces have since been rebuilt as stationary furnaces of 20 tons capacity. The demand for steel castings kept increasing, so that it was necessary in 1910 to erect No. 2 Steel Foundry, which doubled the capacity.

As the demand for locomotive forgings was in evidence the Company built a Forge Shop in 1898. It was necessary to enlarge in 1902; and in 1916, under the stress of war conditions, its capacity and scope were increased by the installation of seven steam hydraulic presses. At the present time (1924) the Company is equipped with a plant of the most modern type, and is able to produce locomotive and marine forgings, shafts, rolls, ordnance forgings and miscellaneous forgings of weights up to 40 tons, which can be handled under presses or hammers.

During the year 1900 plans for the systematic enlargement of every department of the Standard Steel Works were instituted. The bed of the Kishacoquillas Creek was changed to allow uninterrupted space for additional buildings.

The advent of new and greater activities necessitated the installation of increased facilities for the greater production of steel. Consequently, in 1902 Open-Hearth Plant No. 2 was built with one 50-ton open-hearth furnace. Another 50-ton open-hearth furnace was added in 1905, a third in 1907, a fourth in 1910 and a fifth in 1916. Open-Hearth Plant No. 3 was built in 1917 with two 75-ton open-hearth furnaces. The capacity at this time (1924) is approximately 200,000 tons annually.

SOLID FORGED AND ROLLED STEEL WHEEL

Previous to 1903 the Company operated a small iron foundry for the production of its own cast iron wheel centers and miscellaneous castings for its own work. In 1903 two large iron foundries were built for the manufacture of miscellaneous castings. Since then the Company has utilized the foundries for the production of their own centers, ingot moulds and other castings required for their own use, and malleable iron for the trade.

In 1903 a Spring Shop was built, with machinery of the latest and most approved design, especially constructed to meet requirements of this particular class of manufacture. It has been kept modern with the most up-to-date machinery to supply the most exacting demands.

In 1904 the manufacture of the "Standard" solid forged and rolled steel wheels was begun. This was the introduction of this type of wheel into America, and it was at that time offered as a substitute for the cast iron chilled wheel which had become

THE RAILWAYS of Britain felt their own motive power was superior to any American made product, so few American locomotives found their way to the British Isles. Great Northern Railway No. 1200, was one that made the trip. Built in 1900. (Collection of C. A. Brown)

TURN of the century passenger power for the Buffalo, Rochester & Pittsburgh. (Collection of C. A. Brown)

inadequate for modern service. The demand for rolled wheels to replace cast iron chilled wheels under the lightest as well as the heaviest equipment constantly increased, so that in 1910 a second plant was erected, doubling the capacity. In order to meet the increased demands in 1917, a third mill was erected. The preliminary forging operations for this mill are performed on two four-cylinder hydraulic presses of 10,000 tons capacity, especially designed for the work. The furnaces in this mill are heated by pulverized coal supplied from a central pulverizing station.

ROLLING A STEEL WHEEL

Realizing the necessity of improving the steel in every possible manner in order to meet the most exacting demands, the subject of heat treatment has been given careful consideration and extensive experiments have been carried on. In 1910 a large heating plant was built, with further extensive additions in 1911. In 1916 the plant was doubled in capacity and provided with vertical tanks that were required for annealing, quenching, and tempering of gun and howitzer forgings, which were supplied by the Company to the United States Government. The furnaces are equipped with accurate pyrometer control.

The weight of electric equipment and the severity of service were constantly increasing so that cast steel gears and pinions were neither rendering adequate service, nor could they meet

PART OF AN ORDER OF 4,500 STANDARD ROLLED STEEL WHEELS FOR THE ARGENTINE STATE RAILWAYS

the demands imposed upon them. In 1911, therefore, the Company began the manufacture of forged steel gears, which have met all expectations and proved very successful.

FOR THE SHORT LINE with the long name, No. 3 was built in 1900, K. V. Stands for the Kishacoquillas Valley, located in central Pennsylvania. (Collection of C. A. Brown)

The production of the various products necessarily meant constant increase in machine shop capacity, so that now the main shop is 175 feet wide by 1,050 feet long, containing horizontal boring mills for machining tires, wheels and driving-wheel centers, with additional equipment of lathes, planers and other tools for finishing heavy forgings; and equipped with specially designed lathes for hollow boring of driving-axles, wrist pins, etc.

POURING STEEL FROM THE LADLE INTO INGOT MOLDS

Among the specialties produced by the Company, particular mention must be made of built-up crank axles for locomotives. This type of crank axle was originally designed to meet the requirements of the four-cylinder balanced compound locomotive. Solid forged crank axles are in extensive use in Europe, but for lighter locomotives than are used in America. Even with the lighter locomotives, the solid cranks have not proved entirely satisfactory. In addition to the axle designed by the Company for use in the United States, the Company during the War designed and supplied a large number of crank axles built on the same general principle but of different pattern. The majority

of these axles were built up of nine pieces, while others were made in five pieces, the crank-pins and central web being made from a single quenched and tempered forging.

The Standard Steel Works met the demands imposed upon it by the extraordinary conditions caused by the World War. It was found necessary to maintain a full volume of output and at the same time to develop and manufacture shell and gun forgings. Large quantities of 4.7-inch to 12-inch shells were supplied for the British Government and equal quantities of 3-inch

FIVE-PIECE LOCOMOTIVE CRANK AXLE

and 4.7-inch for the United States Government. Upon the entrance of the United States into the War the Government called upon the Company to supply 155-millimeter gun and 155-millimeter howitzer forgings.

The total area covered at the present time by buildings and yard is 119 acres. The main plant lies along the east bank of the Kishacoquillas Creek. Water pipes, connected with a constant and abundant supply of water, are laid throughout the Works, with convenient outlets at various points. A well-drilled fire department is maintained, manned and officered by the employees.

There are 15 miles of track in and around the plant, owned by the Company, on which are operated nine steam locomo-

BIG BOILERED 2-6-0 No. 1766 was built for the New York Central & Hudson River in 1900. (Collection of C. A. Brown)

tives, two electric locomotives, nine locomotive cranes, one self-propelled hoisting engine and 81 cars.

The entire plant is thoroughly modern in every particular with every labor-saving device incorporated. It represents the progress of the iron and steel industry which has been continuous from the little forge of 1795, operated by water power and distributing its products by wagon, river and canal, to the extensively developed plant of 1924 with its diverse industries, capable of producing 200,000 tons of steel yearly and employing 5,000 men.

INDEX

SANTA FE PACIFIC of the early 1900's. Balanced compound cylinders were 17″ & 28″ × 28″ driving 73″ drivers. (Collection of C. A. Brown)

LONG ISLAND No. 7, camelback 4-6-0, built in 1901. (Collection of C. A. Brown)

SANTA FE MOGUL No. 605, shipped from Philadelphia in 1901. (Collection of C. A. Brown)

CB&Q No. 368 was assigned to the Burlington and Missouri River. This odd 2-6-2 was built in 1901. (Collection of C. A. Brown)

JUST TO PROVE that the Big Four had a separate identity at one time. This husky compound ten-wheeler was delivered in 1900. (Collection of C. A. Brown)

CLASSY 4-4-0 for the Buffalo & Susquehanna in the early 1900's. (Collection of C. A. Brown)

FOR THE MARBLE quarries near Rutland, Vt., this 0-4-0 with diminutive tender was built in 1901. (Collection of C. A. Brown)

BALDWIN built but a few engines for the Illinois Central. Among them—this 4-6-0 in 1901, had an early Vanderbilt tender. (Collection of C. A. Brown)

CLASSIC 10-WHEELER of the early 1900's poses on the Baldwin turntable. (Collection of C. A. Brown)

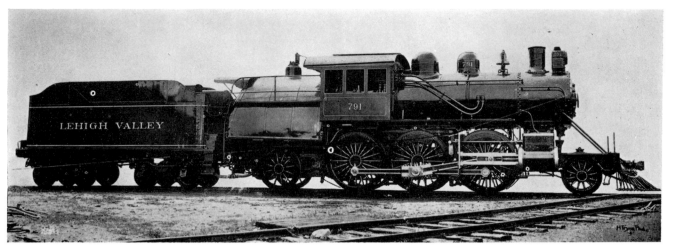

ODD WHEEL ARRANGEMENT for a camelback. Lehigh Valley 2-6-2 was built in 1902. (Collection of C. A. Brown)

ONE OF THE TWO Erie Triplex locomotives built in 1916 was this compound articulated engine with six 36″ × 32″ cylinders. Weight was distributed:

On Driving Wheels	766,300 lb.
On Front Truck	32,050 lb.
On Rear Truck	62,000 lb.
Total	860,350 lb.
Tractive force	160,000 lb.

(Collection of C. A. Brown)

THE GREAT NORTHERN RAILWAY was one of the advocates of the Belpaire firebox as seen applied to this 2-6-6-2 compound Mallet built by Baldwin about 1907. (Collection of C. A. Brown)

THE VIRGINIAN RAILWAY also bought a triplex, their class X-A, in 1916 number 700. The only engine of this class was built as a simple engine with six 34″ × 32″ cylinders and a total weight of 844,000 lbs. ond 166,300 lbs. tractive force. (Collection of C. A. Brown)

1. THE ONE AND ONLY "SMV" of Baldwins in the traditional pose of the engineer "oiling 'round." The Derby and string tie almost simulated Mr. Vauclain's trade mark.

2. CHARLES A. BRINLEY, President of The Baldwin Locomotive Works, speaking at the outshopping of a giant, Southern Pacific "back up" or cab-forward single expansion articulated locomotive. Seated next to Mr. Vauclain is F. E. Russell, Mechanical Engineer of the SP. A rectangular tank replaced the Vanderbilt type formerly used on these engines.

ON THE TEST TRACK at Eddystone a Pennsy Decapod, or bulky "hippo" No. 4471, class I1S, does her "breaking in" exercises. During the years 1922-1923 Baldwin built 475 of these locomotives, sometimes turning out as many as seven in one day. The first one, though, took 57 days to complete from the time of the "go-ahead" order, due to the fact that much tooling up must precede the construction of such a huge machine. But once the first one is out of the way they appear from the erecting shop doors in rapidly increasing number in much speedier succession.

These engines were a real "bread and butter" order for Baldwin and kept shops and offices busy for quite a spell. It was what Baldwin called a "blue print job" that is, the railroad company designed the locomotive at Altoona, and merely supplied blue prints to Baldwin who built the Decapods from them. Little, if any engineering work was done by Baldwin in such instances.

In this scene Norman Suhrie, former traveling engineer of the Philadelphia Terminal Division, wearing a soft hat is seated on the fireman's seatbox.

Pennsy pulled out all the stops on this one, as the Baldwin I1S engines had type "E" superheaters, feedwater heaters, stokers and power reverse gears. Consequently they did a much more efficient job than the earlier non-stoker, non-feedwater heater engines of this type.

Fred Haines, official Baldwin photographer, who took the picture, was an expert at this job, with smoke and steam exuding from the engine as she rolled down the track he captured a splendid example of the "live look" which no other form of railway motive power has ever supplanted.

Cylinders, 30½″ × 32″   Boiler diameter, 82″
Drivers, 62″   Weight, total engine, 386,100 lb.
(Collection of Frederick Westing)

THE MATT H. SHAY, as originally built, in 1914 was numbered 2603. Her performance in heavy pusher service up Starruca grade out of Susquehanna, N.Y. was adequate, but not outstanding. At this time she weighed 845,050 lbs. distributed thusly:

On all drivers:	753,600 lb.
On front truck:	32,050 lb.
On rear truck:	59,400 lb.

Steam was used in two 36″ × 32″ H.P. cylinders which exhausted into four low-pressure 36″ × 32″ cylinders. (Collection of C. A. Brown)

ON JANUARY 2, 1912, George R. Henderson, Consulting Engineer of The Baldwin Locomotive Works, obtained Patent No. 1,013,771, which covered an invention in the field of locomotive construction that created much publicity.

This was a triple articulated compound locomotive generally known as a "Triplex" and to railroaders as "centipedes" due to their 24 driving wheels. The first engine built to Henderson's patent specifications was purchased by the Erie Railroad in 1914 for pusher service on Gulf Summit hill near Susquehanna, Pa.

Named after Matt H. Shay, a veteran Erie engineer with an outstanding service record, this locomotive exerted a tractive force of 160,000 lbs. working compound, and in this respect exceeded any other steam locomotive thus far built. The wheel arrangement was 2-8-8-8-2, the rear group of drivers and the trailer truck being placed under the tender section. Flanged tires were used on all the wheels. The total weight of the locomotive was 853,050 lbs. Approximately 90 per cent of this was available for adhesion. The advantage of this was most apparent in service on heavy grades, where the weight of the tender materially detracted from the net hauling capacity of a locomotive of the ordinary type.

This locomotive had six cylinders, two driving each group of coupled wheels. These cylinders were all the same size, two acting as high-pressure and four as low-pressure. The two high-pressure cylinders drove the second group of wheels. The right-hand high-pressure cylinder exhausted into the two front low-pressure cylinders while the left-hand high-pressure cylinder exhausted into the two rear low-pressure cylinders which were placed under the tender section. The exhaust from the front low-pressure cylinders escaped up the stack, thus creating a draft for the fire: while the exhaust from the rear low-pressure cylinders was discharged through a pipe at the back end of the tank. These cylinders were located at the forward end of the tender section and the exhaust steam, before escaping to the atmosphere, passed through a feedwater heater. The weight carried by the rear group of wheels was necessarily variable and the rear engine was designed to develop less tractive force than either of the other two. This was accomplishd by using different steam laps on the valves, as well as different valve travels. With the water tank and fuel space nearly empty, there would still be enough weight on the rear group of driving wheels to develop full tractive force. Since, however, this locomotive operated chiefly in short runs in pusher service, there was usually an ample supply of fuel and water in the tank when the engine was working at its maximum power.

The boiler was of the conical type. It had a Gaines firebox, in combination with a combustion chamber 54 inches long, which extended forward into the boiler barrel. This construction permitted the use of tubes 24 feet long, this length being within the limits of good practice. This locomotive when working in full power, consumed more coal than could be fired by hand and a Street mechanical stoker was applied. This was an interesting detail of the locomotive and Clement Street's stoker was the first to use steam jets for coal distribution to the grates. A "U" shaped tubular housing on the backhead contained an endless chain conveyor to which were fastened small buckets. To this connected—also in tube-like containers—coal chutes that carried the coal to the center, right and left-hand openings in the backhead from the tender and where steam jets blew the coal onto the grates.

The superheater was of the Schmidt top-header type, composed of fifty-three elements, and presenting the unusually large superheating surface of 1,584 square feet. The Baker valve gear was used throughout, and the three sets of gears were controlled simultaneously by the Ragonnet power reverse mechanism. Two feedwater pumps were used to supply the boiler with hot water from the feedwater heater. Two injectors were also provided for use in case of emergency. A notable feature of this locomotive was that it embodied comparatively few details that had not been fully tried in service. The cylinders cylinder saddles, steam piping and articulated joints closely followed in design best Mallet locomotive practice.

In 1916 the Erie obtained two more of these mammoth engines, but they could not be considered exceptionally successful. Big as that boiler was, it just could not supply those three pairs of cylinders at the long cut-offs associated with pusher service. It used to be said by Erie men that the coolest spot on a hot summer's day was sitting behind the backhead of the Matt H. Shay.

One of Baldwin's most competent elevation engineers, Mr. Elwood C. Shannon, handled the Matt H. Shay assignment. Mr. Shannon told me that when the first "Triplex" was being detailed on the drawing board, for weeks he'd just take ten minutes for lunch so he could get back quickly to that vast amount of detail design required by that job. In those days one man with several draftsmen to help did all the engineering work. Later the "group" system prevailed at Baldwin, and the elevation man or engineer, had the details designed by specific groups which handled cylinders, boilers, valve gears, cabs, and other items.

An interesting sidelight in connection with the Matt H. Shay was the fact that the Baldwin service engineer who put this engine in operation on the Erie was George Fox Johnson, then 88 years of age. George was still on the Baldwin payroll pulling his weight at 95, while both his "boys" over 70, had retired as engineers from the Pennsylvania Railroad. But what George didn't know about getting a steam locomotive tuned up to do her best just wasn't in the book!

In 1916 the Virginian Railway purchased a Triplex from Baldwin of the 2-8-8-8-4 type. Their engine, class X-A also used six cylinders but with simple, or single-expansion steam distribution. It was never duplicated but was later rebuilt.

Cylinders	Boiler diameter, 94″
High-pressure, two-36″ × 32″	Weight, total engine, 845,050 lb.
Low-pressure, four-36″ × 32″	
Drivers, 63″	

(Caption by Frederick Westing)

THE BALDWIN STORY

The Twenties—1924 to 1929

By 1924 the greater part of Baldwin locomotive components were being made and assembled into completed locomotives at Eddystone. All that remained in Philadelphia were the general offices which included the Engineering department, the brass foundry, the machine shop, bolt and stud shop, and facilities for the production of a few other minor items.

During this time and for some years after Baldwin extended their activities to other fields than locomotives. Although many locomotives were built after 1923, that was the last year that Baldwin ever grossed over $100,000,000.00 from locomotive business. A marked decline in railroad traffic was reflected in a reduction of locomotive orders. By 1928, Baldwin's gross for locomotive business was cut to $22,531,000.00. Subsequently a number of acquisitions were made, thereby, forming the Baldwin Group, without impairing Baldwin specialization in the locomotive field. It was hoped that this diversification of products would increase Baldwin sales by creating a greater potential market. Operated under one management as a team, these various acquired companies would—and later did—give strength to one large organization.

Baldwin built its first diesel-electric locomotive in 1925. It used one, two-cycle diesel engine of 1,000 horsepower, being the largest of its kind built in the United States. From then on Baldwin closely followed diesel locomotive progress finally reaching the point where their diesel locomotive production surpassed steam, and finally obliterated it.

Numerous logging companies at this time were supplied with Mallet type locomotives wherein Anatole Mallet's plan of using the articulated main frames and drive with compound steam distribution prevailed.

With the year 1926 came an outstanding event in Baldwin's history, for at that time the Works was ready to build its sixty-thousandth locomotive. To symbolize this event President Samuel M. Vauclain planned and built a huge three-cylinder compound, high-pressure locomotive. It was of the 4-10-2 type and closely resembled engines with this wheel arrangement on the Southern Pacific Railroad. To safely accommodate the high boiler pressure of 350 lb. per square inch, a water-tube firebox was used.

A severe loss was felt by the Baldwin organization with the death of Grafton Greenough, on July 8, 1926, Vice President in charge of the Domestic Sales Department. He had been connected with the Works for forty-one years. His intimate knowledge of the locomotive, and the concern with which he viewed the problems of those who buy, coupled with exceptional ability, and rugged honesty made him an outstanding figure in his field.

Philadelphia's Sesqui-Centennial saw Baldwin represented by a full-size replica of "Old Ironsides," a huge Baltimore & Ohio engine of the Santa Fe type built in 1926, and a Pennsylvania Railroad M1 class Mountain type locomotive. This latter class turned out to be one of the mainstays on the Pennsylvania capable of operating in heavy fast passenger or speedy freight service. Between 1926 and 1927 Baldwin built 175 of these M1 class engines. All were fitted with automatic stokers when built.

During this period Baldwin-Westinghouse electric locomotives were built for many railroads in the domestic and foreign fields. An emphatic sales approach was aimed at interurban railways and small steam roads making connections between trunk lines. The object was to supplement their passenger traffic with the potentialities that could be obtained with clean, speedy freight service. Most of these locomotives were of the standard steeple-cab type long favored by Westinghouse. Many electric mining and industrial plant locomotives were also outshopped. This business proved quite lucrative.

Baldwin was well represented at the Baltimore & Ohio's "Fair of the Iron Horse," in 1927, at Halethorpe, Maryland. Baldwin locomotives of nostalgic and modern eras vied for the crowd's interest.

Early in that year Baldwin built for the Great Northern Railway two double box-cab electric locomotives with electrical equipment furnished by Westinghouse. They were of the motor-generator type which made possible the combined advantages of AC for long distance transmission and DC for the traction motors. These powerful machines produced remarkable operating results. On the section

where they ran a 2.2 per cent grade was encountered. They easily made 6,000 miles a month and handled 80 per cent of all eastbound ton-mileage. The benefits of regeneration, wherein the traction motors brake the train downgrade and pump current back into the line added to their popularity and conclusively proved the value of straight electrification in mountain grade railroading when it is desired to use as few locomotive units as are consistent with the work at hand and eliminate noxious smoke and gas fumes. With a maximum rating of 7,000 h.p. and a continuous rating of 3,500 h.p., they were capable of hauling 200-car freight trains.

A giant move took place in 1928 when Baldwin completed their change of location to Eddystone, Pa. Here a large new office building built to the "cruciform" plan gave a maximum of light and air, to every floor, and in supplying an unusually large area for office purposes, had minimum non-productive space. This brought offices and shops into close contact, thereby, eliminating many former time-consuming methods formerly necessitated by the wide separation between office headquarters and shop.

Samuel M. Vauclain took great pride and pleasure in sponsoring formal dedication ceremonies on June 28, 1928, to officially designate the transfer. Among the distinguished guests was the Hon. James J. Davis, Secretary of Labor.

Baldwin now had plenty of space, to put into figures, the Works including buildings and ground

MANY LOGGING companies used Mallet type engines wherein Anatole Mallet's plan of articulated drive in combination with the compound method of steam distribution was used.

Cylinders 18″ and 28″ × 24″
Drivers 44″
Boiler diameter 66″
Weight, total engine, 209,670 lb.

(Collection of Frederick Westing)

FOR THE FOREIGN MARKET some clean-cut Pacific and Mikado type locomotives were built in 1924, for the Madras and Southern Mahratta Railway, Ltd. in India. Interchangeable boilers were used and many parts of the running gear were suitable for either type. The front of the tender was roofed over and horizontal, movable shutters were applied to both sides of the cab and tender to give protection to the engine crews during the heavy rains of the monsoon season. Track gauge was 5-feet, 6-inches. Engine No. 900, a Pacific type, is shown in the illustration.

Cylinders, 22″ × 28″
Drivers, 74″   Weight, total engine, 184,600 lb.

(Collection of Frederick Westing)

ANOTHER NEAT 4-4-0 American type engine equipped with a superheater, piston valves and Walschaerts valve gear. The low-sided tender contained 4,000 gallons of water and 7 tons of coal.

Cylinders, 17″ × 24″	Boiler diameter, 50″
Drivers, 62″	Weight, total engine, 103,020 lb.

(Collection of Frederick Westing)

IN 1924 THE WORKS built five Pacific type locomotives for the Reading Company. These engines were similar to that Company's G-1-SA class Pacifics built at their Reading shops in 1916. They were the first Reading 4-6-2 type engines built by an outside builder. A repeat order followed in 1925 when the Reading again ordered five Pacifics as illustrated, with 74 inch driving wheels, class G-1-SB. Smaller sized drivers enabled them to cope more successfully with the Reading's hilly sections. The two single-stage 11″ air compressors, instead of one cross-compound air pump was standard practice on Reading Pacifics.

Cylinders, 24″ × 28″	Boiler diameter, 72″
Drivers, 74″	Weight, total engine, 288,160 lb.

(Collection of Frederick Westing)

covered 590.95 acres, with the buildings covering 108.1 acres. The big machine shop wherein were made various details, was directly connected to the erecting shop, the two shops making a single building which alone covered 25 acres.

The year 1928 marked an epochal event in Pennsylvania Railroad history, for President W. W. Atterbury announced plans for a great extension of the railroad's electrified lines. At first this was to cover 325 routes, or about 1,300 track miles. Later, the effect of this momentous decision made its imprint on Baldwin's activities.

On March 28, 1929, George H. Houston became President of The Baldwin Locomotive Works, succeeding Samuel M. Vauclain who was elected Chairman of the Board of Directors.

Baldwin meanwhile, in cooperation with Alco (American Locomotive Company) American Steel Foundries and Pullman, had created the General Steel Castings Corporation. One of its plants was built close to Baldwin's Eddystone Works and was capable of producing gigantic castings embodying main frames, crossties, cylinders, valves and smokebox saddles plus other items in one single casting. One of such a casting provided a chassis of super strength while eliminating much manual fabrication and time consuming operations.

ONE OF THE 3 foot, 6 inch gauge Mountain type experimental locomotives for the South African Railways, built at the same time as the Pacifics. These 4-8-2 type engines acquitted themselves with equal credit and duplicate orders for both types resulted. In 1925, five Pacifics and ten Mountain type locomotives were ordered and these were followed in 1929 by eight duplicate Pacific and four duplicate Mountain type engines. Both locomotives had tenders that contained 7,200 gallons of water and 12 long, or British (2,240 lb. per ton) tons of coal.

Cylinders, 23″ × 28″	Boiler diameter, 76″
Drivers, 57″	Weight, total engine, 227,100 lb.

(Collection of Frederick Westing)

IN DECEMBER 1924, the South African Railways & Harbours placed an order with Baldwin for four locomotives known as "Experimental," for the reason that in these engines were incorporated the best features of South African Railway practice with such features of standard American Railway practice as could be adopted. The order covered two Mountain and two Pacific type locomotives, intended for service on the express trains, the "Union Limited," Johannesburg to Capetown on Thursdays and Sundays, and the "Union Express," Capetown to Johannesburg on Mondays and Fridays. The length of the run was 956 miles and the track gauge 3 feet, 6 inches.

To appreciate the severity of this test it must be noted that the topography of the country is such that in order to reach Johannesburg, which is 5,735 feet above sea level, the train actually climbed a total of 18,636 feet. At one point a grade of 2½ per cent combined with a curve of 300 feet radius is encountered. In fact, at one spot, the train climbed 4,000 feet in twelve miles—this makes the Pennsy's Horseshoe Curve grade between Altoona and Gallitzin where a 1,100 foot rise is met look puny by comparison.

The four "Experimental" locomotives were obtained in 1925 with the idea of reducing the number of locomotives required per run by applying the features which had made the long run successful in the United States; namely hard grease lubrication, self-cleaning front ends, and shaking grates with suitable back-end design.

In trial runs both types quickly demonstrated their ability to run at high sustained speed, and a decisive test showed that Pacific type engine No. 861 could singly make the complete run from Johannesburg to Capetown. Not only that, but it reduced the running time by 101 minutes. The locomotive averaged a speed of 35½ miles per hour for the 956 miles. This was an excellent performance and compared favorably with some standard gauge railroads operating in long distance running.

Engine No. 860, sister of the 861, represents the class of Pacific which made the trial runs.

The English style sandboxes under the running board explain the absence of a sandbox on the boiler top.

Cylinders, 22″ × 26″   Boiler diameter, 72″
Drivers, 60″   Weight, total engine, 192,650 lb.

(Collection of Frederick Westing)

AN EARLIER MOUNTAIN TYPE locomotive operated on the 3-foot-6-inch gauge of the South African Railway.

Cylinders, 22½″ × 26″   Boiler diameter, 69″
Drivers, 51″   Weight, total engine, 203,100 lb.

(Collection of Frederick Westing)

LITTLE "FIUME," built for the Dominican Republic was a wood burning "cabbage stacker" with outside frames, inside driving wheels, and outside cranks and counterweights. The small gauge of 1-ft., 10½ inches and cramped quarters necessitated this arrangement when using inside Stephenson valve gear with space needed for the four eccentric rods and equal number of sheaves.

Another advantage in this method of construction of narow gauge locomotives was in giving a greater width of firebox between the frames, and a greater stability of the engine due to the outside journal bearings.

Cylinders, 8″ × 14″   Boiler diameter, 26″
Drivers, 30″   Weight, total engine, 28,000 lb.

(Collection of Frederick Westing)

IN 1924 and 1925, a group of 36 Mountain type locomotives were built for the Seaboard Air Line Railway. These were designated as class M-2, and with a boiler pressure of 200 lb. could exert a maximum tractive force of 48,200 lb. All had superheaters, power reverse gears, lateral motion, driving boxes on the first axle, flange oilers, mechanical force-feed lubricators and self-adjusting wedges. The Vanderbilt tender held 9,000 gallons of water and 17 tons of coal.

It was Seaboard practice to assign locomotives to specific trains, and under this system all class M-2 engines made fine service records. This was especially so with engines 259 and 260, which ran between Hermitage, and Raleigh, North Carolina, 161 miles. These two locomotives came on the road in 1925.

Two veteran enginemen on trains 3 and 4, operated these two engines, W. R. Bishop on 259 and M. W. Tighe on 260. Up to the end of May, 1928, repective mileages made by 259 and 260 since they began operation, were 135,000 and 140,000. During this time the engines handled an average of eleven cars per train, consuming nine pounds of coal per car per mile.

Seaboard conditions justified this procedure of locomotive assignment, and when backed up by an efficient and energetically pursued maintenance policy could produce splendid steam locomotive performance records.

This is the road of the famous "Orange Blossom Special" and other plush trains which operate over the Seaboard Air Line between Richmond, Va. and points in Florida.

Cylinders, 27″ × 28″   Boiler diameter, 78″
Drivers, 72″   Weight, total engine, 320,900 lb.

(Collection of Frederick Westing)

AS A CONTRAST to the big M-2, we have a superheated Baldwin Pacific which handled the Seaboard's top-name trains before World War I.

Cylinders, 23″ × 28″   Boiler diameter, 71″
Drivers, 71″   Weight, total engine, 211,600 lb.

(Collection of Frederick Westing)

INTRODUCED ON THE BURLINGTON in 1924 these M-4 class Texas type engines gave the most ton-miles-per-hour capacity that had thus far been obtained from a two-cylinder locomotive. Specially designed to meet clearly defined operating conditions the success of their operation was largely attributed to this fact. Standard locomotives, whether steam, diesel or electric, have never been the answer to all operating problems. The steam locomotive's longevity has in great part been due to its being "tailored" for the task. To-day the diesel is seemingly following this policy as evidenced by the many shapes and sizes that range from small, low-powered units up to large single units producing as much as 5,500 horespower—basically the old steam locomotive concept of building the locomotive to suit the specific job!

The M-4 engines most successfully replaced the older Mikados and bulky Santa Fe's, which had plodded along with sizeable loads but at lower speed. Efficiencywise, the M-4's reduced coal consumption 16 per cent, water consumption 22 per cent and the time of engine and train crews by 25 per cent. More cars per train meant fewer train movements while faster time on the road cut engine and train crews overtime. High locomotive horespower played a big part in these direct savings by permitting the locomotive to maintain speed on grades. The large tender capacity of 24 tons of coal and 21,500 gallons of water enabled as many as three water stops to be dispensed with when compared with the older power.

Cylinders, 31″ × 32″   Boiler diameter, 92″
Drivers, 64″   Weight, total engine, 512,000 lb.

(Collection of Frederick Westing)

THE DEVELOPMENT OF DIESEL-ELECTRIC locomotives in the United States was begun in 1925 by two of the established steam locomotive manufacturers. One experimental locomotive was built in that year by The American Locomotive Company in cooperation with the General Electric Co. and The Ingersoll-Rand Co., and the other was built by The Baldwin Locomotive Works. It was not until 10 years later that any other domestic builder undertook development work in this field.

The early Baldwin units were essentially an application of diesel engine-electric generator power plants to tried and proven designs of straight electric locomotives. The internal diesel power generating plant substituetd for an external power source such as trolley or third rail.

Baldwin's first unit bearing construction number which was also its Road No. 58,501, was placed in service June 29, 1925. It weighed 275,000 lbs. on six axles, four of which were powered providing 180,000 lbs. on drivers for tractive purposes. Forty inch diameter wheels were used on all axles. The draft was through the truck frames which were articulated in accordance with acepted straight electric locomotive practice of that time.

A Knudson 1000 H.P., 12 cylinder $9\frac{3}{4}'' \times 12\frac{1}{2}''$, two cycle, solid injection inverted "V" type engine with twin crankshafts geared to a common shaft was used as a prime mover. The common shaft was directly connected to a Westinghouse generator that supplied four Westinghouse 353-D-3, 750 volt D.C. traction motors.

This unit was designed for road rather than switching service and its control system was designed to lend itself to multiple unit operation. (Collection of John F. Kirkland)

A BIG ENGINE for the small Osage Railway. Engine No. 10 was a Decapod type usually found on Class 1 railroads where heavy freight trains can use their heavy adhesive, or pulling power weight.

Cylinders, 24″ × 28″   Boiler diameter, 70″
Drivers, 56″   Weight, total engine, 217,200 lb.

(Collection of Frederick Westing)

IN FAR OFF Australia many years ago a small two-foot gauge "cabbage stacker" worked among the sugar cane.

Cylinders, 7″ × 10″   Boiler diameter, 24⅝″
Drivers, 24″   Weight, total engine, 18,800 lb.

(Collection of Frederick Westing)

A BIG 0-8-0 type switcher built for the Belt Railway of Chicago. An unusual feature was the use of a stoker in switching service.

Cylinders, 23″ × 28″   Boiler diameter, 80″
Drivers, 57″   Weight, total engine, 258,150 lb.

(Collection of Frederick Westing)

WHAT A STEAM RAIL CAR looks like without the car body. Built for the Royal State Railways of Siam, this steam car ran on a 1 meter gauge. A steam brake was used on the leading and driving wheels, while a vacuum brake was applied on the rear car truck. The following dimensions are given in the metric system.

Cylinders, 254mm × 304mm   Boiler diameter, 1.220m
Drivers, 1.016m   Weight, total car, 44,990kgs.

Oil was used as fuel and the tank capacity was 3,028 liters. Water capacity was 7,570 liters. (Collection of Frederick Westing)

WHAT RAILFAN hasn't heard of the "Ma and Pa"? Here we see one of their Consolidations which for years did its duty well as a reliable, efficient freight hauler. With superheater, and a feedwater heater it was enabled to realize its boiler potential.

Cylinders, 22″ × 28″   Boiler diameter, 76″
Drivers, 51″   Weight, total engine, 207,050 lb.

(Collection of Frederick Westing)

ONE OF THE SMALLEST Vanderbilt, or circular tenders, is an interesting part of this Mogul built for the 3 foot, 6 inch Phillippine Railway Company, in the Phillippine Islands.

Cylinders, 15″ × 18″   Boiler diameter, 50″
Drivers 44″   Weight, total engine, 78,200 lb.

(Collection of Frederick Westing)

A BELPAIRE FIREBOX was used on this engine built for the Havana Central Railroad of Cuba. The 11″ Westinghouse air compressor almost dwarfs the smokebox. This engine was operated in passenger service on standard (4′8½″) gauge track. Fuel used was the 2,100 gallons of oil in the tank.

Cylinders, 18½″ × 24″   Boiler diameter, 55″
Drivers, 68″   Weight, total engine, 119,600 lb.

(Collection of Frederick Westing)

IN 1925 the American Locomotive Company brought out a three-cylinder single expansion Mountain (4-8-2) type locomotive which was put into service on the Lehigh Valley Railroad. Its fine performance stimulated a revived interest in this method of steam distribution. Soon Baldwin was building such engines for domestic and foreign use.

Conforming to this three-cylinder trend were ten engines of the Mountain type, class M-75, for the Denver & Rio Grande Western in 1926. The road's "Scenic Limited" was often hauled by one of them. In the movement of fast freight the M-75's were equally successful.

Cylinders (3) 25″ × 30″   Boiler diameter, 92″
Drivers 67″   Weight, total engine, 419,310 lb.

(Collection of Frederick Westing)

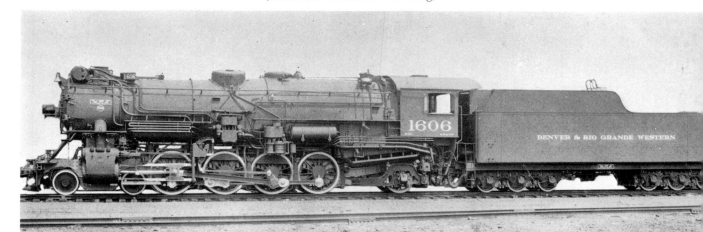

JUST THE THING for the "gentleman farmer" to help gather in the crops. This 0-6-0 side tanker built in 1927 is another illustration of the fine finish given to Baldwin locomotives whether built for the four-billion dollar Pennsylvania—as it was in the days of steam—or a single farm owner! Two sandboxes, top feed injector checks and electric headlight (note that tall exhaust pipe from the steam turbine section of the generator) were used on this engine. The metal plate over the stack was to give some protection against rain when the engine stood outside for long periods. Some French locomotives had a similar arrangement over the stack which could, however, be turned aside or flipped open and shut to suit. A free exhaust is desirable, but where heavy rains are prevalent and engines stored outside the damage done by water to the smokebox interior was to be avoided if possible. (Collection of Frederick Westing)

A REAL WESTERN HERO of the silent film days, William S. Hart, poses at the throttle of the first eastbound "Chief" of the Santa Fe as it prepares to leave Los Angeles on November 14, 1926. The engine is No. 3748 of the Mountain type built by Baldwin in 1924.

The two sandboxes, typical of Santa Fe practice, are quite prominent as is the number box in back of the stack, a feature unique with this road. These were placed on both sides of the engine. The "Chief" was scheduled to make the run from Los Angeles to Chicago in 63 hours, cutting five hours off the former schedule.

Cylinders, 28″ × 28″
Drivers, 69″   Weight, total engine, 361,600 lb.

(Collection of Frederick Westing)

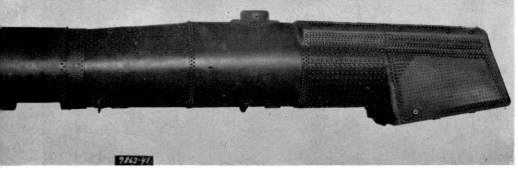

BOILER for Pennsylvania Railroad class M1 locomotive showing how third course top embodied Belpaire firebox roof sheet; unlike, the classes K4, L1, and I1, steam dome is on second course of boiler instead of third. Third course served as combustion chamber while 69.9 square feet of grate area roughly the 70 square feet, standard of the K4, L1 and I1 engines was retained. (Collection of Frederick Westing)

A GOLIATH of the rails was this single expansion 2-8-8-2 built for the Chesapeake & Ohio Railway in 1926. Four cylinders 23″ × 32″ were used, boiler diameter was 93⅞″ with 57″ drivers, and total engine weight was 565,000 pounds. Two of the air drums were located near the boiler top in back of the sandbox. Vanderbilt type tenders were used. (Collection of Frederick Westing)

THESE FINE-LOOKING and splendid performing Pacifics were built in 1926 for the Reading Company. Five of these engines were built carrying road numbers 175 to 179, class G-2-SA. They were built for heavy high-speed passenger service, and represented a marked increase in size over the road's earlier Pacifics of the G-1-SA class. All were hand-fired.

Cylinders, 25″ × 28″ Boiler diameter, 74″
Drivers, 80″ Weight, total engine, 306,360 lb.

(Collection of Frederick Westing)

IN 1923 the Pennsylvania Railroad built and began tests of a large Mountain type locomotive numbered 4700. The basic thought motivating its construction was the desire to obtain a dual service locomotive for freight and passenger traffic.

Although its overall size made it suitable for operation on most Pennsy main line divisions, its primary field of service was to be the haulage of freight trains on the Middle Division, covering 130.8 miles between Harrisburg, and Altoona, Pa.

Numerous tests on the Altoona test plant indicated the need for some detail changes, particularly to the boiler; these were made and class M1 was the result.

The Pennsy then placed an order for 200 class M1's of which Baldwin received an order for 175 units. These were completed between 1926 and 1927, carrying road numbers 6800 to 6974.

While many of the details of these locomotives were similar to those of previously designed Pennsylvania power, a number of features deserve special mention. First of these was the boiler. It was of the Belpaire type, with tubes 19 feet long between tube sheets, and a combustion chamber eight feet two inches long.

To properly provide for expansion and contraction in a furnace of this length the crowns of the firebox and combustion chamber were united by a corrugated plate which constituted an expansion joint. The corrugation was made with a two-inch radius and formed a trough about five inches deep across the crown sheet. To make similar provision in the lower part of the firebox a crescent-shaped corrugation, with a maximum depth of two inches at the center, was formed in the front tube sheet below the tubes. The forming of these corrugations called for some unusual flanging operations. Other interesting flanging jobs were that of forming the hip joints for the Belpaire firebox connection on the top of the second boiler course, after the course had been rolled to a circular shape; and the flanging of the lower half of the rear boiler course in one piece with the outside throat sheet. The latter arrangement eliminated the usual throat seam, and permitted the height of the boiler above the rail to be reduced.

In accordance with Pennsylvania standards, the machinery details were of minimum weight consistent with good practice, Walschaerts valve gear was applied and was controlled by a power reverse mechanism. The main and side rods had thin webs and flanges, and floating bushings were used on the main rod back ends and the main and third pin bearings on the side rods. The stubs had a design of grease cup which was new when applied. It consisted of a horizontal cavity closed by a plug, and communicated with holes drilled through the brass so that the pin could be lubricated.

The frames were separate castings of massive construction, seven inches wide throughout the greater portion of their length and 9½ inches wide above the pedestals. The transverse bracing was correspondingly substantial. A one-piece rear frame cradle was used, in combination with a trailing truck of the so-called KW type, similar to the trucks previously used on the Pennsylvania's Atlantic, Pacific and Mikado type locomotives. Duplex stokers with their two feeding barrels simulated the letter "V" and were a prominent part of the cab's interior.

Original tenders, class 110-P-75 were quite similar to those on the K4 Pacifics and were patented by William F. Kiesel. Capacity was 11,000 gallons of water, and 35,000 pounds of coal.

The M1's large 72 inch drivers were unusual for a freight engine at that time, but they worked out very well in handling 4,200 ton trains, up to 125 cars when they bucked the grades on the westbound run over the Middle Division. They could take such trains over the road in about four hours, substantially surpassing class L1 in tonnage moved and speed. Coming east with the grade in the train's favor 140 hopper cars loaded with coal were routine for an M1.

A total of 201 of these locomotives was built, including the original No. 4700 which was modified to suit standard M1 practice and was renumbered 6699. They proved to be the most versatile steam locomotives used in road service. Many were the top-name passenger trains they hauled as well as freight, performing equally well in both services.

Cylinders, 27" × 30"   Boiler diameter, 84½"
Drivers, 72"   Weight, total engine, 382, 400 lb.

(Collection of Frederick Westing)

A REAL "CHATTANOOGA CHOO-CHOO" was this stoker-fired Mountain type locomotive built for the Nashville, Chattanooga & St. Louis Railway. Cylinders were 27″ × 30″, *boiler diameter was 78″, drivers 69″ with a total engine weight of 326,950 pounds. Built in 1925 a group of these engines did excellent work on the Cumberland Mountain grades where a 2.35 per cent grade southbound, and a 2.50 per cent northbound grade challenged engines and passenger trains usually made up of 10 to 13 cars of old heavyweight stock, running on friction bearings. Known as J-1-B-54 they were based on the roads United States Railroad Administration design of light Mountain type and, this road's class J-1-54. Running 288 miles between Nashville and Atlanta, with a crew change at Chattanooga, they rolled up impressive monthly mileages and allowed 13 locomotives on the Atlanta Division to be released for other service. The neatly curved cap that topped the stack gave a pleasing touch to their appearance and was applied to most of their locomotives after 1913. Vanderbilt tenders, a standard part of the road's new power contained the fuel and water.

* In accordance with Baldwin practice the boiler diameter referred to the diameter at the first course of the boiler barrel. (Collection of Frederick Westing)

A STAR STEAM locomotive salesman, was Grafton Greenough, Vice President in charge of domestic sales, who died in 1926. (Collection of Frederick Westing)

REAL BRUTISH POWER built in 1927 for the Western Maryland Railway. These Decapods carried a heavy driving wheel load and with a working pressure of 240 pounds per square inch, developed a tractive force of 96,300 lb. This was a high figure for a non-articulated rigid-framed engine. Most of their work was done on the 171.4 miles of heavy grade line between Hagerstown, Md. and Connellsville, Pa. The Western Maryland 2-10-0's exceeded the Pennsy's famed Decapods by quite a margin in every respect. The huge tender contained 30 tons of coal and 22,000 gallons of water. Stokers and power reverse gears with "A" type superheaters were part of their equipment.

Cylinders, 30″ × 32″   Boiler diameter, 92″
Drivers, 61″   Weight, total engine, 419,280 lb.

(Collection of Frederick Westing)

A PERKY LITTLE 4-4-0 built as late as June 1927, for the Chicago & Illinois Midland Railway, equipped with an "A" type superheater, Walschaerts valve gear and 8″ piston valves, her basic dimensions were 18″ × 24″ cylinders, 56″ for the boiler diameter, 63″ drivers, and an engine weight of 118,400 pounds. (Collection of Frederick Westing)

IN 1927 heavy traffic on the Pennsylvania Railroad prompted that company to order one-hundred of their K4S class Pacific type locomotives. With 27″ × 28″ cylinders, a boiler diameter of 78½″, drivers 80″ and a total engine weight of 308,890 pounds, these engines represented the Pennsy's standard type for heavy high-speed passenger service. Baldwin was given the order for 75 engines, road numbers 5400 to 5474. This was the first and only time any outside builder ever received an order for this world famous class. The remaining 25 were built by the railroad at Altoona. Featured with these engines was a new design of tender which had been applied in 1926. Patents for the tank and its trucks were granted to William F. Kiesel, Pennsy's Mechanical Engineer at Altoona. Weight reduction and less costly construction were his objectives, and this he achieved by a light single-casting underframe which eliminated the side and end sills while using short body bolsters. The trucks also emphasized simplicity with superior riding qualities and Kiesel tenders were used on the M1's. The Baldwin K4's had fine service records and one No. 5436, hauled the westbound Broadway Limited for years between Manhattan Transfer and Harrisburg. Class K4 had remarkably high capacity for a hand-fired engine (Collection Frederick Westing)

A HAND-FIRED BALDWIN K4, No. 5406, hauling a 17-car train on the Pennsylvania Railroad, near Linden, New Jersey, while bound for Washington, D.C. On the road east of Pittsburgh the K4's were hand-fired well up into the 1930's. Finally came the I.C.C. edict which forced stoker applications on all road engines which exceeded a specific weight on drivers. Value of the stoker on the K4's was apparent in their twilight years when they made records never envisioned by their creators. (Collection of Frederick Westing)

IN 1927 the Baltimore & Ohio Railroad ordered 20 Pacifics from Baldwin. These engines, class P-7, were based in great part on the Pennsy's K4 class Pacific in their vital proportions. Painted olive green with gold leaf lettering and striping, they were named for Presidents of the United States and, for which they received much favorable publicity. The first engine of the class was appropriately named President Washington, road number 5300, and shown here resting at the Communipaw enginehouse in Jersey City after bringing in a train from Washington. Unlike the Pennsylvania's K4's the Presidents were equipped with automatic stokers. The top inverted tank collar on the tender was applied by the railroad years after their initial appearance.

I have a vivid recollection of the speed capabilities of these P-7 engines, for I had, through the courtesy of the railroad, the pleasurable experience of riding the cab of the Royal Blue between Philadelphia and Jersey City. It probably represented the highest speed at which I have even ridden in a locomotive cab, either steam, electric, or diesel. As I recall, the speedometer dial gave a reading up to 95-mph. and over the New York short line cut-off, between Olney and Parkland Junction, the needle was glued to this maximum 95-mph. reading.

At this time the Royal Blue featured special light-weight equipment and was normally hauled by the Hudson type engine Lord Baltimore, but the big V-2 class engine was out for boiler wash, so President Pierce, No. 5312, took over—and did we roll! Again the value of the automatic stoker was clearly shown; hand firing with that 8-car train and pace would have been "some" job. But our fireman in a most relaxed manner, just adjusted his stoker valves to suit steam demands and kept her about two pounds from the "popping-off" point all the way.

Cylinders, 27" × 28"   Boiler diameter, 78"
Drivers 80"   Weight, total engine 326,000 lb.

(Collection of Frederick Westing)

BALTIMORE AND OHIO

DOWN IN MARYLAND class P-7 engine President Taylor, No. 5310, has a good roll on the ten-car National Limited as it heads west for Washington and St. Louis. This locomotive was later fitted with the Emerson water-tube firebox in 1939, thereby, becoming class P-9-B. (Collection of Frederick Westing)

FREQUENTLY switching locomotives run backwards about as often as they operate in forward motion. Thus the slope back tank is of greater value in providing a clearer rear lookout than a rectangular tender tank. While this sloping tank reduces water storage space such a condition is not vital in yard service where water is readily available within a short distance at all times. This locomotive was built in July 1927, and was fitted with power reverse gear, a decided boon to an engineer in switching service.

Cylinders, 20″ × 24″   Boiler diameter, 65″
Drivers, 51″   Weight, total engine, 147,700 lb.

(Collection of Frederick Westing)

AN EVEN LARGER SWITCHER was this huge 0-10-0 built in 1927 for the Duluth, Missabe & Northern Railway. Also stoker fired, it included two thermic syphons, power reverse, limited cut-off, and a tender booster estimated to develop 14,500 lb. tractive force and applied to the front tender truck. A one-piece locomotive bed, with air brake operation on all driving and tender wheels with air pumped by two 8½″ cross-compound compressors illustrated the progress made even in the lowly steam switcher.

Cylinders, 28″ × 30″   Boiler diameter, 88″
Drivers, 57″   Weight, total engine, 352,250 lb.

(Collection of Frederick Westing)

RETURN OF THE "BALDWIN BOOMER". After numerous tests on railroads where No. 60,000 ran successfully on coal or oil as fuel, the big three-cylinder compound with its water-tube firebox came home to Eddystone. Engine 60,000 attained the highest power ever developed up to that time on the Altoona test plant, namely, 4,500 horsepower. This, at the time, exceeded the plant's capacity and restricted attempts to obtain greater power with additional tests.

Cylinders (3) High-pressure (1) inside 27″ × 32″   Boiler diameter, 84″
Low-pressure (2) outside 27″ × 32″   Weight, total engine, 457,500 lb.
Drivers, 63½″

(Collection of Frederick Westing)

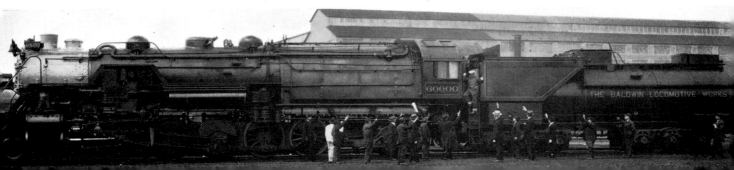

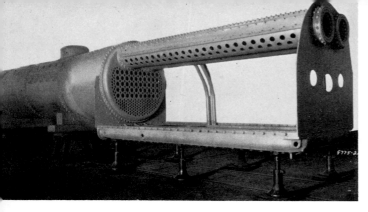

THIS ILLUSTRATION clearly shows the constructional features of the water-tube firebox of engine No. 60,000. The foundation, or mud ring, was a huge steel casting, covered by a United States patent. (Collection of Frederick Westing)

SMOKEBOX INTERIOR of No. 60,000. Headers at top of superheater flues fed steam to front-end throttle valve from whence it flowed to the center, or high-pressure steam chest and cylinder. Exhaust from this cylinder entered two low-pressure cylinders and exhausted through two outside pipes leading to the exhaust nozzle. (Collection of Frederick Westing)

BILLED AS THE WORLD'S tiniest actor, Paul Del Rio, of Spain possibly also qualifies as the smallest engineer to handle the automatic brake valve on No. 60,000 the big 4-10-2 at the Franklin Institute in Philadelphia. (Collection of Frederick Westing)

THE GLORY THAT WAS BALDWINS! A comprehensive view of the Baldwin Eddystone Works as it appeared from 1928 to the 1950's. Even this large overall scene does not include the huge tender shop wherein many tender, electric locomotives and diesels were built. The cruciform construction of the eight-story office building with the one-story cafeteria building to its right is clearly discernible. Today nearly everything east of the main line of the Pennsylvania Railroad has been razed, including the erecting, tender and forge shops. (Collection of Frederick Westing)

A STRIKING CONTRAST to the gigantic Eddystone Works is "Matty" Baldwin's first locomotive building shop in Philadelphia's Lodge Alley. (Collection of Frederick Westing)

EARLY IN 1929 the Great Northern Railway announced their intention of operating a new train named the "Empire Builder" to decrease the running time of the fastest schedule then in use by five hours which included the Rocky Mountain crossing. To meet this formidable task the 4-8-4 type of engine was selected as most suitable.

Here we have a picture of one of these massive machines, class S-1 graced by some pretty girls. It was one of six engines built in 1929 for operating over the Continental Divide in Montana. The maximum grade on the east slope was 1.8 per cent, and passenger trains were handled over these grades without helpers. These engines burned oil for fuel and had a Belpaire firebox with a grate area of 108 square feet. The boiler had a maximum diameter of 98-inches, and carried a pressure of 250 lb. Main drivers were cross balanced and Walschaerts valve gear was arranged to give a variable lead increasing from 3/32" in full gear forward to ¼" in mid-gear. This was an unusual feature with this valve gear. The equipment included an exhaust steam injector. These locomotives could traverse curves as sharp as 16 degrees. Their tractive force was 22 per cent greater than that of the Mountain type locomotives formerly used in this service.

Cylinders, 28" × 30"   Boiler diameter, 88"
Drivers, 73"   Weight, total engine, 472,120 lb.

(Collection of Frederick Westing)

AT THE MAIN ENTRANCE to the office building at Eddystone stands Matthias W. Baldwin. Another statue of Baldwin, who was one of Philadelphia's most distinguished citizens, also honors him on the north side plaza of Philadelphia's City Hall. (Collection of Frederick Westing)

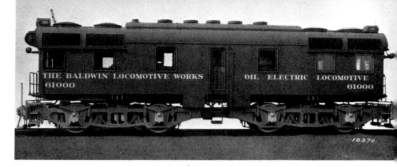

ON MAY 15, 1929, Baldwin released to railroads for demonstration service a diesel electric switching locomotive bearing construction number which was also its Road No. 61,000.

This locomotive's running gear followed tried and proven electric locomotive articulated designs and was of 0-4 + 4-0 wheel arrangement using 48″ diameter wheels. The locomotive weighed 270,000 lbs. all on drivers.

A Krupp 1,000 H.P., 6 cylinder 15″ × 15″, four cycle solid injection super-charged engine was directly connected to a Westinghouse 478A generator that supplied four Westinghouse 355, 600 volt D.C. traction motors. Oil cooled pistons were used. The engine was cranked by admitting high pressure air to the cylinders. (Collection of John F. Kirkland)

IN 1928 the Texas & Pacific Railway obtained five Mountain type locomotives from Baldwin. These were handsome engines, and the neat copper cap that topped the stack, a unique item in modern American steam locomotives, enhanced the eye-pleasing effect created by their appearance.

Cylinders, 27″ × 30″   Boiler diameter, 78″
Drivers, 73″   Weight, total engine, 361,400 lb.

(Collection of Frederick Westing)

IN AN ATTEMPT to produce a Pacific capable of matching a Hudson, the Pennsylvania Railroad designed and ordered two super-Pacifics, class K5. One No. 5699, was built by Baldwin in 1929, and equipped with the Caprotti poppet valve gear invented by Senor Arturo Caprotti, of Italy. The other K5, No. 5698, was built by the Pennsy at Altoona and used Walschaerts gear. Each K5 rated 54,675 lb. tractive force surpassing their own K4 class and the New York Central's Hudsons, despite the latter's use of a booster trailing truck. But the K5's ponderous size restricted operating locations and, in upper speed ranges the Central's Hudsons out-performed them. How the Pennsy could have expected a hand-fired, muzzle-loading Pacific to equal or beat a superbly designed and built New York Central Hudson, appears to be a high point in engineering naivete!

Pennsy's dogged insistence on hand-firing these huge locomotives (even in the early L1's I1's and first M1 engine were hand fired) borders on unjustifiable obstinacy. Naturally, the full potentialities of that big well designed K5 boiler (for it was all of that) could not be realized by one pair of human arms.

In time the Caprotti gear gave way to the Walschaerts on the 5699 as the latter seemed sturdier and more effective in meeting American operating conditions. Suffice to say class K5 stopped with these two engines and after a comparatively short and uneventful career disappeared from the scene.

Cylinders 27″ × 30″   Boiler diameter 84½″
Drivers 80″   Weight, total engine, 331,555 lb.

(Collection of Frederick Westing)

THE BALDWIN K5, No. 5699, in action between Narberth and Wynnewood, Pa., on the main line of the Pennsylvania Railroad. The train is headed west Pittsburgh bound, and is climbing a fairly stiff grade. This particular engine was known to Pennsy railroaders as "Mussolini" due to the Italian invented Caprotti poppet gear. Note the absence of external valve motion. Engine No. 5698, on the other hand, was called "General Butler" due to some controversial incident that was publicized between Premier Mussolini, and General Smedley Butler. (Collection of Frederick Westing)

A GROUP OF THE LARGEST and most flexible steam locomotives were thirty-five, 4-8-4 type engines delivered to the Chicago & North Western Railway in the fall of 1929. These were known as class H, and the objective of their design was to attain maximum capacity within the restrictions of imposed weight and clearance limits.

Originally built with safety valves set for 250 pounds, this figure was raised to 275 pounds, and at this pressure the tractive force from the main cylinders was 71,800 pounds. When using the booster applied to the rear axle of the trailing truck this figure was raised to 84,200 pounds tractive force. With their high starting tractive force, and 76 inch driving wheels, these engines were well suited for dual service operation and were equally satisfactory in freight or heavy high-speed passenger service. High boiler capacity coupled with the use of efficient auxiliary equipment contributed much to this result. An unusual feature of these engines was the outside bearings on the front truck which was something rarely encountered in American locomotive practice.

For the protection of the public, class H, was fitted with continuous automatic train control which was operative between Chicago and Omaha. It represented, at the time, the longest installation of this kind in the United States. The General Railway Signal Company supplied the apparatus, and used color light signals in the cab. If restrictive indications appeared and no acknowledgment made by the engineer, speed was automatically reduced and a warning horn sounded in the cab. A contactor then had to be acknowledged or an automatic brake application stopped the train. This device permitted removal of all wayside signals, except at terminals and interlocking plants.

Cylinders, 27" × 32"   Boiler diameter, 90¾₁₆"
Drivers, 76"   Weight, total engine, 498,000 lb.

(Collection of Frederick Westing)

BUILT FOR the Akron & Barberton Belt Railroad, this 0-6-0 type switcher bore some resemblance to Pennsylvania Railroad practice. The cab, Belpaire firebox, stack and safety valves with whistle in back of the steam dome were all suggestive of the Pennsy's B-6-SB class switchers of this type. One departure was the rather large tender. (Collection of Frederick Westing)

NO OTHER RAILROAD in the United States had engines like them; they were a distinct Southern Pacific trademark. The sight of a cab-forward 4-8-8-2 type single expansion articulated as it climbed the Sierra Nevada Mountain ranges or gracefully rounded Tehachapi's loops, was an inseparable part of the S. P.

Not the first to run an engine cab with the tender on the smokebox end, the North Pacific Coast, a 70 mile narrow gauge line had run such a lone engine patented by William Thomas. Also some time before World War 1, the Southern Railway of Italy, ran some four-cylinder compounds of the 4-6-0 type, cab first with a rigid six-wheel cylindrical tender at the smoky end.

The Italian locomotives were quite successful and performed with equal facility in freight or passenger service. As with the Southern Pacific "back ups" (so called on this road) a clear view was obtained by the engine-men, something that was becoming a problem with the coming of the larger high-pitched boilers. Unlike the oil burning Southern Pacific engines, the Italian "back ups" burned coal stored in tank-like side bunkers.

Nevertheless, no railroad used this form of motive power so plentifully and successfully as the S.P., or concentrated so much power in such locomotives. Conventional Mallets with cabs in the rear and coupled to the tender at that point had preceded them. These had proved their ability to outperform any rigid frame engine on their road in pulling power.

But the smoke problem when running through the necessary snow sheds which abound on a line noted for traditionally heavy snowfalls was terrific, especially at drag freight speeds on an uphill run. Smoke splitters—a "V" shaped metal wedge placed lengthwise over the stack did something to split up the smoke concentration, but left much to be desired.

At this point officials of the Southern Pacific recalled the North Coast Pacific "cab-firster" and with oil as fuel the idea of a train coming down the track with firebox end leading presented no great problem. Another change was made in the Mallets in that they were "simpled" from compounds into four-cylinder single expansion articulated locomotives, and the result pepped up performance so much that Baldwin and Southern Pacific got together to plan a large version of this design.

Originally built to run between Roseville, California and Sparks, Nevada, approximately 139 miles, where rugged grades were a severe problem, they finally found their way on various other parts of the S.P. where they served equally well. Baldwin was the only locomotive builder to construct these giant "back-ups" for the S.P.

In 1928 ten of these 4-8-8-2 type single-expansion articulateds, class AC-5, were built for the Southern Pacific, and the writer had the pleasure of riding one up and down the test track one afternoon at Eddystone. The following year 16 more were built and delivered. Originally set with valves for a 70 per cent maximum cut-off, they developed 112,760 lb. tractive force. Later this was changed to 81.6 per cent when operating in full gear, thereby upping the tractive force to 116,900 pounds. In 1930, 25 similar units were built which were a bit heavier and carried a pressure of 250 lb. which increased the tractive force to 124,300 lb.

Cylinders (4), 24" × 32"   Boiler diameter, 94 1/16"
Drivers, 63½"   Weight, total engine, 622,600 lb.

(Collection of Frederick Westing)

SOUTHERN PACIFIC LINES

Depression Years—1930 to 1941

Despite the 1929 stock market crash and its subsequent impact on the business world, Baldwin did get orders in 1930 for various types of steam locomotives from several railroads.

In 1931 The Baldwin Locomotive Works purchased the George D. Whitcomb Co. which had been in business since 1878 as manufacturers of coal mining equipment. This company had also been the builders of the first successful gasoline locomotives used in coal mines since April 1906. From then on they built many narrow gauge gasoline locomotives for mines and industrial plant operations. Their first electric trolley locomotive was built in 1921, and in 1929 Whitcomb designed and built the largest gasoline-electric locomotive constructed for service on American railroads.

After becoming a Baldwin subsidiary they operated under the name of The Whitcomb Locomotive Company. As such they produced many diesel-electric locomotives for various forms of service in narrow and standard gauge sizes.

Another series of acquisitions took place in 1931 when Baldwin-Southwark Corporation was formed for the purpose of carrying on the heavy machinery business of The Baldwin Locomotive Works. The divisions of Baldwin-Southwark were Southwark Foundry and Machine Company; I. P. Morris & De La Vergne, Inc.; and the Pelton Water Wheel Company.

Among the products manufactured by the Baldwin-Southwark Corporation, were scale cars for calibrating railroad track scales. These were in weights of 40,000 to 100,000 pounds.

A novel experience for Baldwin occurred early in 1932 when the Works built their first locomotive for Persia. This was an order received from the Imperial Government for Persia for four locomotives to be operated on the Southern Persian State Railways. These engines were of the Mogul type and ran on a standard gauge track. With Persia an oil producing country, the locomotives were designed for burning oil as fuel.

An important project initiated at this time by Thomas R. Cook of Baldwin was a detailed investigation regarding the economic value of old steam locomotives still in service. It was clearly established that maintenance costs rose correspondingly with a locomotive's age. Proving that new locomotives could pay for themselves in maintenance cost reduction was Mr. Cook's basic concept.

Elaborate studies illustrated with tables and diagrams based on actual operating experience of many years, proved this point overwhelmingly. The effect of these studies did cause some railroads to re-evaluate their motive power situation and subsequently purchase new steam locomotives.

In this period the necessity for higher train speeds became more important. In some cases freight train schedules equalled those of passenger trains. To meet this condition, driving wheel diameters increased from a 63-inch standard size of 1925 to 70 and 76 inches in 1930.

With higher piston loads to be provided for to produce the required tractive force, more weight was added to the driving machinery and weight available for the boiler was, in order to keep within reasonable axle loads, correspondingly reduced. The four-wheel trailing truck was the natural result of this situation and brought forth the 2-8-4 Berkshires, 2-10-4 Texas type, 4-6-4 Hudsons, and 4-8-4 type Northerns or Mohawks.

The degree of superheated steam was raised during these years, and some locomotives obtained a superheat of 700 degrees. This was provided by the "E" type superheater wherein an installation of superheater units covered the entire flue sheet. Front-end throttles offered decreased steam consumption and the use of superheated steam in the locomotive's auxiliary equipment brought economical gains. These latter were small, but a decided advantage was derived from lower maintenance on the E type superheater unit.

Increased carrying capacity of the trucks made it possible to apply boilers of ample capacity and likewise provide large grates needed to obtain maximum evaporation from boilers using a poor grade of coal.

Greater use of cast-steel locomotive beds, which extended to the tender in the form of solid cast-steel frames, or tank bottoms became nearly standardized on all trunk lines.

While some of these improvements taken individually effected seemingly insignificant economies, their cumulative effect helped create steam locomotives capable of producing powers at speeds little short of marvelous when compared with locomo-

FOUR ENGINES built for the Baltimore & Ohio in 1930 were of particular interest. Two, classes T-1 and T-2 were of the mountain type, while the other two classes KK-1 and KK-2 were of the single expansion 2-6-6-2 articulated type.

Featured on one articulated class KK-1, and one Mountain class T-1 was the Emerson water tube firebox invented by George H. Emerson, Chief of Motive Power and Equipment. Boilers of the KK-2 and T-2 engines were of the conventional type. Tenders on all these locomotives were identical and of the Vanderbilt or circular tank form. An objective of its design was to have, despite its capacity of 18,000 gallons of water and 20 tons of coal, a tender with an unusual load to dead weight ratio. The fact that 2.16 pounds of coal and water were carried per pound of light tender weight, shows how well this goal was achieved. Being of the lightest possible construction, two four-wheel trucks were sufficient to carry its weight.

Mr. Emerson had the greatest respect for Mr. Vauclain's opinions on locomotives, and whenever he visited Baldwin's insisted on doing business with Mr. Vauclain in person.

Cylinders, 27½″ × 30″   Boiler diameter, 89⅝″
Drivers, 74″   Weight, total engine, 384,000 lb.

(Collection of Frederick Westing)

THE TREND toward the Hudson (4-6-4) type was indicated when twelve such engines were built for the Chicago, Burlington & Quincy Railroad in 1930. Overall sizes in height and width, by eastern standards appear quite large; from the top of the rail to the top of the stack the distance was 15 feet, 10 inches, with an overall width of 10 feet, 9½ inches. A load of 69,200 lbs. was carried on each pair of driving wheels. On the rear axle of the trailing truck a booster was applied, thus increasing the starting tractive force from 47,700 pounds to 59,400 pounds. In common with many locomotives then built and for some time to come, the one-piece bed with cylinders cast integral was used.

Performance records showed the S-4 engines averaging 12,042 miles per month, though at one time in a 30 day period several S-4's accumulated more than 16,500 miles each.

Later, Engine No. 3002 was streamlined, named "Aeolus" and renumbered "4000". On one occasion Aeolus made a 431 mile run from Minneapolis to Chicago, went to the roundhouse where it received routine servicing and inspection, and departed 38 minutes later on the 1,034 mile run to Denver. These two runs, totaling 1,465 miles, were made on the diesel-powered Zephyr schedules averaging better than 60 miles an hour.

Cylinders, 25″ × 28″   Boiler diameter, 82″
Drivers, 78″   Weight, total engine, 391,830 lb.

(Collection of Frederick Westing)

HERE, we have, the T-2 class Mountain type engine, No. 5550 built 1930 for the B&O with its conventional, radial, or round-top firebox boiler. And speaking of boilers it might be pertinent at this spot to explain that all boiler dimensions in this book refer to the diameter of the boiler shell at the first course. Baldwin's measurement at this point referred to the outside diameter.

Cylinders, 27½″ × 30″   Boiler, diameter, 89⅝″
Drivers, 74″   Weight, total engine, 385,000 lb.

(Collection of Frederick Westing)

FOURTEEN 4-8-4 type locomotives were built for the Southern Pacific in 1930, and assigned to passenger service. Use of a four-wheel trailing truck allowed a larger firebox. At this time the boiler pressure was raised from 210 to 250 pounds so that these new engines developed 62,200 lb. tractive force at about 75 percent cut-off. A booster engine drove the rear pair of trailing truck wheels adding another 13,710 lb. tractive force. The driver load per axle was rather high for steam power, being 65,500 lb.; heavier than former Southern Pacific practice. But any additional track stress due to this heavier loading was somewhat offset by cross counter-balancing the main drivers. Riding qualities of these locomotives were noticeably smooth and they were among the first engines on the S.P. to have a cast steel engine bed with the cylinders cast integral.

Cylinders, 27″ × 30″   Boiler diameter, 86″
Drivers, 73½″   Weight, total engine, 442,300 lb.

(Collection of Frederick Westing)

IN 1930 ELEVEN LOCOMOTIVES Nos. 5001 to 5011, of the single expansion articulated 2-8-8-4 type, were built for the Northern Pacific Railway. Class Z-5, or the "Yellowstones" as they were called, were of exceptional interest, for up to that time they were the largest steam propelled units ever built. From rail top to stack top they measured 16 feet, and were 11 feet, 6 inches in width. Length over the engines and tender bumper faces was 120 feet, 6¾ inches. Total weight of engine and tender was 1,125,400 pounds, and total starting tractive force with the booster was 153,400 pounds. These figures are even more impressive when it is understood that these locomotives were built to traverse curves as sharp as 22 degrees.

The Z-5's burned Rosebud coal, which was a species of lignite found in Montana. It occurs close to the surface and was obtained by strip mining. As mined, the moisture in the coal varied between 24.6 per cent and 30 per cent, and the ash between 11.9 per cent and 14 per cent. The heating value approximated 6,200 to 7,000 B.t.u. per pound, but when the coal was dried the heating value rose to about 10,000 B.t.u. per pound.

Cost prices of the strip-mined coal ranged from 50 to 98 cents per ton, delivered on the tender. Later, one of the most reliable and oft quoted estimates placed this cost at 69 cents per ton. This figure also represented the fuel cost for this railroad's 4-8-4 Northern type locomotives of the "A" class.

The boilers of the Z-5 class when working at maximum capacity, had to evaporate over 90,000 pounds of water an hour, necessitating the consumption of 22,000 pounds of fuel. As it was desired not to exceed a maximum combustion rate of 125 pounds of coal per square foot of grate per hour, the grate area required would be at least 180 square feet. This presented a stoker problem which was unprecedented as no stoker then in use had the capacity required. The stoker companies, however, built dummy fire-boxes and experimented with Rosebud coal, and evolved a successful stoker which could handle 45,000 pounds of coal an hour.

These huge engines operated in freight service between Glendive, Montana, and Mandan, North Dakota, a distance of 216 miles, where it was required to haul 4,000 ton trains. This line traversed the so-called "badlands" and at one time relocation of this route was considered, but the cost was prohibitive and the Z-5's were the result. A pilot model of this 2-8-8-4 type locomotive was built by the American Locomotive Company in 1929. Proving successful the eleven Baldwin Z-5's followed plus some minor changes only from No. 5000 the first Yellowstone type.

An interesting problem was posed by the grate of these engines due to their length which measured over 22 feet. To rake such a grate with a firehook was impractical, therefore, two small openings, one on each side of the firebox were made near the front end. To permit raking the fire so far from the backhead firedoor, a small folding platform something like an "outrigger" was located under each firebox side opening. This gave safer and easier accessibility than could have been obtained otherwise.

Proof of the success of class Z-5 was the fact that twelve of these engines replaced twenty-eight former rail giants in doing a better job more economically. Multiple operation by Mikado type locomotives and Mallets formerly used in this service indicated that the Yellowstones showed a clear saving of at least 15 per cent in coal required to move equivalent tonnage. By making better time and handling heavier trains over the division, there was also a saving of between 42 and 45 per cent in the cost of engine and train crew wages. Running time over the 216 mile division was 10 hours, with a maximum allowed speed of 35 miles an hour. Average monthly mileage per locomotive was about 4,000 but considerably greater mileage at the time would have been possible except for depressed business conditions, which greatly reduced tonnage movement.

Cylinders (4), 26″ × 32″   Boiler diameter, 103¼″
Drivers, 63″   Weight, total engine, 723,400 lb.

(Collection of Frederick Westing)

FOR THE SANTA FE a huge 2-10-4 Texas type locomotive was built in 1930, and numbered 5000. It was quite a favorite with the engine crews and received the sobriquet of "Madam Queen." Up to the appearance of diesel power, No. 5000 assisted many a multiple-unit diesel locomotive in lifting its train over the severe Raton Pass.

Cylinders, 30″ × 34″   Boiler diameter, 92″
Drivers, 69″   Weight, total engine, 502,260 lb.

(Collection of Frederick Westing)

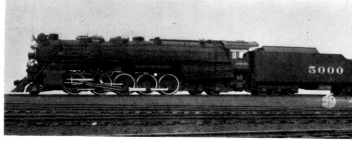

tives of twenty-five years before. Fuel consumption was reduced per ton mile, maintenance was appreciably reduced with longer runs between stopping. With one locomotive unit able to run over several divisions, increased mileage per month was obtained and made possible the elimination of older units. This meant that fewer locomotives with auxiliary devices such as stokers, feed-water heaters, coal pushers, mechanical lubricators and exhaust steam injectors, could deliver more work in ton-miles—the basic commodity of a railroad—than was possible with two or even three older units. In this fashion the auxiliaries justified their application, and still permitted the steam locomotive while providing great power to remain the simplest and most rugged self-contained locomotive ever built to this day.

These new locomotives equipped with modern auxiliary devices proved the truth of Baldwin's studies which had pointed out that continual repairing of old locomotives, or a "pants patching" policy to keep them running at about half of their efficiency was bad business. Such action was far more costly than getting fewer new and larger units to replace two or three times as many old locomotives to do the same work. The maintenance costs alone associated with the older power made the purchase of newer locomotives justifiable.

As previously referred to, the Pennsylvania Railroad in 1928, officially committed itself to extending main line electrification by hundreds of track miles. This action was due to the fact that Westinghouse Electric & Manufacturing Company (later Westinghouse Electric Corporation) had in 1927 produced an alternating current traction motor which used in a twin combination could provide 1,000 horsepower per driving axle, and yet, fit within the main frames of the locomotive.

The project as first announced in 1928, intended to cover the trackage beginning at New York where connection was made with New Haven Railroad trains from New England, and extending West and South. Westward from Philadelphia the main line was to be electrified from Paoli to Atglen Pa., and the low grade freight lines which join at Columbia, Pa., thereby connecting the cities of New York, Philadelphia and Wilmington, with electrified train operation.

TWO ENGINES for the Maine Central built in June 1930, gave Baldwin its first order for the Hudson type.

Cylinders, 23″ × 28″   Boiler, diameter, 78½″
Drivers, 73″   Weight, total engine, 312,590 lb.

(Collection of Frederick Westing)

The intimate association of Baldwin with the Pennsylvania's original locomotives in this electrification plan, and their subsequent development makes it fitting to record some of its background.

In accordance with previously expressed views, it was intended to use the alternating current single-phase system of electric traction, similar to that used in the Philadelphia suburban area since 1915. For suburban service multiple-unit car equipment was to be used, but through passenger and freight service was to be handled with electric locomotives.

Following the decision to electrify, such operation was extended to Wilmington, Delaware, and West Chester, Pa., in 1928, from Philadelphia. In 1929 this service was lengthened to Trenton, N.J., and Norristown, Pa.

Prior to and coincidental with electrification of these Philadelphia suburban lines, an investigation was being made concerning the best type of road service electric locomotive to meet service requirements. This resulted in a new approach to electric locomotive design and construction indicated by the three new types as follows:

Class O1 of the 4-4-4 type, for passenger service
Class P5 of the 4-6-4 type, for passenger service
Class L6 of the 2-8-2 type, for freight service

No class O1 or L6 electric locomotives were built by Baldwin. Both classes were considered unsuitable for future service conditions and their construction was discontinued.

Meanwhile the Pennsylvania decided to electrify their main line between New York and Washington, D.C., a distance of 226 route miles. Preliminary work on this began late in 1931, and by December 1932, the section between Sunnyside Yards, Long Island, and New Brunswick, New Jersey, was ready for operation. This left a gap between New Brunswick and Trenton which was soon electrified.

During this time the P5A locomotives and engine crews had been "breaking in" on various sections of the Pennsylvania, some hauling trains between Wilmington and Trenton, including the K4 at the head end, while others ran in the New York tunnel and terminal area.

149

On January 16, 1933, through electrified service was inaugurated between New York and Philadelphia with a P5A class locomotive heading the first trains, east and west. Fitting ceremonies were held in New York and Philadelphia to signify the importance of this new mode of operation.

Soon the sturdy, blunt-nosed box cab units were speedily shuttling between New York, Philadelphia, Wilmington and Paoli, with "clockers" and top-name trains for the West and South.

In attempting to provide a locomotive superior to class P5A, Baldwin and Gibbs and Hill were the motivating forces. Between them was created and built a 4-6-6-4 articulated type electric locomotive, No. 4899 later renumbered 4800, which in wheel and chassis arrangement bore striking resemblance to a class of electric locomotive on the New Haven Railroad. The main difference was in the cab's construction which on the New Haven was of the box-type form while the Pennsylvania used a combined

SUCCESS OF THE MOUNTAIN type locomotives on the Pennsylvania Railroad led this road to the development of a revised design known as class M1A. These engines featured several changes among which was that of the cylinder construction. Whereas class M1 cylinders were cast iron, each cast in one piece with a half saddle, in M1A the entire cylinder assembly was formed in a single casting, including the forward truck center pin. Width of the saddle bearing beneath the smokebox was so great that steam pipes could be kept entirely within the boiler shell minimizing danger of air leaks. A feed water heater was used on class M1A, and placed on top of the smokebox just back of the stack. Instead of the double-barreled Duplex stoker, a single coal conveying trough Standard Stoker model was used. This gave more room in the cab and under test proved its ability to feed as much as 22,656 pounds of coal per hour. The M1A's had twelve-wheeled tenders carrying 22,090 gallons of water and 63,000 pounds of coal. Water capacity was twice that of the former M1 class tenders. This high capacity was of special value when making long runs on divisions not equipped with track tanks.

The Pennsy ordered 100 of the M1A engines of which Baldwin built 50 in 1930. Tests were made in 1931 with M1A engine 6706 and contrasted with those of an M1 engine No. 6872. A wide range of speed and power output was covered by these tests with the M1A decidedly showing higher efficiency and capacity. The feed-water heater and improved draft conditions due to smokebox modifications materially contributed to this result. Actual increase in maximum steam capacity of the M1A over the M1 was 16.6 per cent, of which 59 per cent was due to the feed-water heater, and 41 per cent to increased boiler power.

Working at full capacity with 63 per cent cut-off at a speed of 240 rpm's engine 6706 showed the following:

Indicated horsepower, 4,662
Drawbar horsepower, 4,034

As for efficiency this is how the M1A stacked up against the M1;

Class M1	Class M1A
40 rpm., 4.7 per cent	5.5 per cent
200 rpm., 6.1 per cent	7.0 per cent

Such low figures do not look good when the conventional steam locomotive is compared with contemporary locomotives, such as steam turbines and diesels. But years ago railroad management believed that the locomotive that could stand up to the sledge hammer work of everyday railroading and be shopped infrequently was a better investment than, say, a costly steam turbine locomotive with 18 per cent thermal efficiency which spent over 200 days a year in the shops—and how right they were.

Ten of the Baldwin engines were intended for passenger service, and were painted and equipped accordingly; five went to the Middle Division and five to the Panhandle Division, while the remainder were assigned to freight service.

Cylinders, 27″ × 30″	Boiler diameter, 84½″
Drivers, 72″	Weight, total engine, 390,000 lb.

(Collection of Frederick Westing)

THE WESTERN PACIFIC RAILROAD, whose main line extends from San Francisco, California, to Salt Lake City, Utah, handles a large tonnage of perishable freight which moves eastbound on fast schedules. The most difficult part of the run is the 117 miles from Oroville to Portola, in the Sierra Nevada Mountains of Calif. For a distance of over 100 miles in the Feather River Canyon there is a practically continuous ascending grade of one per cent. On this section of the line there are 33 tunnels and 385 compensated curves.

Six single-expansion articulated locomotives of the 2-8-8-2 type were built by Baldwin for service in the Feather River Canyon in 1931. They were designed to handle "fruit blocks" approximating 70 cars or 3300 tons each, from Oroville to Portola, at a running speed of 18 to 20 miles an hour. Previously the tonnage per train had been limited to 3100 tons, handled by one Mallet compound 2-6-6-2 type with a heavy Mikado (2-8-2) type as helper. The two locomotives consumed approximately 16.28 gallons of fuel oil per 1000 gross ton-miles.

The articulated locomotives handled their increased tonnage with a consumption of approximately 14.01 gallons per 1000 gross ton-miles, saving about 22 barrels of oil per trip; while the elimination of the helper saved an additional 700 gallons, burned when running light down the grade.

In view of the fine service rendered by the first group of articulated locomotives, four additional units, differing somewhat in details but of the same general dimensions, were built by Baldwin early in 1938. These ten large locomotives proved a notable success in this difficult service.

Cylinders, 26″ × 32″	Boiler diameter, 104″
Drivers, 63″	Weight, total engine, 663,100 lb.

(Collection of Frederick Westing)

box and steeple-cab design.

Meanwhile electrification between Wilmington, Delaware, and Washington, D.C., was completed in January 1935. Before establishing regular service a demonstration run was made on January 28, 1935, between Washington and Philadelphia and return. Locomotive No. 4800 headed the nine car train in both directions. Southbound, the GG-1 covered the 134 miles in 110 minutes at an average speed of 73 miles-per-hour. During this run a speed of 102 miles an hour was reached and easily held, though no effort was made at any time to push the locomotive to its limit.

Freight service between Washington and New York commenced in May 1935, and was built up as quickly as electric locomotives could be delivered. As the GG-1 locomotives came on the road the box-cab, and later the streamlined P5A's took over the operation of freight trains. Class L6 as previously referred to had proved unsuitable for the task. So the P5A passenger units had 70-mph. gears applied, thereby, replacing the original 90-mph. gears.

The freight line by-passed the Washington Union Station connecting with its electrified termination at Potomac Yards, in Virginia. By this time the entire electrification embraced some 1,405 miles of track with 364 route miles.

With the completion of the New York Washington electrification which by virtue of its traffic density had received prior consideration, attention was turned to the extension of electrified trackage, westward from Philadelphia, and also upon some incidental lines.

We have seen that the 1928 plans called for electrifying the road as far West as Atglen and Columbia, Pa. Subsequent plans, however, were made to carry electrification as far West as Harrisburg, Pa., and amplify these earlier ideas in general.

These newer plans included the Main Line, or Philadelphia Division, from Paoli to Harrisburg for passenger service to and from the West. The low grade freight line from Morrisville, Pa.; near Trenton, N.J., via Columbia to Enola Yard near Harrisburg, the freight line from Columbia, Pa., following the Susquehanna river to Perryville, Md., and the freight line from Monmouth Junction to South

Amboy, N.J., with connecting branches and yards.

A bond issue of $52,670,000 was authorized by the Company to finance the huge project, which added 315 miles of line (or route) and 773 miles of track to its electrified trackage. Despite the magnitude of the project, and it involved the placing of 11,000 wayside steel poles, set in concrete foundations; the stringing of more than 3,600 miles of heavy bronze and copper wire, and the building of 21 new electrical sub-stations, it was accomplished in less than a year's time. Work was begun early in 1937, and electrified passenger train operation went into effect on the Philadelphia Division on January 15, 1938.

The first train to operate under electric power between Philadelphia and Harrisburg was "The Metropolitan" train No. 25, from New York and Philadelphia for Harrisburg, Pittsburgh and the West.

Less than one month after the electrification of the Philadelphia Division the writer had the pleasure of riding the cab of a GG-1, between Philadelphia and Harrisburg when hauling train 25. At that time the schedule used with steam operation was effective, and the GG-1 duplicated it with ease. It was quite apparent from "head end" observation, that the locomotive had plenty of reserve power on hand for accelerating the schedule consistent with

safety and operating efficiency. Subsequently, this was done, not only on train No. 25, but others as well.

The first regularly scheduled Eastbound train to operate electrically out of Harrisburg, on January 15, was "The Pennsylvania Limited," train No. 2 from Chicago, St. Louis and Pittsburgh to the East. It was operated in two sections that day, and the first section left Harrisburg at 1:06 P.M.

With the completion of this electrified extension, the Pennsylvania had 2,677 miles of electrified track. This gave it the distinction of being the possessor of more tracks under catenary and trolley than any other railroad in the United States.

Electrification on the Pennsylvania has proved a success. This result on a railroad of such magnitude, and beset with many complex problems, is a striking indorsement of the value of straight electrification. It has produced a faster, better and more reliable service with fewer locomotive units and greater economy than is possible with steam or diesel operation.

Despite the diversion to electric locomotive construction on a mass production basis, Baldwin continued to build steam locomotives during this time. Many were of the 4-8-4 type which had proved its ability to handle heavy passenger and freight trains at speed. Single-expansion articulated locomotives

FOR THE HEAVIEST FREIGHT runs on the Lebanon Valley and East Penn Branches of the Reading Company, Baldwin built, in 1931, ten class K-1-S-B engines of the Santa Fe type. These locomotives had unusually large tenders supported on two six-wheel trucks. With a capacity of 19,000 gallons of water and 26 tons of coal, the trucks twelve wheels had to carry a weight of approximately 189 tons. This called for wheels that would render maximum service with longest life, and it is interesting to note that another Baldwin subsidiary, Standard Steel Works Company, of Burnham, Pennsylvania, supplied these wheels. One of the Reading Santa Fe type engines was equipped with the Caprotti valve gear. This gear was of Italian origin and was similar to that used on the Pennsylvania's K5 class Pacific. Basically it was of the poppet valve type.

Cylinders 30½" × 32"   Weight, total engine, 451,000 lb.
Drivers, 61½"   Tractive force, 92,570 lb.

(Collection of Frederick Westing)

were also prominent in the construction schedules.

Quite a few locomotives were shipped for export directly from Eddystone's "Wharf 251" which stretched out into the deep waters of the Delaware River. South American countries accounted for much of this business.

Streamlining of locomotives was quite the vogue in the 1930's and Baldwin made a contribution to this fancy in 1937 when it built ten streamlined Hudsons for the New Haven. In general the technical value of streamlining proved negligible and such locomotives were, in general shorn of their streamlined shrouding all over the world.

On April 25, 1935, Robert S. Binkerd, Vice President of Baldwin, gave a talk before the New York Railroad Club entitled "Muzzle Not The Ox That Treadeth Out The Corn." In this he made illustrated presentations to show how steam power was still most suitable for main line operation. Mr. Binkerd compared the operation of trains using interchangeable all-steel Pullman cars and passenger coaches of customary size and weight, with the sensationally publicized light-weight streamlined diesel-powered trains with rigidly limited seating capacity and non-interchangeable equipment. He pointed out that speedwise, steam powered trains in the "nineties" had surpassed some high-speed spots of the diesel streamliners and, that a locomotive hauled train could adjust itself more flexibly to variable load conditions than one dependent upon a small diesel power plant.

The diesel won the fight in the closing rounds of the battle, but Mr. Binkerd did put over one good point and, the diesel locomotive builders utilized it by using locomotive hauled trains to retain the advantage of using interchangeable equipment so that trains—especially those handling mail and express traffic—could be made up to suit conditions of service with conventional rolling stock.

During this time Baldwin produced an automatic oil-fired one-man operated steam 0-4-0 type saddle tank locomotive for switching service. Its fire was so regulated that when the safety valves were ready to "pop" the intensity of the fire was automatically reduced. Thus in this respect no steam or fuel was wasted. Low cost Bunker C oil was used at a rate of about four gallons per hour. Compared to the regular switching locomotive at the Works, only about 35 per cent of the B.T.U.'s were used in doing the same work as the coal-fired switcher.

The oil-fired automatic switcher was one of Mr. Binkerd's pet projects, and although he was a most persuasive salesman, in this field of slow speed switching and transfer work, the diesel was even then competitively impregnable.

By 1938 nearly 1,000 Baldwin disc driving wheel centers had been ordered since their introduction in 1936. Advantages were reduced weight and improved counterbalancing. A report issued by the Association of American Railroads in 1937, plainly stated that these two points had been fully realized adding that the Baldwin disc wheels yielded a marked reduction in dynamic augment, conducive to superior locomotive riding qualities.

Another Baldwin subsidiary, the Cramp brass and Iron Foundries Company, did a good business meanwhile in supplying some of the largest steamships with propellers. Among these was the S. S. America launched on August 31, 1939 at Newport News Shipbuilding and Dry Dock Company, Newport News, Virginia. The America was a twin screw ship of 34,000 shaft horsepower developed by two triple series of turbines driving the propellers through reduction gears. The propellers were of Parsons' manganese bronze and were chosen by the shipbuilders for use on the S. S. America.

An interesting fact in connection with and other propellers made by Cramp, is that they are produced by the Randupson Process of molding, which is the pouring of molten metal in cement bonded molds rather than in sand molds ordinarily employed by foundries. Cramp was the only foundry in the United States that fabricated propellers by this method.

During this period of lowered business activity Whitcomb gasoline and gasoline-electric locomotives were steadily put into service in increasing numbers. This was due to many railroads, particularly those of small size coming to a realization of

A GOOD EXAMPLE of the Santa Fe 2-10-2 type. Introduced on the Santa Fe in 1903 by Baldwin, this type achieved much popularity on many railroads. (Collection of Frederick Westing)

A STRING OF REEFERS follow a 2-10-2 Santa Fe type engine on the railroad of the same name. Train was running through Cajon Pass, and the double sandboxes and number indicator behind the stack are all in the best tradition of Santa Fe steam power. (Collection of Frederick Westing)

the need for a readjustment of motive power and attendant facilities. Railroad executives were vitally cost conscious at this time and Whitcomb mechanical drive locomotives from 3 to 30 ton sizes showed savings over steam operation hitherto considered impossible. In the larger fields of heavy switching and interurban operation, Whitcomb again proved its point of low-priced efficient service unattainable with steam in these power ranges.

In the construction of the San Francisco-Oakland bridge, where the most effective equipment was essential, Whitcomb locomotives were chosen. Here many feet above the waters of San Francisco Bay, Whitcomb gasoline-mechanical drive locomotives hauled concrete from the loading hopper to the paving operations on the bridge. Also built by Whitcomb were seven box-cab diesel-electric road locomotives for the Texas-Mexican Railway. These were of the 0-8-0 type arranged for double-end

operation, and rated 660 horsepower. In that part of the country sand is a problem, therefore, all air entering the engine compartment was filtered to keep out sand.

By 1940, Baldwin was deeply engrossed in building diesel-electric switchers (normally aspirated) in both 660 and 1,000 horsepower ranges on a production line basis. Many of the country's most prominent class 1 railroads were among the purchasers. Numerous repeat orders gave striking evidence of satisfactory performance. In this area of railroad operation Baldwin switchers were second to none. To this day one can see (now supercharged) Baldwin switchers working on railroads throughout the United States.

Apart from propellers, Baldwin was also represented in the marine field with Baldwin-De La Vergne diesel engines which powered ships. These engines were known for ruggedness and reliability

154

and were the prime movers on Baldwin switchers.

On February 4, 1940, Samuel M. Vauclain, Chairman of the Board, died. The following fine tribute to a great leader of American industry was written by Malcolm K. Wright, Advertising Manager of Baldwin.

Around this time it was found that the big 4-6-4 and 4-8-4 type locomotives which were built for high sustained speeds coupled with great hauling capacity created problems in driving wheel counterbalancing. Damaged or kinked rails resulted in some instances. Wheel slipping tests made by some railroads showed that under certain conditions driving wheels would oscillate and lift from the rails. This action caused the kinks, and removal of certain quantities of the overbalance corrected this effect as proved in later wheel slip tests.

Prominent in investigating this question was Charles D. Damsky, of the Engineering Department. From his studies Baldwin formulated counterbalance rules to meet modern high speed steam locomotive operation.

A great loss was suffered by Baldwin with the death of William Holland Winterrowd, Vice President in Charge of Operations, on December 7, 1941.

THIS LITTLE Baldwin-Westinghouse locomotive is blocked for shipment on a New Haven 34 ft. flat car with Fox trucks typical of the early 1900's, for the 3 ft. gauge Whitehall Railway. It weighed 20,000 lbs., had a top speed of 6 MPH when fully loaded. (Collection of C. A. Brown)

Mr. Winterrowd was a world renowned authority on locomotives which coupled with his exceptional gift for obtaining harmonious relations among the workers at Baldwin made his loss irreparable. His unique talents were never replaced, and the opinion of many was, that if Mr. Winterrowd had lived Baldwin would still be successfully and profitably building locomotives in which they could have taken pride.

THE PITTSBURGH & WEST VIRGINIA RAILWAY COMPANY operated 132 miles of road that made connection with the Western Maryland, New York Central, Pennsylvania and Baltimore & Ohio. Their main field of activity was the great iron and steel area in the Pittsburgh district, and in this connection they carried all sorts of freight in considerable volume. Baldwin Mikados had handled this traffic for years, but in 1934 they purchased three 2-6-6-4 type, single-expansion articulated locomotives for heavy freight hauling. When completed these engines traveled from Eddystone to Pittsburgh under their own steam instead of the usual procedure of being shipped "dead on own wheels" accompanied by a messenger.

Railroaders usually called these engines "Malley's" though strictly speaking Anatole Mallet's patent specified the compound system of steam distribution. Nevertheless, the articulated running gear, or chassis were alike, so the name does not appear to be a misnomer regardless of the arrangement in using the steam in the cylinders.

There was a Pennsy look about these engines due to the huge Belpaire firebox boiler, and more than a hint of that road's class M-1's with its long 74" combustion chamber that extended into the boiler barrel. This boiler was known as the straight-top, wagon bottom type, which indicated that the top was straight, but the bottom tapered in width as it approached the firebox—just the opposite of the wagon-top, or conical connection boiler where the reverse occurred.

An interesting feature on these locomotives was the use of a Bethlehem auxiliary locomotive unit applied to the rear tender truck which added 16,000 pounds of starting tractive force. This was basically a locomotive booster such as were used on the trailing trucks of numerous locomotives. Four duplicate engines were ordered in 1936, but omitted the auxiliary locomotive booster on the tender truck.

Cylinders (4), 23" × 32"   Boiler diameter, 94"
Drivers, 63"   Weight, total engine, 528,040 lb.

(Collection of Frederick Westing)

THE YEAR 1932 saw the construction of ten 4-8-4 type locomotives, Nos. 5101 to 5110 for the Lehigh Valley Railroad. These were the road's T-1 class, first introduced in March 1931 with Baldwin engine 5100.

These engines known on the "Valley" as "Wyomings", were designed to operate 3,000 ton trains on a fast freight schedule over the entire main line from Buffalo and Suspension Bridge to Jersey City. This run covered about 450 miles, with helper service on Wilkesbarre Mountain where there is a 21 mile climb with a maximum grade of 68.5 feet per mile. Eastbound on this run, there is a 42 mile hill with a maximum grade of 21.12 feet per mile, affording an excellent opportunity to work the locomotive at full capacity for a considerable distance. On these heavy grades west of Easton, Pennsylvania, the T-1's proved outstandingly suitable.

Class T-1 fully met and exceeded expectations in speed and tonnage. Compared with Mikados on the Seneca Division in the same service, they hauled 500 tons more per train with a 20 minute reduction in running time. A decided decrease in operating costs resulted, and this can be better appreciated when it is understood that the ten T-1's replaced twenty old locomotives.

The Lehigh Valley Railroad operated through a region of rare scenic beauty, and in 1932 in order to stimulate business during this time of lessened passenger traffic, the road operated special excursion trains to give residents of the communities it served a chance to view points of interest on the line. One of the Baldwin engines handled a 30 car train.

Cylinders, 27″ × 30″   Boiler diameter, 86″
Drivers, 70″   Weight, total engine, 413,170 lb.

(Collection of Frederick Westing)

SUCCESS of the T-1 class engines of the 4-8-4 type prompted the Lehigh Valley to order five more which were built in 1934. These locomotives carried road numbers 5125 to 5129. Changes involved increasing the drivers from 70 to 77 inches, and elimination of boosters. Fine work was done by these engines in passenger and fast freight service up to the time of the engulfing diesel tide.

Cylinders, 27″ × 30″   Boiler diameter, 86³⁄₁₆″
Drivers, 77″   Weight, total engine, 435,000 lb.

(Collection of Frederick Westing)

WHILE THE 0-1 CLASS ELECTRIC LOCOMOTIVES (none were built by Baldwin) were first on the road, the real big electric road service locomotives in main line service were the box-cab P5A class units of the 4-6-4 type. These locomotives operated on 11,000 volts single-phase current at 25 cycles. This potential in the trolley had been settled upon as early as 1915 when the Philadelphia-Paoli line was electrified at that time. It is the road's standard to this day.

Electrical equipment design was fully coordinated between Westinghouse and General Electric, thereby, permitting speedy replacement of parts on the locomotive and in the stocked inventory as two concerns could simultaneously supply identical equipment. Thirty-seven of the box-cab locomotives were of Baldwin-Westinghouse manufacture. Each driving axle was driven by two 625 horsepower motors embodied in one external frame by a gear and quill drive. The twin-motor combination thus rated 1,250 horsepower, or 3,750 continuous horsepower for the locomotive up to 90 miles per hour at the driver rim. Class P5A—in common with all electric locomotives—could, and did, develop peak ratings of 6,500 horsepower for short periods of time. This ability to momentarily surpass itself is unique with the straight-electric locomotive. No self-contained locomotive of any form can duplicate this action; only the use of additional units can enable such locomotives to obtain more power.

The picture shows locomotive No. 4739 in 1933 at Eddystone almost ready to be coupled onto the Broadway. Take note of those stainless steel handrails.

Horsepower, continuous, 3,750	Motors (6), 625 hp. each
Drivers, 72″	Weight, total engine, 392,000 lb.

(Collection of Frederick Westing)

PENNSYLVANIA RAILROAD'S original GG-1 was built by Baldwin in 1934 at the Eddystone tender shop. Charlie Siegal, tender shop foreman at the time, likes to recall the exasperating comment of Mr. Loewy as the locomotive was first put on public display: "What are all those buttons?" All later GG-1's were welded, and 4800 has the distinction of being the only one of the class "buttoned" together with rivets. This is the renumbered GG-1. (Photo by C. A. Brown)

THIS IS HOW the GG-1's looked after Raymond Loewy restyled them. The "cats whiskers" striping was long a prominent part of their appearance. Now a single wide band chrome-yellow stripe in place of the costlier genuine gold leaf striping is used. Driving axles are powered by geared twin motors through double-end quill drive. Of the first grouped order of 57, Westinghouse received an order for 34 units. All told a total of 139 GG-1's were built through the years. In passenger service these locomotives can momentarily attain 9,000 horsepower for a short time. All locomotives of classes P5A, R-1 and GG-1, operated on a line voltage 11,000 and a frequency of 25 cycles single-phase current. (Collection of Frederick Westing)

IN 1934 studies were made of larger size motive power units than the P5A in anticipation of heavier trains to come with a consequent need for more power. In order to obtain greater power and lighter axle loadings than with the P5A, class R-1 was designed and built in 1934 with a 4-8-4 type wheel arrangement. It was really a beefed-up P5A, for each driving axle developed 1,250 horsepower at 100 mph. Baldwin mechanical and Westinghouse electrical equipment was used on the R-1. Some engineers of Baldwin, Pennsy and Westinghouse were so favorably inclined toward this locomotive, that it received road number 4800, as it was thought it would be the first of a fleet of such locomotives and was numbered accordingly.

On the test track at Claymont, Delaware, the R-1 proved to be the closest competitor of the GG-1, reaching a speed of 120-mph. thus topping the GG-1's, 115 mph. But at higher speeds it couldn't quite match the tracking flexibility of the GG-1. Unquestionably the GG-1 was safer at high speed and smoother riding than anything on rails. The R-1 had the distinction of being the first and only 4-8-4 type ever owned by the Pennsy, and in its time carried three road numbers, 4800, 4899, and 4999. For several years it was regularly assigned to the Broadway Limited. The picture shows the R-1 ready to go out onto the Pennsy main line at Eddystone. Building in the background is part of the Baldwin office headquarters.

Horsepower, continuous, 5,000   Motors (8), 625 horsepower
Drivers, 62″   Weight, total engine, 406,900 lb.

(Collection of Frederick Westing)

THIS WAS IT, the locomotive that won the day on the Claymont test track. Also built in 1934, the 4899 as she was first numbered represented the first of the famous fleet of class GG-1. Its ability to run at high speed with the least damage to the track won the day. George Gibbs Consulting Engineer of Gibbs and Hill, which organization electrified the Pennsy had long held the view that lighter axle loads were one of the advantages of the electric locomotive, and that it should not exceed 50,000 lb. per axle. This load the P5A's had greatly exceeded. Mr. Norman Litchfield, G&H Vice President, suggested to Mr. Gibbs that the New Haven had an electric locomotive with an axle load that just about met this figure, and pointed out that it might be a good idea to borrow one of these locomotives and try it out on the test track. The New Haven locomotive besides having the lighter axle loading was articulated which gave superior flexibility in tracking. Mr. Gibbs suggested this to the Pennsylvania where it was accepted. Tests showed its superiority over all the rigid wheelbase locomotives, and class GG-1 was built with a wheel arrangement duplicating that of the New Haven locomotive. The first locomotive was built and numbered 4899 since No. 4800 had already been taken by the R-1. At the tests conclusion fifty-seven additional GG-1's were ordered and the R-1 and GG-1 swapped numbers. Raymond Loewy, industrial consultant was then called in, and a welded cab with more rounded contours replaced the riveted cab of No. 4800. Through the years additional GG-1's were built and their splendid operating performances have obtained world-wide acclaim. No. 4800, was the first one to be permanently re-geared for freight service, and others have followed. In this work they match their ability against the much newer E-44's and appear to do just as good a job.

Horsepower, continuous, 4,620	Motors 12- 385 horsepower
Drivers, 57″	Weight, total locomotive
	460,000 lb.* and 477,000 lb.**

*Geared for 90-mph. when first built.   **Geared for 100-mph as was No. 4800.

(Collection of Frederick Westing)

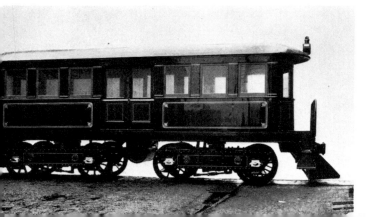

THIS ELECTRIC LOCOMOTIVE was built in 1895 for exhibition and later sold to the Lackawanna & Wyoming Valley (Laurel Line). First Baldwin-Westinghouse electric locomotive. (Collection of C. A. Brown)

IN THE EXPERIMENTS conducted by the PRR to develop a standard Electric locomotive, Baldwin built the only 4-8-4 on the PRR: Class R1, No. 4999. (C. A. Brown photo)

AFTER A DISASTROUS crossing collision with a truck at Deans, New Jersey on January 3, 1934, construction of the box-cab P5A's was discontinued. A revised, or "modified" design was prepared which put the cab in the center of the locomotive. A total of twenty-eight of these steeple-cab locomotives was built completing the original order for ninety of this class. Baldwin-Westinghouse furnished locomotives 4743 to 4754. These were known as electric locomotives of the Modified P5A class. Improvements were made in their spring equalization system and somehow from my own experience with them they apeared exceptionally speedy in accelerating a heavy train. The scene shows a Modified P5A at the head end of a heavy New York bound train from Washington taken in January 1935. Smoke is from train heating boiler in No. 1 end which was trailing.

Horsepower, continuous, 3,750
Drivers, 72"
Motors, 6, 625 horsepower
Weight, total engine, 394,300 lb.

(Collection of Frederick Westing)

A BOX CAB P5A at speed on the Maryland Division heading a heavy Washington-New York train. (Collection of Frederick Westing)

EARLY IN 1935 the Seaboard placed in service five single-expansion articulated locomotives of the 2-6-6-4 type (Class R-1) which were built by the Baldwin Locomotive Works. The locomotives were specially intended for fast freight service between Richmond, Virginia, and Hamlet, North Carolina, a run of 252 miles. The country was hilly and the line had an undulating profile with frequent curves. Northbound, the tonnage consisted largely of fresh fruits and vegetables, and the running time for the 252 miles was 10 hours and 20 minutes. South of Hamlet, conditions were less severe, and a Mikado (2-8-2) type locomotive, handled, Northbound, 2700 tons. A Class R-1 locomotive took this same tonnage through to Richmond, and could in fact handle 3500 tons as far as Raleigh, 96.6 miles from Hamlet with a helper over Southern Pines Hill, where the grade was 1.1 per cent.

On the Hamlet-Richmond run, two locomotives of Class R-1 replaced three of Class Q-3, each of the new engines handled about 50 per cent more tonnage per train than one Mikado. Due to the success of Class R-1, five additional locomotives of the same general design were built in 1937. To better fit them for the requirements of the service, certain changes in details were made; and the new group was designated Class-R-2.

These articulated locomotives carried an average load of 55,000 lbs. on each pair of drivers; and could maintain a speed as fast as 60 miles an hour under favorable conditions. This was a notable case in which a specific design of locomotive successfully met difficult requirements.

Cylinders (4), 22″ × 30″   Boiler, diameter, 84″
Drivers, 69″   Weight, total engine, 480,000 lb.

(Collection of Frederick Westing)

WHEN THE BOSTON & MAINE RAILROAD purchased five Mountain type locomotives from Baldwin in 1935, it represented an innovation on their road. So satisfied were they with their operation that by 1941 when five more such units were supplied by Baldwin, they brought the total up to eighteen 4-8-2's in service on the road.

The last five engines, class R-1-D, were equipped with roller bearings throughout and featured a fourteen wheel "centipede" tender with a water capacity of 23,000 gallons—3,000 gallons in excess of former B&M Mountain type tenders—and 21 tons of coal. Advantages of this style tender were greater capacity for a fixed wheel-base, combined with lower tender weight and better distribution of this weight. Wheels 42-inches in diameter showed increased mileage per wheel turning. Plainly (and similar results were obtained on other roads) centipede tenders were easier on operating and maintenance costs.

But the B&M went diesel and in 1947 Baltimore & Ohio took thirteen of these engines into their fold. On the B&O the Mountains were put into two groups, class T-4, Nos. 5650 to 5662, and class T-4-A, Nos. 5660 to 5662. Only slight differences in the firebox area made the distinction between them. In fast freight service on the Chicago and Akron Divisions, they supplemented the B&O's class T-3 engines in that territory.

Cylinders, 28″ × 31″   Boiler, diameter, 84″
Drivers, 73″   Weight, total engine, 415,200 lb.

(Collection of Frederick Westing)

IN AN EFFORT at cost reduction to make the diesel locomotive more competitive with steam locomotive manufacturing costs, the conventional straight electric locomotive box cab double end design was dropped in favor of a single end cab design with automotive type engine and radiator compartment hoods and mounted on conventional swivel trucks.

Baldwin's first locomotive manufactured to these designs was construction No. 62,000, completed on April 23, 1937. This unit was sold to the Santa Fe and was assigned their Road No. 2200. For many years this locomotive performed switching service in downtown Chicago.

During World War II this 600 H.P. locomotive was traded back to Baldwin in exchange for a new locomotive of what had by then become a standard design 1000 H.P., 120 ton type of switching locomotive on the Santa Fe. Road No. 1 was assigned by B.L.W. to this pioneer locomotive in recognition of its being the first of all the long line of Baldwin standard designs of switching locomotives that were to be subsequently manufactured. Locomotive No. 1 served out its life in service at Eddystone as a plant switcher for many years that followed through World War II and the Korean War effort.

The unique feature embodied in the design of this locomotive was its carry over from steam locomotive practice of using a single unit cast steel underframe which housed the batteries for engine cranking, provided space for fuel storage, and also served as the bed and crankcase for the diesel engine to which the engine's "A" frame or engine block was attached. The unit weighed 100 tons.

This locomotive was powered with a DeLaVergne 600 H.P., 6 cylinder in line 12½" × 15½", 600 RPM solid injection engine. Motors, generator and control equipment was of Allis-Chalmers Manufacturing Co. design. (Collection of John F. Kirkland)

WITH THE OPENING of the Huey P. Long Memorial Bridge at New Orleans, the New Orleans Public Belt Railroad was called upon to perform heavy transfer service between railroads located on the east and west banks of the Mississippi River. The adverse grade on the bridge required locomotives with greater weight on drivers and greater continuous tractive effort capability than possessed by existing steam locomotives owned by N.O.B.P., and, accordingly, three 900 H.P., 120 ton diesel electric locomotives with multiple unit controls were purchased from Baldwin.

The design of these units generally followed Construction No. 62,000, only with greater weight and horsepower. The unit cast steel underframe features were retained.

A DeLaVergne 900 H.P., 8 cylinder in line 28½" × 15½", 600 RPM solid injection engine was used. The first of these three units was completed at Eddystone December 15, 1937. (Collection of John F. Kirkland)

INTRODUCED ON THE SANTA FE by Baldwin in 1927, the 4-8-4 type showed marked superiority over the 4-8-2 Mountain type in capacity and efficiency. Main drivers were cross-balanced with a resultant decrease in track stresses for locomotives of their weight and capacity. In 1938 eleven 4-8-4's, road numbers, 3765 to 3775, were delivered to the Santa Fe for heavy high-speed passenger service. These locomotives were operated in the mountainous area encountered between La Junta, Colorado, and Los Angeles, California, a run of 1,235 miles, on which grades as steep as 3½ per cent are met with. With their large 80-inch driving wheels, they successfully met the faster schedules that were adopted at the time of their construction.

Cylinders, 28" × 32"   Boiler diameter, 90"
Drivers, 80"   Weight, total engine, 499,600 lb.

(Collection of Frederick Westing)

SINCE 1927 THE SANTA FE used Baldwin-built Hudsons, but in 1937 they received six Baldwin Hudsons numbered 3460 to 3465, that differed so much in proportions that they could hardly be considered direct developments of the earlier engines of this 4-6-4 type.

Here we have an illustration of one of these Santa Fe Hudsons, No. 3462 on the Baldwin test track at Eddystone, taken during its "break-in" runs. One of the engines No. 3460, was streamlined and known as "Mae West." Later, however, the streamlining was removed. Boilers were of nickel steel with safety valves set to lift at 300 pounds pressure, but the design permitted a 310 pound pressure to be safely used. They were tested with steam at 330 pounds and with hot water (hydrostatic test) at 414 pounds.

To permit turning the locomotives on a 90-foot turntable, the tenders were of rather high rectangular shape in order to contain the 20,000 gallons of water and 7,000 gallons of oil. The Hudsons were intended primarily for service on the Eastern Lines, between Chicago and La Junta, Colorado, where the grades are moderate.

But, nevertheless, in an effort to demonstrate the high availability of the Hudson type steam locomotives, No. 3461 of this group on December 12, 1937 completed what was believed to be the longest continuous run ever made by a steam locomotive in regular scheduled passenger train service, when it pulled into Dearborn Street Station, Chicago, with express and mail train No. 8, after a run of 2,227.3 miles from Los Angeles, Calif. The train was made up of a dynamometer car, and 10 to 12 conventional steel cars, comprising a total trailing load of 757 to 939 tons. The run with this train normally required four locomotives plus helpers.

No attempt was made at a speed record, the elapsed time was 53 hours, 40 minutes of which about 4 hours, 35 minutes were spent at stations en route. This time was consumed in loading and unloading mail and express, cutting cars in and out of the train, etc. This left a running time of 49 hours, 5 minutes, giving an average speed of about 45.4 mph. for the entire run. The maximum speed was 90 miles per hour.

Helper service was provided on four severe grades. Force feed lubrication supplied by a four-feed mechanical lubricator played a big part in the success of this achievement by providing adequate lubrication. The combination of seven-foot diameter drivers with a tractive force of 49,300 pounds enabled these locomotives to combine speed and hauling capacity to a degree unusual in a six-coupled engine.

Cylinders, 23½" × 29½"   Boiler, diameter, 88"
Drivers, 84"   Weight, total engine, 412, 380 lb.

(Collection of Frederick Westing)

SANTA FE'S ONLY streamlined steam power was Baldwin-built #3460, later dubbed "Mae West" because of her curves. Built in 1937, No. 3460 became the stand-in for the early diesels on the extra fare "Super Chief." She was cut up in 1955. (Collection of C. A. Brown)

SIX ADDITIONAL 4-8-4 type locomotives were built for the Richmond, Fredericksburg & Potomac Railroad—or "Capital Cities Route"—in 1938. These followed the "Generals" and were named after former Governors of the State of Virginia. The locomotive illustrated, No. 602, was named Governor Thomas Jefferson. The Governors were somewhat lighter than the Generals, and were assigned to passenger service. Six more Governors were added to the roster in 1942.

Cylinders, 27" × 30"   Boiler diameter, 84"
Drivers, 77"   Weight, total engine, 406,810 lb.

(Collection of Frederick Westing)

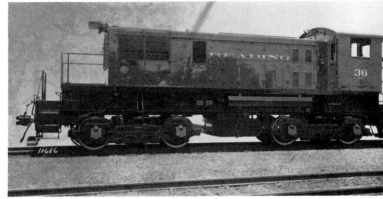

THIS RAILROAD appropriately known as the "Capital Cities Route" formed the connecting link between the Pennsylvania and the Baltimore & Ohio, terminating at Washington, D.C., and the Atlantic Coast Line and the Seaboard Air Line, which terminated at Richmond, Virginia. Southern fruits and vegetables constituted a large proportion of the freight tonnage and most of the road engines were suitable for use in either fast freight or passenger service.

Early in 1937 the Richmond, Fredericksburg & Potomac received five locomotives of the 4-8-4 type from the Baldwin Locomotive Works. These engines, named after noted Generals, were placed in freight service between Richmond and Potomac Yard near Washington. An idea of the savings that they had effected may be obtained from the fact that during the months of February to May 1936, inclusive, 657 double-header freight trains were operated; while during the same months of 1938, with the new locomotives in service, only 199 double-headers were run in spite of the fact that the freight car miles increased from 11,615,924 during the 1936 period, to 14,729,910 in 1938. On the basis of eliminating 600 double-headers a year, the direct saving from this source alone amounted to more than $55,000 per annum.

During the period of peak traffic the "Generals" averaged 52 oneway trips a month; the monthly mileage in freight service often exceeded 5600.

Following are the road numbers and names of these locomotives:

No. 551—General Robert E. Lee
No. 552—General T. J. Jackson
No. 553—General J. E. B. Stuart
No. 554—General A. P. Hill
No. 555—General J. E. Johnston

Cylinders, 27″ × 30″ Boiler, diameter, 86″
Drivers, 77″ Weight, total engine, 466,040 lb.

(Collection of Frederick Westing)

A FURTHER EFFORT at cost reduction resulted in construction of a fabricated steel underframe locomotive for the Reading Railroad bearing Road No. 36, which was completed and delivered June 22, 1939. This unit carried Baldwin Construction No. 62,300. It was equipped with a 600 H.P. DeLaVergne 6 cylinder in line 12½″ × 15½″ 600 RPM solid injection engine. The anticipated economies from the fabricated underframe design failed to materialize, and as a result the integral cast steel underframes were continued as standard until approximately 1950, at which time increases in casting costs made it desirable to adopt the fabricated design of underframe as standard. Beginning with this locomotive the diesel engine was equipped with a conventional crankcase independent of the underframe. Separate fabricated fuel tanks and battery boxes were used, these items being eliminated from the cast steel underframes that followed this locomotive. With this unit, Westinghouse electric equipment was standard and remained so at Baldwin until 1954 when Westinghouse made the decision to withdraw from the future manufacture of heavy traction electric equipment. (Collection of John F. Kirkland)

IN 1938 five 4-8-4 type locomotives were built for the Denver & Rio Grande Western. They were designed to develop maximum capacity with an axle load of 70,000 pounds. Up to July, 1939 the average mileage for each engine of the 4-8-4 type was 113,896. The maintenance cost per mile was 3.42 cents for classified and 11.62 cents for running repairs, or a total of 15.04 cents. Comparing 1938 with 1937 there was a decrease in the cost of fuel per train mile of 8.33 per cent, and in helper and light locomotive mileage of 29.90 per cent, due to the use of the new power. The Denver & Rio Grande Western affords an excellent illustration of the economies that were effected by using modern power specially designed for the work to be done.

Cylinders, 26″ × 30″ Boiler diameter, 92″
Drivers, 73″ Weight, total engine, 479,360 lb.

(Collection of Frederick Westing)

TEN STREAMLINED LOCOMOTIVES of the 4-6-4, or Hudson type, were built by Baldwin in 1937 for the New Haven and designated as class I-5. They handled the road's fast trains between New Haven and Boston, a run of 156.8 miles over the Shore Line. Grades were comparatively light but curves abounded in profusion. For 20 years prior to their construction, the heaviest and fastest trains were handled by Pacific (4-6-2) type locomotives of Class I-4, which were rapidly becoming out-classed because of heavier train loads and increased speeds. A locomotive was desired which could maintain a speed of at least 60 miles per hour on an ascending grade of from 0.6 to 0.7 per cent, with 12 cars aggregating 830 tons behind the tender. To determine the amount of power necessary to accomplish this, tests were made with a 12-car train and dynamometer car, using two Class I-4 locomotives to maintain the desired speed up the grade. Based on the results of these tests, a 4-6-4 type locomotive of the necessary capacity was designed. The conditions to be met were especially difficult because of the many curves and consequent speed restrictions on the line, and to make fast schedules, a locomotive capable of rapid acceleration was necessary. The new locomotives proved particularly satisfactory in this respect and materially exceeded the calculated acceleration rate.

Cylinders, 22″ × 30″   Boiler diameter, 82⁷⁄₁₆″
Drivers, 80″   Weight, total engine, 365,300 lb.

(Collection of Frederick Westing)

166

FOLLOWING CANADIAN practice the Government owned Alaska Railroad, provided the engine crew with a cab suitable for defying arctic blasts of wind and snow met with in that country. The 8½" cross-compound air pump was encased and located on the pilot beam extension platform. This Pacific was built in December 1940. During the war years additional units were built and served our Government well.

Cylinders, 22" × 28"   Boiler diameter, 72"
Drivers, 63"   Weight, total engine, 248,980 lb.

(Collection of Frederick Westing)

LATTER DAY Baldwin Mallet on the Western Maryland, No. 1207, represents a class of fine 4-6-6-4 simple Mallet engines, delivered just before W.W. II for high speed freight service. (C. A. Brown photo)

TEN ARTICULATED LOCOMOTIVES of the 4-6-6-4 type, with single-expansion cylinders, were built by Baldwin for the Denver & Rio Grande Western and placed in service early in 1938. They were used in both fast freight and heavy passenger service over mountain grades in Utah and Western Colorado. Between Salt Lake City, Utah, and Grand Junction, Colorado, a distance of 295 miles, the rating for one locomotive was 2,750 adjusted tons, with a pusher over the 30 miles of two per cent grade between Thistle and Soldier Summit. Between Helper, Utah, and Grand Junction, a distance of 177 miles over an undulating profile, the schedule allowed 5 hours 40 minutes with one stop for coal and two stops for water. This run has actually been made in 4 hours 50 minutes with 2870 tons, representing an increase in ton-miles per hour of 22 per cent as compared with the scheduled performance.

During the month of October, 1938, a period of peak traffic, nine of the new locomotives, in service as outlined above, averaged 7397 miles per locomotive. As compared with the 4-8-2 and 2-10-2 type locomotives formerly used in this service, there was an increase in gross ton-miles per train-hour of 18.4 per cent and a decrease in helper and light locomotive miles per thousand gross ton-miles of 15.6 per cent.

One locomotive of the 4-6-6-4 type has been used in heavy passenger service between Salt Lake City and Helper, over the Wasatch range of mountains. Fifteen cars were handled westbound over a ruling grade of 2.4 per cent, while eastbound 16 cars were handled over a grade of 2.0 per cent. Up to July 1939 the locomotive had made 76,089 miles in this service, the cost for classified repairs was 5.62 cents a mile and running repairs 19.38 cents, or a total cost of 25 cents.

These 4-6-6-4 type locomotives could be operated at speeds up to 70 miles an hour. Dynamometer tests have shown a tractive force of approximately 60,000 pounds at a speed of 50 miles an hour.

Five more Baldwin built engines of this type, class L-105 were built in 1941 for this railroad. They carried road numbers 3710 to 3714. On the tender tank they carried the road's new title designation and style of lettering.

Cylinders (4), 23" × 32"   Boiler diameter, 94½"
Drivers, 70"   Weight, total engine, 641,700 lb.

(Collection of Frederick Westing)

EARLY IN 1938 Baldwin delivered to the Atlantic Coast Line twelve locomotives of the 4-8-4 type, designated by the Railroad Company as Class R-1. They were used in through passenger service between Richmond, Virginia, and Jacksonville, Florida, a run of 650 miles, replacing Class-P-5-B locomotives of the Pacific (4-6-2) type formerly used. Double heading was frequently necessary with the latter locomotives.

The Class R-1 locomotives with driving wheels 80 inches in diameter and a steam pressure of 275 pounds were notable examples of modern power. To minimize the time lost in making fuel and water stops they had large capacity tenders carrying 24,000 gallons of water and 27 tons of coal. These were the first tenders built with eight-wheeled trucks.

After the locomotives had been thoroughly broken in, a test run was made with Engine No. 1800, hauling train No. 76, the Havana Special, from Jacksonville to Richmond. The train was composed of 20 cars, weighing 1500 tons. Deducting time consumed in stops, average speed was 53.8 miles an hour. Particular attention was paid to the rate of acceleration—an item of importance on a fast run involving intermediate stops. Here the locomotive exceeded expectations, reaching a speed of 70 miles an hour in 11½ minutes while covering 11 miles. The water evaporated per pound of coal varied between 7.50 and 7.69 pounds on different sections of the run. The speed capacity with such a heavy train is indicated by the fact that north of McIntosh, Georgia, an average of 73.6 miles an hour was maintained for 13 miles; while near Benson, North Carolina, the average was 84 miles an hour for 5 miles. In passenger service these locomotives have made as high as 18,000 miles per month.

Class R-1 locomotives were also used by the Coast Line to haul perishable freight which must be moved at high speeds.

Cylinders, 27″ × 30″   Boiler diameter, 86³⁄₁₆″
Drivers, 80″   Weight, total engine, 460,270 lb.

(Collection of Frederick Westing)

READY TO LEAVE Jacksonville, Florida, the Atlantic Coast Line's Havana Special is headed by a new 4-8-4 type, class R-1, No. 1804 at the head end. With trains such as this speeds of 80-mph. were reached on certain parts of the run. (Collection of Frederick Westing)

IN 1941 BALDWIN DELIVERED twelve 4-6-6-4 type single-expansion articulated locomotives, Road Nos. 1201 to 1212, to the Western Maryland Railway. These engines were put to work on the Hagerstown-Connellsville run where they replaced the older 2-10-0 Decapods.

Grades on this run were severe and at one section for 23 miles there is a 1.75 per cent grade. With the Decapods this 171.4 miles run was made in two separate runs which terminated at Cumberland Md., 91.4 miles east of Connellsville, and 80 miles west of Hagerstown.

The big articulateds singly ran right through between Hagerstown and Connellsville, hauling heavy freight trains at speeds up to 50 miles per hour.

One of the new locomotives, number 1208, on its first run in through service, handled 155 loaded coal cars—total tonnage 11,738—between Cumberland and Hagerstown. This is said to have been the greatest tonnage ever handled out of Cumberland in a single train. On their initial runs, locomotive 1205 hauled 11,208 tons while locomotive 1201 was assigned to a train of 10,550 tons.

All of the locomotives were delivered from Eddystone to Hagerstown under their own steam and went into active service without delay. Thorough inspection of the locomotives, after their initial runs with tonnage trains, showed them to be in excellent condition.

Cylinders (4), 22″ × 32″   Boiler, diameter, 98½″
Drivers, 69″   Weight, total engine, 601,000 lb.

(Collection of Frederick Westing)

A WESTERN MARYLAND 4-6-6-4 hauls a heavy load of coal through the Maryland countryside.
(Collection of Frederick Westing)

W. M. 1208 tackles the grade near Frostburg, Md., with 100 empty coal cars in the summer of 1947.
(Collection of C. A. Brown)

VIEW OF THE SCALE HOUSE at Eddystone. On a scale 100 feet long, and 27½ feet wide, with a capacity for weighing anything up to 900,000 pounds, it was able to accommodate the largest locomotives with size and weight to spare. (Collection of Frederick Westing)

A BIG A-4 CLASS ENGINE built in October 1941 for the Northern Pacific Railway Company, enters the scale house ready to "tip the beam." The individual scales alongside the locomotive were·used to give the weight on each wheel. Weighing a steam locomotive was quite a secretive affair. Only the regular staff connected with the scale house and specifically authorized observers were permitted inside during the "weighing-in" ceremonies. Like many ladies the steam locomotive appeared sensitive about its weight being publicly known—probably another reason why we referred to it as "she!"

This "cloak and dagger" routine was necessitated by the fact that railroads paid their engine crews according to engine weight, besides mileage and time. For example, on the Pennsylvania Railroad an engineer and fireman received more for operating a K4, than an E6 or K2, when hauling a passenger train. Railroad management was, therefore, averse to publicity regarding engine weight. Publicized weight given by Baldwin was based on an engine in working order which left some lee**way** as to what that might constitute on certain roads; for instance, some based that on one or two gauges of water in the boiler and other roads might figure otherwise. By Baldwin standards the tender weight was figured at two-thirds full. (Collection of Frederick Westing)

CLOSE-UP of how they got the exact weight bearing on a driving wheel with the movable scales. Bubble levels and special adjusters aided in this work of precision. (Collection of Frederick Westing)

IN 1941, the Bessemer & Lake Erie Railroad obtained five 2-10-4 type locomotives of unusual capacity. These were known as class H-1-E. Since 1929, Baldwin's 2-10-4's had moved exceedingly heavy tonnage trains of iron ore between Lake Erie ports and the Pittsburgh area.

Steam being the life blood of a locomotive, the Bessemer engines had boilers of great steam producing capacity, being able to evaporate 84,300 pounds of water per hour. With a steam pressure of 250 pounds per square inch, and 250 degrees of superheat, the potential boiler horsepower was about 4,690.

These Texas type engines had boilers of the straight-top, wagon bottom design, with a 49½" combustion chamber extending into the boiler. Three thermic syphons were used, two in the firebox, and one in the combustion chamber. They were also equipped with "E" type superheaters, exhaust steam injectors, power reverse, limited cut-off, Baldwin disc main driving wheels, and air brake on all driving and tender wheels. Two 8½" cross-compound pumps "squeezed" the air for the brake system.

Tractive force of the H-1-E class, road numbers 631 to 635, was 96,700 pounds, with about 13,100 pounds added from the trailing truck booster, giving a total of 109,800 pounds starting tractive force. And they surely needed it with 100 car trains of ore weighing 12,000 tons. The trains these locomotives moved—with one engine pulling and one pushing such huge loads—were among the heaviest found anywhere.

Ore trains are noted for exceptional weight and you may have noticed on some railroads that cars smaller than conventional hopper cars are used for the movement of ore. This is done to prevent overloading with its probable result of hot boxes, broken axles and possible derailment. By using a smaller car carelessness in loading will still permit the car's trucks to meet the weight of the load. But if a large hopper car were used and filled to a "heaped-up" loading, it could cause serious trouble, because a given quantity of iron ore filling a specific amount of space is considerably heavier than the same amount of coal in identical conditions. One way to use hopper cars was to restrict the loading to a certain point. This was not always carried out, hence the need for smaller cars. On the Bessemer, however, conventional sized hopper cars were used and this road took great care to see that the ore contents were well below the top of the car indicating close and commendable control of the situation.

Cylinders, 31" × 32"   Boiler diameter, 92"
Drivers, 64"   Weight, total engine, 519,740 lb.

(Collection of Frederick Westing)

A SCENE that clearly illustrates the mammoth size of the Bessemer's huge 2-10-4 type ore train haulers. (Collection of Frederick Westing)

A MORE UNUSUAL VIEW of a Northern Pacific class Z-5 locomotive, taken at Eddystone. Note the rectangular shaped sandbox with its three filling lids over the headlight. (Collection of Frederick Westing)

WHILE NOT GENERALLY KNOWN, for it was never publicized, Baldwin built steam locomotives for the Duluth, Missabe & Iron Range Railway that in some vital respects exceeded Alco's well-publicized "Big Boy" built for the Union Pacific. Speed was not the main objective but heavy haulage was and this the Baldwin giants accomplished to the full satisfaction of the railroad. With a starting tractive force of 140,000 pounds to "Big Boys" 135,375 pounds, they unquestionably had the edge in this respect.

In 1941 the Duluth, Missabe & Iron Range Railway operated 542 miles of road with 95 per cent of its traffic representing the transportation of iron ore to the Lake Superior ports. Such traffic as seen by the mammoth locomotives of the Bessemer is most grueling and called for the best in motive power.

As early as 1910, traffic became so heavy that a number of Mallets of the 2-8-8-2 type were obtained from Baldwin. Heavier Mallets followed in 1916 and 1917, and several of these were later converted to single-expansion engines and continued in service. The great tonnage of ore necessary to meet demands of the National Defense Program, called for more powerful locomotives and early in 1941, the road placed in service eight Baldwin locomotives which were among the most powerful in the world.

The new locomotives, Class M-3 were of the single-expansion articulated 2-8-8-4 type with cylinders 26 × 32 inches, driving wheels 63 inches in diameter and a working steam pressure of 240 pounds per square inch. They developed a tractive force of 140,000 pounds. Weight on drivers was 560,257 pounds, total weight of engine 695,040 pounds and total weight of engine and tender was 1,131,675 pounds. They had one-piece cast steel locomotive beds with integral cylinders and all wheels of both engine and tender were fitted with roller bearings. The tender had a capacity of 25,000 gallons of water and 26 tons of coal.

In referring to these engines P. M. Sullivan, Superintendent of Motive Power and Cars of the Duluth, Missabe and Iron Range Railway stated:

"The locomotives broke in with practically full tonnage and were released for pool service after three supervised trips. No trouble was encountered during the break-in or subsequent trips. No alterations and very few adjustments were necessary. The locomotives steamed perfectly and exceeded the expected fuel performance.

"The 25,000-gallon tender permitted through runs from docks to mines, eliminated intermediate water stops, while the coal capacity of 26 tons would generally be sufficient for a round trip. The roller bearings, force-feed lubrication and type of side-rod lubrication made it unnecessary for enginemen to service the locomotives at terminals as required with previous types."

Great public interest was aroused by the sight of these huge engines and hundreds of people actually gathered at stations and trackside to see them in action. This interest stemmed partly from the perennial fascination steam locomotives ever have had, and partly for practical reasons, for bigger locomotives meant more iron ore hauled from the mines and this, in turn meant greater prosperity for Northern Minnesota where iron is gold.

The M-3's handled all the ore on the Iron Range Division from the mines to the docks at Two Harbors. This included the 80-mile run from Ely in the Vermilion Range and the 65-mile haul from Virginia, in the Mesabi Range. The round trip from Ely to Two Harbors and back occupied 12 hours and the round trip out of Virginia took about ten hours.

Contrary to public opinion the haul from the mines to the lake shore is not mostly down grade. There are numerous adverse grades, the heaviest grade against the load being one of 0.62% for a distance of about three miles.

The new engines were handling better than 6,000 gross tons of ore per trip in short high ore cars, some of which held 50 tons and some 75 tons of ore. This is an increase of at least 25% over the best tonnage handled by the converted Mallets. The new power steamed freely and proved its ability to handle heavy tonnage with worth-while reduction in the fuel and water required per 1000 gross-ton-miles as compared with the locomotives previously used.

ALCO'S "BIG BOY" of the 4-8-8-4 type built for the Union Pacific in 1942. (Collection of Frederick Westing)

To check out certain data let us contrast the Duluth engines with "Big Boy" of the Union Pacific.

Builder	Baldwin	Alco
Railroad	Duluth, Missabe & Iron Range	Union Pacific
Type	2-8-8-4	4-8-8-4
Cylinders	(4) 26″ × 32″	(4) 23¾″ × 32″
Boiler, diameter	104″	95″
Boiler pressure	240 lb.	300 lb.
Drivers	63″	68″
Wheelbase, driving	45′7″	(2) 18′3″
Wheelbase, engine	67′2″	75′5½″
Wheelbase, engine & tender	113′5⅞″	117′7″
Weight, on drivers	560,257 lb.	540,000 lb.
Weight, total engine	695,040 lb.	762,000 lb.
Weight, engine & tender	1,131,675 lb.	1,104,200 lb.
Tractive force	140,000 lb.	133,375 lb.

(Collection of Frederick Westing)

BALDWIN'S single-expansion articulated 2-8-8-4 type locomotive built for the Duluth, Missabe & Iron Range Railway. (Collection of Frederick Westing)

Final Years from 1942 to 1954

With the bombing of Pearl Harbor on December 7th 1941, the full resources of The Baldwin Locomotive Works were placed at the Government's disposal. It was recognized that locomotives would be a pressing need particularly, for use overseas. Here operating conditions would vary from ours and motive power would have to be built accordingly.

First of the standard United States Government locomotives built for the War Department, was a 2-8-2 type Mikado. Progress in locomotive design prompted Colonel Howard R. Hill—then a Major, and active participant in the project, to suggest this wheel arrangement. For in some quarters the Consolidation type was favored especially in view of the fine reputation of the "Pershing" Consolidations of World War I fame. Later a standard US War Department Consolidation was designed and hundreds were built for use overseas.

Important executive changes occurred at Baldwin during the war years. On April 1, 1943, President Charles E. Brinley was elected Chairman of the Board. He was succeeded as Baldwin's President by former Vice-President Ralph Kelly.

It was a proud day for Baldwin on April 16, 1943, when Colonel D. N. Hauseman, District Chief, Philadelphia Ordnance District, United States Army, made the Army-Navy "E" Production Award.

In accepting the award, Charles E. Brinley, Chairman of the Board of Directors, addressed Colonel Hauseman and Captain H. E. Haven of the U.S.N., saying, "I promise you, Sirs, a continuous, sustained and ever increasing effort." That Baldwin employees and officials lived up to that promise was proved by the flow of locomotives that were outshopped at an ever increasing tempo from the works.

But while foreign orders were being filled in profusion, many railroads in the United States staggering under the load of unprecedented traffic conditions were brought to a realization of their own motive power requirements. Recognizing this situation, the Government in certain cases granted priorities to domestic railroads and Baldwin thereupon built locomotives where the need was pressingly vital.

It was at this time that Baldwin began mass production of 0-4-4-0 type diesel-electric switchers with electrical equipment supplied by Westinghouse.

With the war's cessation in September 1945, activities at the Works were somewhat curtailed, but a vast backlog of foreign and domestic orders gave Baldwin plenty to do in the locomotive business for awhile.

From 1946 Baldwin steadily increased diesel-electric locomotive production, and steam locomotive construction correspondingly declined. A few notable examples of steam power were built and received quite some prominence, such as the steam-turbine locomotive built by Baldwin with Westinghouse equipment, and the Duplex T-1 class engines of the Pennsylvania.

Meanwhile, Baldwin in view of the dieselization trend, went into this field of locomotive production with vigor and commendable enterprise, bringing over a century of locomotive "know how" to their aid they produced locomotives in sizes which they knew eventually must predominate the field. The foresight and accuracy of this viewpoint is to be seen today in the high-powered diesel locomotive units which have replaced the puny power-package, "building block" concept of locomotive operation.

Baldwin was the first to envision 6,000-hp. in one diesel locomotive unit—and build one. Today locomotive manufacturers are furnishing units quite

SOME mighty fine Hudsons were built for the Chesapeake & Ohio Railway Company in 1942. Eight engines, on what is sometimes referred to as George Washington's railroad, carried road numbers 300 to 307. Big as the C&O Pacifics were in 1913, the six-coupled Hudsons plainly showed how locomotive design had progressed through the years.

Cylinders, 25″ × 30″
Drivers, 78″
Boiler, diameter, 86″
Weight, total engine, 439,500 lb.

(Collection of Frederick Westing)

comparable in power range to this Baldwin "first." Baldwin was also the first to pack 3,000-hp. into one cab, and this locomotive went to work on the Seaboard. Baldwin also put 2,000-hp. into a "hood" model long before anyone else, with their novel road transfer diesel-electric locomotive. In this unit they also realized the value of six pairs of driving wheels when compared to four pairs, when there was rugged work to be done.

Ralph P. Johnson, Chief Engineer at Baldwin, once remarked that "the best line of endeavor for the diesel locomotive builders was to get higher concentration of power from the diesel engine." Unfortunately at the time conditions had not progressed to a point where one diesel engine could singly provide enough power to haul conventional weight cars in competition with steam and electric locomotives. Baldwin did the next best thing, they doubled more powerful supercharged engines in one cab or under one hood than had been previously used and obtained more powerful locomotive performance for their day.

While disparaging remarks were made about the high-powered diesels by some—especially the 4-8-8-4 type "centipede" they had more than an equal number of adherents. These particular locomotives saw service on the Seaboard where they were entrusted to the road's top-name luxury trains, and did much work on the National Railways of Mexico. On the Pennsylvania Railroad they were arranged to operate in tandem and provide 6,000-hp., thereby cutting four 1,500-hp. units down to two 3,000-hp. units. It is now conceded, that regardless of size, inspection and maintenance costs per unit are about the same. In such case this could result in a cost reduction of approximately 50 per cent.

In 1947-1948 the Chesapeake & Ohio ordered three mammoth steam turbine-electric locomotives. As a road greatly involved in the heavy movement of coal they understandably enough, wanted to use a fuel from which they derived much revenue, and had "on their front door step." Baldwin and Westinghouse had been pondering such a design for a good time. The result was a steam turbine-electric locomotive using a conventional locomotive boiler. This supplied steam to a turbine-electric generator set which through control equipment fed current to the traction motors. Three such units were built but were ineffective in retaining steam on the C&O, to the exclusion of diesel.

Baldwin meanwhile, continued to build a standard line of diesel locomotives which represented a policy they began in 1940. Through the years until the conclusion of their locomotive building activities, external appearance changed but little although installed horsepower in all the various types was progressively increased.

The far-sightedness of Samuel M. Vauclain is once again attested to by an address which he presented on January 29, 1926, at Chicago, Illinois, before the Mid-West Power Conference. His subject was "Internal Combustion Locomotives and Vehicles." His concluding remarks are quoted herewith: "The internal combustion locomotive unit, whether constructed with direct drive, hydraulic transmission, or electrical transmission, is yet in its infancy. The best engineering talent of the world is bending its energy to a successful solution of the problem, and

SCENE in Baldwin erecting shop as a big Chesapeake & Ohio Hudson type locomotive takes shape. Frame has been lined up, sandbox fitted, and boiler shell lagging partially applied. Baldwin shopmen could turn out as many as twelve such locomotives in a single day—and often did. (Collection of Frederick Westing)

THE YEAR 1942 saw fourteen powerful Berkshire (2-8-4) type engines built for the Louisville & Nashville Railroad, class M-1, road numbers 1950 to 1963. In common with locomotives all over the United States, these engines were faced with a record-breaking volume of wartime traffic in freight service. This was performed so well, that after the war, duplicate units were ordered from Baldwin and operated until the diesel take-over.

Cylinders, 25″ × 32″   Boiler, diameter, Front 88″ Back, 98″
Drivers, 69″   Weight total engine, 447,200 lb.

(Collection of Frederick Westing)

we will not know what new difficulties in operation will be encountered or what the anxieties of the future may be in the matter of safety until the actual operation of some appreciable number of engines gives us a thorough experience."

It was not until over twenty years later that a successful diesel hydraulic commercial design of locomotive was manufactured in the United States. This was a Baldwin 70 ton, 600-hp. locomotive. It was powered by a Caterpillar diesel engine and equipped with a Mechydro hydraulic transmission for which Baldwin had obtained the American rights in Germany. As of present writing this locomotive is still in successful daily operation without benefit of design changes. It serves as a switcher at the Eddystone, Pa., manufacturing plant of what has become Baldwin-Lima-Hamilton Corporation.

On May 4, 1949, Marvin W. Smith, a Westinghouse official, who had been serving Baldwin as Executive Vice-President, was elected President of The Baldwin Locomotive Works. Some time before Westinghouse had acquired a substantial stock interest in Baldwin. Ralph Kelly, retiring Baldwin President and former Westinghouse official had suggested both the stock acquisition and Mr. Smith for the Presidency.

On December 4, 1950 a merger was consummated between Baldwin and Lima-Hamilton Corporation. The new merged corporate name was Baldwin-Lima-Hamilton Corporation. Marvin W. Smith was named President, and George A. Rentschler, Chairman of the Board of Directors.

The Mechydro transmission drive having proved itself on the switcher previously referred to, Baldwin proceeded to design a full line of diesel hydraulic drive locomotives. Three high-speed passenger locomotives were subsequently built in 1956. One for the New York Central, and two for the New Haven of 1,000 hp. each. These units were powered with Maybach "V" type solid injection turbo-charged engines brought from Germany. These engines featured a very high ratio of horsepower to dead weight. It was not until years later, that any other locomotive builder in the United States offered a successful diesel hydraulic locomotive to American railroads.

The New York Central locomotive had the distinction of hauling their new light-weight train, the

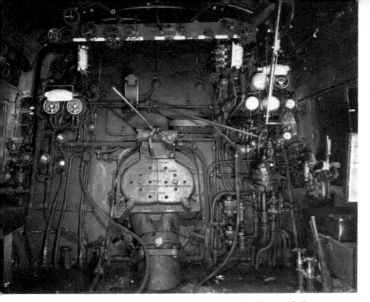

CAB INTERIOR of the Louisville & Nashville Berkshire type locomotive. Stoker feed conveyor underneath the butterfly type fire door can be seen protruding from the floor. Grapevine type throttle was used on these engines. (Collection of Frederick Westing)

ANOTHER AUTOMATIC BUTTERFLY fire door with stoker housing feeding coal to the distributor plate just below the floor opening is seen in the Frisco 4-8-4 type locomotive cab. The lowest of the valves on the left-five in number controlled the steam jets which blew the coal to various locations in the firebox. The bar type throttle lever was used here but instead of the usual angular position was placed in a horizontal line. (Collection of Frederick Westing)

Xplorer which went into service on the 260 mile run between Cleveland and Cincinnati. Outwardly the locomotive resembled a standard diesel, though it was "pushed down" in height to harmonize with the train's smaller cars.

Finally the time came when locomotive building was discontinued and other items were concentrated upon. Additional markets were created when Austin-Western in 1951, came into the Baldwin Lima-Hamilton organization. Dump cars and heavy earth moving equipment took up some of the lag left by the cessation of locomotive business.

Today Baldwin is a subsidiary of Armours of Chicago, world famous in the field of meat products. Baldwin-Lima-Hamilton, nevertheless, operates independently with its own President and operating personnel.

But locomotive building days at Spring Garden Street and Eddystone have gone into the shadows of the past; this record attempts in some measure to portray the glory that once was Baldwin's!

E N D

INSIDE THE CAB of the little Mysore engine. Like a big Pennsy K4 when first built, the sight-feed lubricator is suspended from the backhead on the fireman's side, a screw reverse gear was used, and the drip gauge funnel under the throttle lever, with its three try-cocks is also reminiscent of the Pennsy. A fireman on this locomotive meant "fireman" for three tons of coal were carried in the tender with room for 3,000 gallons of water. Construction No. 64,349, is clearly discernible on the old-style Baldwin circular badge plate. (Collection of Frederick Westing)

AFTER TWO EXPERIMENTAL RIGID FRAME 4-4-4-4 type Duplex locomotives class T-1 built by Baldwin for the Pennsylvania Railroad in 1942, Nos. 6110 and 6111, fifty more units were ordered. A few changes were made, among other things the cowling was removed in great part to allow easier access to the running gear. Baldwin received an order for twenty five Nos. 5525 to 5549, and Altoona Works built the balance Nos. 5500 to 5524. Again the Pennsy was striving to retain steam power and these T-1 engines were supposed to duplicate the performance of the GG-1 electrics. But it was all too late. The best of everything went into these locomotives and like the first two all were equipped with Franklin poppet valve gear. But the incoming diesel tide soon swamped the Pennsy as it did other roads and all T-1's have been scrapped.

Cylinders (4) 19¾″ × 26″   Boiler diameter, Ft. 91½″
Drivers, 80″   Boiler diameter, Bk. 100″
                            Weight, total engine, 502,200 lb.

(Collection of Frederick Westing)

A TRIM SINGLE NARROW GAUGE SUPERHEATED ENGINE built in September, 1942, to operate on a two-foot gauge railway. Ordered by the Mysore Iron & Steel Works, India, this comparatively tiny "Mike" with outside frames and counterbalanced cranks extending beyond the driving wheels were distinguishing features. Note the size of the locomotive in comparison with the man alongside. Just the thing for the railfans!

Cylinders, 12″ × 18″   Boiler, 48″
Drivers, 33″   Weight, total engine, 66,800 lb.

(Collection of Frederick Westing)

THE FIRST UNITED STATES GOVERNMENT standard locomotive built for the War Department was a 2-8-2 type Mikado, built in April 1942. A most prominent participant in the designing and building of this locomotive was Colonel Howard G. Hill, USAR (Ret.) Colonel Hill told me of the many difficulties he faced in getting out this design under intense pressure. Our British Allies favored the old Pershing's of the Consolidation type of World War I fame, but as Colonel Hill pointed out, good as those engines had been and though some were still working, progress had been made in steam locomotive construction. Experience on American railroads had outmoded the Consolidation in favor of the Mikado type years before, but to British eyes a trailing truck on a freight locomotive "just wasn't done." A few had been tried, and Sir Nigel Gresley, one of the most progressive of British Locomotive Engineers had produced a good Mikado, but in general, forward and trailing trucks were omitted on British "Goods" or "Mineral" locomotives—the latter denoting engines used on coal drags, as we'd say in the U.S.A.

Colonel Hill stuck to his guns because for a locomotive that would quickly fit into the picture and take over the duties assigned to it, this design appeared best. The Mikado, therefore, won out, and the locomotive pictured herewith was the result.

Cylinders, 21″ × 28″   Boiler, diameter, 68″
Drivers, 60″   Weight, total engine, 200,000 lb.

(Collection of Frederick Westing)

SUCCESS OF THE "GENERALS" built in 1937 prompted the Richmond, Fredericksburg & Potomac Railroad, to add six more 4-8-4 type engines to their roster, in 1942, Nos. 607 to 612. These were named after "Governors" of the State of Virginia, and were duplicates of six such engines built in 1938. Unlike the "Generals" which had rectangular tender tanks, the "Governors" used tanks of the Vanderbilt or circular type. These engines instead of dual service operation, were built for use in passenger train operation, though with the pressing demands of wartime conditions they found themselves "drafted" into freight service as well. In both fields their service gave satisfaction to the railroad company.

With their blue coloring, lined in gold leaf striping and lettering the appearance of these locomotives was a treat to the eye.

Cylinders, 27″ × 30″   Boiler, diameter, Front, 84″ Back 95″
Drivers, 77″   Weight, total engine, 408,400 lb.

(Collection of Frederick Westing)

CLASS A-5 OF THE NORTHERN PACIFIC built in June 1943. This was one of ten engines, road numbers 2680 to 2689. These were the last of the road's 4-8-4 type engines and represented the ultimate of their fine "A" class.

Baldwin locomotives were no strangers to this road. As early as 1890, a Baldwin 4-6-0 type locomotive hauled the North Coast Limited on the western end of its run to the Pacific. Since 1934, powerful locomotives of the 4-8-4 type were used on this famous train. Four lots of these engines were furnished by Baldwin. Ten class A-2 locomotives were built in 1934; eight class A-3 in 1937, eight class A-4 in 1940; and ten class A-5 completed in the spring of 1943.

There was little change in the various lots of locomotives and all were especially successful in the severe service in which they were engaged. These locomotives—like the enormous class Z-5's—were designed to successfully burn a semi-bituminous fuel known as "Rosebud" coal, which was strip-mined near Forsyth, Montana. The large, well designed boiler gave ample steaming capacity, and the engines were capable of delivering maximum horsepower for sustained periods.

They established an enviable record in high-speed, long distance passenger service. For many years they hauled the North Coast Limited, up to 18 cars in length, between St. Paul, Minnesota, and Livingston, Montana. This run of 1,008 miles, one of the longest in the world, was made without changing locomotives.

One of the appealing features of these locomotives was the fact that they delivered as much as 4,000 horsepower at the drawbar, and rated a starting tractive force of 69,800 pounds, while burning coal that cost but sixty-nine cents per ton delivered to the locomotive tender!

Class A-5 was equipped with type "E" superheaters, feedwater heaters, stokers, six circulators, power reverse, one-piece cast-steel locomotive bed with integral cylinders. Air brakes were applied to all wheels on engine and tender with air supplied by two 8½″ cross-compound pumps bracketed to the left side of the boiler.

Cylinders, 28″ × 31″   Boiler diameter, 88″
Drivers, 77″   Weight, total engine, 508,500 lb.

(Collection of Frederick Westing)

FOLLOWING THE LOUISVILLE & NASHVILLE BERKSHIRES came fifteen 4-8-4 type locomotives numbered 4500 to 4514, for the St. Louis-San Francisco Railway. These were dual service locomotives with comparatively large drivers enabling them to work in passenger and fast freight service on the Frisco.

The new engines built 1942, operated on the Eastern Division from St. Louis, to Monett, Missouri, and over the Southwestern Division to Tulsa, Oklahoma. In this service they joined heavy Mountain type locomotives and permitted the release of a number of Mikado and medium weight Mountain type locomotives for service on other divisions.

Cylinders, 28″ × 31″   Boiler, diameter, Front 88″, Back 100″
Drivers, 74″   Weight, total engine, 462,500 lb.
Numbers 4500 to 4502—oil fuel
Numbers 4503 to 4514—coal fuel

(Collection of Frederick Westing)

FIVE EXCEPTIONALLY POWERFUL Baldwin Westinghouse electric locomotives were built for the New Haven during the war in 1943. Wheel arrangement was of the 4-6-6-4 type with twin-motor, gear and quill drive. Built primarily for freight service between the New Haven's New York freight terminal and the yard at Cedar Hill, New Haven, they could be used in passenger service and handle twenty 85-ton Pullman cars between New York and New Haven on any schedule then in existence. As they operated without train heating boilers, special train heating cars with a boiler, oil fuel and water tanks were coupled to the engine whenever they were used in passenger service during the winter. Some concession to streamlining was made in rounding the ends of the double-end operating superstructure which was essentially of the box-cab type.

Drivers, 57″   Weight, total engine, 500,000 lb.
Line voltage, AC. 11,000 volts single-phase 25 cycles.
Continuous horsepower at 65-mph. 4,860
Maximum horsepower, 9,100
Maximum tractive force—25 per cent adhesion, 90,000 lb.

This high horsepower enabled these locomotives to take 5,000 ton freight trains, of 125 cars, over the road at a speed of 55-mph; a 41 per cent increase over the best performance previously made by electric power on this road.

(Collection of Frederick Westing)

LIKE TO TAKE OUT the Broadway? Despite the prolific display of gauges, valve handles and levers, the S-2 was a comparatively easy locomotive to handle. One master control lever drove the locomotive and also was used for reversing. (Collection of Frederick Westing)

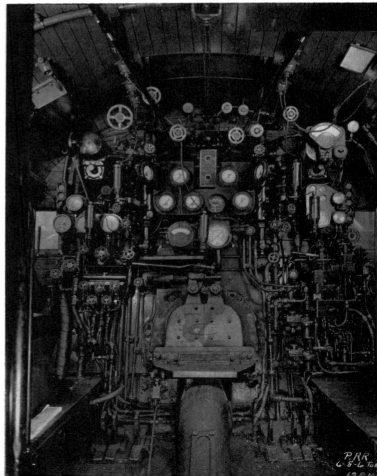

IN 1944 AN INNOVATION took place when Baldwin entered the diesel-electric locomotive field with a powerful 2,000 horsepower road service locomotive. This was as powerful as any built at that time and embodied latest improvements in diesel engines and electrical equipment. This locomotive presented a colorful display with its streamline blue, cream, and white cab superstructure. It was soon a familiar sight on many American railroads where it was assigned to regular trains while performing in a most creditable manner.

This Baldwin-Westinghouse diesel electric was intended for high-speed operation of both passenger and freight trains up to 90 mph. Its 80-foot cab contained, as its power plant, two standard 1,000-hp normally aspirated (non-supercharged) diesel engines driving two DC generators, supplying power to four geared-traction motors, each one-third larger than any heretofore used with 2,000-hp. diesel electric locomotives. The cab was mounted on two trucks, which had the merit of simplicity, yet were satisfactory for locomotives of moderate tractive force.

Weight on drivers for freight locomotives should be as large as possible because high starting tractive forces are necessary. Yet since the locomotive was to be used in high-speed passenger service, the weight per axle had to be limited so as to minimize damage to track. To accommodate these two conflicting requirements the load per axle was fixed at about 60,000 pounds which necessitated six-wheel trucks. Under good rail conditions, the starting tractive force per driving axle was 18,000 pounds or a total of 72,000 pounds for the locomotive.

Front and rear axles of each truck were power driven and the center axle was idle. Motors were of the nose-suspended type driving the axle through a pinion and gear. An operating cab was located at one end.

Drivers, 40″	Motors, 4 Westinghouse, 370-B
Diesel engine, 2-1,000-hp at 625 rpm.	Weight, total, 381,000 lb.

(Collection of Frederick Westing)

AS A HEAVY COAL HAULING RAILROAD and with coal available on "its own door step" the Pensylvania Railroad wanted to retain coal as locomotive fuel. In an effort to combat the thermal efficiency selling point of the diesel, attention was focused on the steam turbine. The direct drive geared steam-turbine locomotive, class S-2, built by Baldwin with Westinghouse furnishing the forward and reverse turbines of 6,900 and 1,500 horsepower rsespectively, was outshopped in 1944. Originally planned as a 4-8-4 type, wartime priorities intervened and required heavier steel for the boiler shell with a considerable addition of weight. For supporting this greater weight two six-wheel trucks were used providing a locomotive of the 6-8-6 type. Though No. 6200 hauled top-name trains, including the Broadway Limited, heavy steam demands at low speed—greatly in excess of that required by the reciprocating type—caused harmful results on the boiler staying and No. 6200 was the only S-2 ever built for the Pennsy.

Forward turbine, 6,900-hp.	Boiler diameter, Ft. 93″
Reverse turbine, 1,500-hp.	Boiler diameter, Bk. 102″
Drivers, 68″	Weight, total engine, 580,000 lb.

(Collection of Frederick Westing)

A MIGHTY 2-10-4 Texas type engine built for the Santa Fe in 1944. Though Lima is credited as the originator of this wheel arrangement, it was Baldwin which built the first 2-10-4 in the United States when they out-shopped engine No. 3829 for the Santa Fe in 1919. Data on engine 5012 is as follows:

Cylinders 30″ × 34″   Boiler diameter, F. 94″ B. 104″
Drivers, 74″   Weight, total engine, 538,000 lb.

(Collection of Frederick Westing)

MALLETS on the Baltimore & Ohio have almost been synonymous. Ever since John E. Muhlfeld, the road's Supt. of Motive Power back in 1904, introduced a Mallet of the 0-6-6-0 type, first in the United States, the B&O became Mallet conscious. Operating conditions on their road made the use of such engines exceptionally appropriate.

In the turmoil of the war years the B&O found themselves faced with a need for more power and quickly. By this time the B&O had diesel road service locomotives in use and would have preferred such locomotives. But at that time diesel power to match a big steam locomotive would have called for about three times as much metal—not to count the vital copper needed for generators and traction motors. War priorities therefore, ruled out the diesels and a four-cylinder single-expansion steam locomotive of the 2-8-8-4 class EM-1 was built instead. Between 1944 and 1945 thirty of these locomotives were turned out by Baldwin.

They immediately went into service without any "breaking in" for pressing war traffic demanded quick action. Not only in freight did these EM-1 engines out-perform anything in steam on the B&O but in passenger service also. On 18-car passenger trains, doubleheading and pusher service on the severe grades were entirely eliminated. The B&O stated that for the work these engines were built for, they considered the EM-1 class unexcelled.

Cylinders (4) 24″ × 32″   Boiler diameter, Front 96⅛″
Drivers, 64″   Boiler diameter, Back 100³⁄₁₆″
Weight, total engine, 628,700 lb.

(Collection of Frederick Westing)

BECAUSE OF THE TREND toward applying higher total horsepower to the haulage of mainline trains, Baldwin designed and built in 1942 for test purposes a radically advanced design of road diesel locomotive. This unit had an articulated running gear arrangement which had been tried and proven in straight electric locomotive applications consisting of a 4-8 + 8-4 wheel arrangement. This locomotive carried the forces of buff and draft through its trucks rather than through the car body. This single end box cab streamlined locomotive was 91'6" over couplers. It was equipped with an automatic oil fired train heating boiler and was powered by a complement of 8 radically new engines of BLW design. Eight cylinder "V" engines rated 750 H.P. each were used. These were 9½" × 9½" 910 RPM engines supercharged by Roots mechanically driven blowers providing a total installed horsepower in a single locomotive of 6000. It was not until 24 years later in 1966 that any other builder offered to the railroads a single locomotive unit of this installed horsepower.

All 12 axles were capable of being powered for freight service, however, for passenger service the leading and trailing truck axles were not powered.

Although the locomotive proved entirely successful, it was never put in production for the trade, because its cost of manufacture exceeded the cost of equivalent horsepower installed in smaller standard locomotive units operating in multiple unit.

This locomotive was rebuilt in 1945 at which time it was equipped with two 1500 H.P. Baldwin 608SC, 12¾" × 15½" supercharged engines and sold to the Seaboard Air Line where it was assigned Road No. 4500. Thirteen other similar 3000 H.P. units were subsequently purchased by the Seaboard Air Line Railway in 1947 to complete their ownership of 14 units. Fourteen similar units were purchased by National Railways of Mexico in 1948. During 1947 the Pennsylvania Railroad purchased 24 of these units which were arranged in pairs coupled back to back by means of draw bars rather than couplers to form 12 locomotives of 6000 H.P. each.

(Collection of Frederick Westing)

(Caption by John Kirkland)

BALDWIN'S unique shark-nose diesel locomotive is well illustrated by this four-unit Pennsylvania Railroad 6,400 horsepower locomotive. Each A and B unit had two four-wheel trucks with all axles motorized. When this quartet operated in unison they developed a combined starting tractive force of 295,200 lb. The following data applied to each A and B unit:

Diesel engine, 1-8 cyl. 1,600-hp.
Traction motors, 4 Westinghouse, type 370
Drivers 42"
Weight, total unit, "A" 248,000 lb.
Weight, total unit, "B" 244,000 lb.

(Collection of Frederick Westing)

WHEN SKIES DARKENED for steam power on our American railroads attempts were made by some railroads to combat the high thermal efficiency argument of the diesel locomotive. On some roads coal was cheap and the supply prodigious so recourse was made to some technological tool with which to match the diesel. This brought to mind the steam turbine, for here was a machine operated by steam that showed decided thermal advantages over the conventional type of steam engine. Turbines had been tried in Europe, and thermal-efficiencywise had proved their point while burning coal as fuel.

We have seen how the Pennsylvania tried to do the job but neither the Pennsy or any other American Railroad ordered a similar turbine-drive locomotive. Nevertheless the turbine bug became quite virulent at this time and the Chesapeake & Ohio were bitten by it. In 1947-48 they got themselves three steam turbine-electric locomotives from Baldwin. One Westinghouse steam turbine of the forward impulse type with 6,000-hp. shaft horse-power at a speed of 6,000-rpm. drove four 1,000 KW, DC, generators which through suitable control equipment fed current to eight axle-hung traction motors.

Steam was supplied by a locomotive type boiler, with a working steam pressure of 310 lb. per square inch. It was equipped with a type "E" superheater, feed water heater, stoker, three thermic syphons in the firebox, and two 8½" cross-compound compressors. But as European railways had learned, the steam turbine tho a superb machine in stationary power plant practice and aboard ship where conditions are just right for its use, on a locomotive it was a different story. For on a railroad operating conditions hamper its best efforts. One pilot model would have shown a more realistic approach, considering bugs and kinks bound to be part of such a gigantic experiment, but the railroad wanted three right off. They got them, tried them, and speedily scrapped them. Thus bluntly endeth the sad story of Chessie's attempt to stave off the complete take-over by diesel power.

> 1 steam turbine, 6,000-hp. Boiler, diameter, Front, 93" Back, 102"
> Drivers, 40" Traction motors, 8-Westinghouse type 370-F
> Weight, total engine, 857,200 lb.

> (Collection of Frederick Westing)

WHEN LARGE STEAM LOCOMOTIVES were shipped to nearby roads, they were frequently delivered under their own power as is the RF&P 4-8-4 shown here backing on the B&O lead at Eddystone. 1947 (C. A. Brown Photo)

A CLOSE-UP VIEW under part of the casing of the Chesapeake & Ohio steam turbine-electric locomotive. On such a locomotive when a failure occurred it took three days to find what was wrong and three minutes to fix it. On the reciprocating type steam locomotive it took three minutes to find what was wrong and three days to fix it. (Collection of Frederick Westing)

PRESIDENT RALPH KELLY of Baldwin delivered the first J-1 class 4-8-4 type locomotive to C. J. Wolfe, Superintendent of Motive Power of the Western Maryland Railway in 1947. Nevin Watt and L. W. Metzger, Baldwin officials look on.

Cylinders, 26½″ × 32″   Boiler diameter, Ft. 92″ I.D.
Drivers, 69″   Boiler diameter, Bk. 102″ O.D.
                         Weight, total engine, 506,500 lb.

(Collection of Frederick Westing)

AMONG THE LAST steam locomotives built by Baldwin were a group of four 3'3⅜" (Meter) gauge Mikados (the 2-8-2's were always a sturdy breed) for the India Supply Mission for the Government of India. These engines were built in March, 1950, were equipped with "A" type superheaters, one thermic syphon, hand screw reverse, cast-steel cylinders, and steam brake, with vacuum brake on tender and train, with train connection front and rear.

Cylinders, 16¼" × 24"   Boiler diameter F. 57" B. 62"
Drivers, 48"   Weight, total engine, 129,400 lb.

(Collection of Frederick Westing)

AN EXCEPTIONALLY SUCCESSFUL Baldwin-Westinghouse diesel-electric locomotive was the 0-4-4-0 type switcher. In this field many railroads said no other diesel could match a Baldwin diesel switcher in pulling capacity and overall dependability. A long-time customer purchased this one. They came in sizes from 800-hp. to 1,200-hp. (Collection of Frederick Westing)

LAST MAIN-LINE electric locomotives built by Baldwin went to the Pennsylvania Railroad. They featured ignitron rectifier tubes which converted trolley-fed AC into DC for the traction motors—really a mobile sub-station and locomotive all in one. Basic objective was to use AC in the transmission and distribution system and DC traction motors like those used on diesels. Two units were operated in tandem to form one complete locomotive. In the picture we have the 4-4-4 type locomotive with three four-wheel trucks per unit. The other ignitron locomotive was of the 0-6-6-0 type with two six-wheel trucks per unit. Neither type was duplicated. Data on locomotive shown is as follows:

Type, B-B-B   Drivers, 44"
RR class, E3B   Motors, 12-Westinghouse type, 370-DZ
Weight, total locomotive, 756,000 lb.
Maximum starting tractive force, 189,000 lb.

A MOST POPULAR MODEL, another Baldwin "first." Baldwin was putting 2,000 horsepower (later this was upped to 2,400 horsepower) in a "hood" model long before anyone else. And long ago they recognized the value of six pairs of powered wheels per locomotive compared with four pairs. Starting tractive force was 106,200 lb.

Diesel engines, Two, 6-cylinder in line
Drivers, 42"
Traction motors, 6 Westinghouse Type 370.
Weight, total engine 354,000 lb.

(Collection of Frederick Westing)

ANOTHER VIEW of the same type diesel switcher sold to a good customer over the border. Fine visability with a roomy comfortable cab were a part of these locomotives. (Collection of Frederick Westing)

THE **SOUTHERN PACIFIC** received forty 4-8-8-2 type "back-ups" in 1942, to meet a gigantic tonnage challenge created by the impact of World War II. For on this road the burden was probably greater especially in the earlier days, due to its strategic Pacific Coast location which served as a springboard of the Nation's offensive in the Pacific area. These engines were numbered in the 4200's, one group Nos. 4205 to 4244, and an additional lot of thirty in 1943, Nos. 4245 to 4274. All these engines had rectangular tender tanks in place of the former Vanderbilt form.

Prior to the first locomotive reaching El Paso, Mr. Ray E. Bedford, Baldwin Service Engineer, conferred with Southern Pacific's Mr. R. U. Lipscomb, Supt. of Motive Power, and Mr. M. J. Gunther, Supt. of the El Paso Shops, in order to work out a program to be followed in setting up these locomotives.

The first locomotive to reach El Paso arrived at 1:40 am. At 2:30 pm that same day, less than 13 hours after its arrival, the locomotive was ready to go out on its break-in trip. This was considered record time for that class of heavy power, but the record did not stand for long. On subsequent engines this was reduced to ten hours, then eight hours and finally only seven hours were needed to do the job. A truly remarkable achievement of speed and efficiency yet with no compromise in safety and thoroughness.

Following was the work performed:

Brick firebox, apply main rods and other motion work, put up connections between engine and tender, test and oil air brake system, check feedwater heater, remove oil cellar boxes and change oil, trace all pipes for correct tagging, clean boiler with hot water, take oil and water, fire up boiler and test all steam pipes and valves under pressure, test all air pipes with house pressure.

As soon as each locomotive was set up it was given a 178-mile break-in run to Alamogordo and return to El Paso and then placed in westbound revenue service handling 75 to 80 empty refrigerator cars 148 miles to Lorsburg, New Mexico.

Cylinders, (4), 24″ × 32″	Boiler, diameter, Front—94$\frac{1}{16}$″
Drivers, 63½″	Boiler, diameter, Back—106⅛″
	Weight total engine, 657,900 lb.

(Collection of Frederick Westing)

DESPITE THE FINE WORK done by the 2-8-2 type Mikados, it was the old Consolidations built in 1942 on and for some time after that exceeded in quantity any of the other wartime engines. In Great Britain and Continental Europe these locomotives saw much service. One of them No. 2737, turned out of the erecting shop on Saturday, December 4, 1943, was the recipient of Baldwin construction number 70,000, which put it in the honored company of other ten-thousandth Baldwin milestoners, such as the Pennsy K3S Pacific, No. 40,000, the 2-8-8-2 type Mallet for the Southern Railway, No. 50,000 and the three-cylinder compound with watertube firebox, bearing Baldwin construction number 60,000.

These sturdy Consolidations brought the famed Pershing 2-8-0 type engines up to date, and were a modernized version of those doughty machines of World War I fame. All were equipped with "A" type superheaters, hand-lever reverse,° cast-iron cylinders, and steam brake on all driving and tender wheels. One 9½″ air pump was on the left-hand side of the smokebox front; air and vacuum brake on train.

Cylinders, 19″ × 26″	Boiler diameter, 70″
Drivers, 57″	Weight, total engine, 161,000 lb.

° This particular group.

(Collection of Frederick Westing)

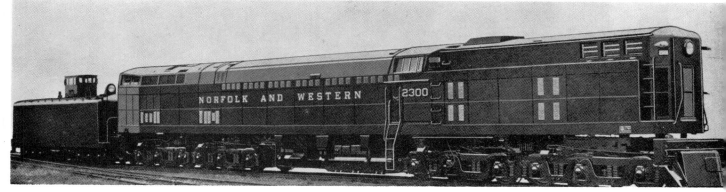

"JAWN HENRY" was the last valiant attempt of a coal hauler to find a more efficient coal burning machine. Most of the difficulties which were encountered in the earlier C & O turbines such as inaccessible electrical equipment and the contamination of traction motors by cinders were eliminated, but she was too late, and too expensive. (Collection of C. A. Brown)

NOTE: *In 1954 Baldwin built what was said to be the largest single unit locomotive in the world for another big coal hauling railroad, the Norfolk & Western. Again it was of the steam turbine-electric type.*

On this railroad steam operation was superb and its locomotive availability matched and even bettered that on some diesel operated roads. This was due to the excellence of the locomotives and the care taken in their maintenance. On this road steam power was treated with the same consideration given to diesels, which hitherto had not been the case.

This huge locomotive received the name "Jawn Henry" a legendary figure possessed of superhuman strength according to the mountain folk along the N&W. One good point of Jawn Henry was the fact that his sponsors saw fit to use a higher boiler pressure, one that popped the safety valves at 600 pounds per square inch. At this pressure steam temperature would be quite high especially when superheated. Steam then rotated the turbine blades at a 2,000-mph. speed with really hot steam that approached that pure gaseous state sought for by engineers. To safely use this pressure a water-tube boiler was built by Babcock & Wilcox because pressures in this range ruled out the locomotive type boiler.

After being put in service in 1954 Jawn Henry showed that he could rate 175,000 lb. tractive force at starting, and at 9 mph. had a continuous tractive force of 144,000 lb. Maximum speed was 60 mph. Four six-wheel trucks with each axle power driven with a total of twelve traction motors turned the turbine generators power into work at the wheels.

A large tender containing a Zeolite water softening plant held 22,000 gallons of water. Twenty tons of coal were located in the coal bunker which was at the front of the locomotive as on the C&O turbine locomotives. When running forward firedoor and stoker were in back of the engine crew. Also like the C&O turbines it was arranged for single-end operation and called for a lengthy turntable. One point that was stressed was the fact that these turbine-electrics could—like diesels—use dynamic braking.

But while great things were expected from Jawn it became clear that in handling trains at speed the N&W's latest single-expansion articulateds could out-run the turbine. True, Jawn showed up better in burning less coal for distance traveled and load hauled, but not in speed. And the ability to move tonnage at speed is vital in modern railroading. Hauling more cars with a bit higher efficiency but taking longer to do it is less of a selling point than getting cars speedily over the road with a bit less efficiency. Another thing plain to see was that the slower moving Jawn Henry was much more complicated, vastly more costly to build and maintain than any of the N&W's latest articulateds of comparable power.

Absence of a condenser was a serious handicap to all the steam turbine-electric locomotives. Aboard ship and in riverside stationary steam power plants they are an inseparable part of turbine operation. Here a prolific supply of water for condensation and adequate space permit this. But on a locomotive this set of circumstances did not obtain. Air-cooled condensers using fans were featured on the Ljungstrom direct drive turbine locomotives, but the huge quantities of steam to be condensed on these American locomotives were enormous in comparison to the much smaller European condensation demands of their turbine locomotives.

1 steam turbine, 4,500 shaft horsepower. Drivers, 42″
Type 6-6-6-6 Traction motors, 12 Westinghouse, DC diesel type
Weight, total engine, 807,000 lb. Weight, tender, 365,000 lb.
Weight, total engine and tender, 1,172,000 lb. (586 tons)

(Caption data above by Frederick Westing)

Samuel Matthews Vauclain

BORN, MAY 18, 1856   DIED, FEBRUARY 4, 1940

When Samuel Matthews Vauclain passed away, our Country lost one of its distinguished citizens. The Railroad World, which he loved so well and which loved and honored him, lost a man whose energy and genius had served it for more than sixty-five years.

With his death, The Baldwin Locomotive Works lost a leader whose guiding genius was one of the most potent factors in the development of Baldwin as a great industrial plant. The name "Vauclain" will always be associated with this Company which he served for fifty-seven years as Superintendent, Partner, Vice-President, President and Chairman of the Board.

Not only in the United States, but throughout the world, wherever there are railroads, the news of Mr. Vauclain's death was received with sorrow by those who had known and worked with him. Nowhere was this sorrow more profound than among his associates at Baldwin to whom he was fellow-worker as well as Chief.

To think of Mr. Vauclain is to think of those who shared his labors, for he was essentially a worker. He was proud of the fact that he had started his career as an humble apprentice; proud, even when he headed the Baldwin organization, to join his men in the shops and put his shoulder to the wheel.

Mr. Vauclain often remarked that the man who liked his job and who "worked for the work's sake", not only found contentment but material success as well. With him this was not merely a theory, it was the rule by which he regulated his entire business life. In his success it found its highest fulfillment.

This man, whose great character we attempt so feebly to portray, was a devoted husband, father and grandfather, philanthropist, world traveler, business executive, salesman, mechanic, and public-spirited citizen. He was an optimist in the best sense of the word. Not only did he believe in the future of his Country and his fellow man, he devoted his best energies to the task of making his dream come true.

With the death of Samuel Matthews Vauclain, there passed one of the truly great men of our time.

SAMUEL M. VAUCLAIN—"Mr. Locomotive" served Baldwin for 57 years.

OWNED BY THE MARBLECLIFT Quarries No. 7615 was the last of the long line of Baldwins